Your
Poodle's
Life

Also Available from PRIMA PETS™

The Allergy Solution for Dogs by Shawn Messonnier, D.V.M.

The Arthritis Solution for Dogs by Shawn Messonnier, D.V.M.

Your Beagle's Life by Kim Campbell Thornton

Your Border Collie's Life by Kim D.R. Dearth

Your Boxer's Life by Kim D.R. Dearth

Your Cat's Life by Joanne Howl, D.V.M.

Your Chihuahua's Life by Kim Campbell Thornton

Your Dog's Life by Tracy Acosta, D.V.M.

Your German Shepherd's Life by Audrey Pavia

Your Golden Retriever's Life by Betsy Sikora Siino

Your Lab's Life by Virginia Parker Guidry

Your Rottweiler's Life by Kim D.R. Dearth

Your Yorkshire Terrier's Life by Elaine Waldorf Gewirtz

VIRGINIA PARKER GUIDRY
Joanne Howl, D.V.M., Series Editor

Your POODLE'S *Life*

Your Complete Guide to Raising Your Pet from Puppy to Companion

PRIMA PETS

An Imprint of Prima Publishing
3000 Lava Ridge Court • Roseville, California 95661
(800) 632-8676 • www.primalifestyles.com

Interior photos by Kent Lacin Media Services
Color insert photos © Isabelle Français and Tara Darling
Chapter 6 illustrations by Pam Tanzey

Special thanks to the beautiful dogs who appear in this book and their wonderful owners: Frankie, owned by Sharron Rennert; B.J., Susan Diehm; Skoshie, Hsiu Lairamore; C.C. and Patrick, Margaret Kohler; Tio, Jean Hunt.

Library of Congress Cataloging-in-Publication Data
Guidry, Virginia Parker
    Your poodle's life : your complete guide to raising your pet from puppy to companion / Virginia Parker Guidry.
        p. cm. — (Your pet's life)
    ISBN: 0-7615-2537-8
    1. Poodles I. Title. II. Series.

SF429.P85 G87 2000
636.72'8—dc21   00-031370

00 01 02 DD 10 9 8 7 6 5 4 3 2 1
Printed in the United States of America

How to Order

Single copies may be ordered from Prima Publishing, 3000 Lava Ridge Court, Roseville, CA 95661; telephone (800) 632-8676 ext. 4444. Quantity discounts are also available. On your letterhead, include information concerning the intended use of the books and the number of books you wish to purchase.

Visit us online at www.primalifestyles.com

To Mom

Contents

Acknowledgments

Writing *Your Poodle's Life* has been a privilege and an awesome opportunity to meet, chat, and learn from a host of dedicated and wise Poodle enthusiasts. Truly, I couldn't have done it without you! Special thanks to Versatility In Poodles co-founder Grace Blair, M.D., and Diann Ellis and the Poodle Club of America. Thank you to all members of the PSG online mailing list, especially Winona Kuhl, Caroline Hair, Michelle Mace, Lisa Haidle, Irma Shanahan, Tracey Kaul, Belinda Hankins, Linda Smith, Tracey Raby, Susan Sloane, Deb Johnson, Claudette Vatore, Linda Hargett, Kadelia Hamilton, Julie Borst, Sandy Marshall, and Rhonda Le'Bilron. And, sincere appreciation to the Prima Pets staff.

Introduction

The Poodle is quite possibly one of God's finest creations. Most Poodles are extremely intelligent, good-
natured, sophisticated, fun-loving, beautiful, adaptable to a
variety of lifestyles and activities, sensitive, highly trainable
and, of course, have the most incredible coat found on any
canine breed. The Poodle comes in three sizes—small,
medium, and large—and is suitable for any lifestyle. As one
Poodle enthusiast says, "Ranging from three to ninety
pounds, Poodles are a terrific package of brains, beauty,
brawn, and bang for your buck! What more could you want
in a canine companion? Nothing! The Poodle is the best of
the best of the best." This is probably why you're a Poodle
owner or are thinking of acquiring a Poodle—and why
you're reading this book.

You probably need no convincing of the Poodle's merits,
but need more information about living with and caring for
this splendid breed that can do almost anything—earn obedience titles, compete in field and agility trials, pull a sled or
cart, prance in the breed ring, play with kids, or participate
in flyball competition. There's little the Poodle cannot do if
he is given proper instruction and encouragement. That's
why the Poodle is so popular, and has been for many, many

years. The breed has, in fact, ranked in the top five of American Kennel Club (AKC) registrations for two decades.

Not only is the Poodle popular in the United States, but the breed has enjoyed worldwide appreciation for centuries. According to the AKC's *Complete Dog Book*, few breeds have ever been regarded in such high favor in so many different countries as has the Poodle, and few purebreds can claim so many references in art and literature through the ages.

What It Means to Have a Poodle in Your Life

When writer John Steinbeck traveled across the United States in a pickup camper, he was accompanied by Charley, a fun-loving Standard Poodle. Steinbeck later wrote of his travels, and his thoughts about the nation, in *Travels with Charley*. The book expresses Steinbeck's fondness for the big Poodle and shows the unique relationship between Charley and Steinbeck. When you become a Poodle owner, you may not become famous like Charley and Steinbeck, but you will have the opportunity to enjoy a similar friendship as the one they shared.

Poodles cannot speak words—though it seems like they should—but their actions tell you they are loyal and devoted companions, anxious to please. Poodles are also sensitive. Should you feel ill, you can depend on your curly-coated companion staying by your side. Your Poodle is a playful friend, sure to give you a tickle or a belly laugh. She's a smart companion, too, able and willing to learn anything you can teach her. A Poodle in your life means having the best companion you've ever had!

Dog Ownership:
The Many Sacrifices, the Many Joys

You'll pay a price for your friendship with a Poodle—not entirely in dollars (though money is essential to caring for your dog). Owning a Poodle means changes, adjustments, additions, and subtractions to your lifestyle. You may be required to make some *sacrifices*. What changes might you expect? If you normally sleep until 11 A.M., your sleepy mornings may be over. Your Poodle will expect you to rise early to feed and walk her. Regular grooming is a must, and you'll have to fit it into your busy schedule. You'll also need to make time for training. In case of emergency, you will need to drop everything and rush your Poodle to the animal hospital. You can't just take off on a Caribbean vacation without booking dog-friendly accommodations either at home or abroad. If you have small kids, you must constantly supervise dog-child interactions for the safety of both parties. Then, of course, there's the mundane (and sometimes smelly) tasks of kennel cleanup, yard cleanup, and bed washing. Get the picture? Owning a Poodle will impact your life! Are you prepared to accept that reality?

How Much Thought
Have You Given to Owning a Poodle?

Perhaps you haven't given dog ownership that much thought. Lack of forethought is the most common reason so many owners relinquish their companion animals to shelters. People imagine that owning that cute pup will be nothing but fun, and that's the extent of their thinking. They buy the little bundle of fur, take her home and expect to live together happily ever after. After all, how much work can an adorable puppy be? A lot! Just keeping up with a Poodle's grooming regimen can be overwhelming. Then, of course, you'll encounter all those normal, but annoying puppy behaviors—chewing, barking, stealing—that you must tolerate until they are trained away.

Owners who do not carefully consider the costs of dog ownership often end up dumping the dog at a shelter. They have little emotional investment so throwing it away means nothing.

Carefully think through the costs of owning a dog before you acquire one by answering these questions:

❍ *Why do you want a dog?* Is it an impulse decision because you saw a cute pup or adult dog? Are you lonely and in need of a companion? What is your true motivation for owning a dog?
❍ *Why do you want a Poodle?* Does your neighbor have a Poodle or do you like the breed? Did you see one you admire on TV or in a magazine ad?
❍ *What do you really know about the breed?* Did you read a book or magazine article about Poodles that sparked your interest? Have you talked with a Poodle owner or breeder? Does what you think you know match true descriptions of the breed?
❍ *Can you afford a pet?* Can your budget handle the cost of supplies, food, medical care, grooming costs, and so on?

Carefully consider these questions before you acquire your Poodle. It's only fair. Why bring home a dog when you're ill-prepared to take care of her and may decide not to keep her? That is what will happen if you don't plan ahead.

We're Here to Help

The Poodle is a wonderful breed of dog, and deserves the best of care from you. That's why we've published *Your Poodle's Life*—so you can fully prepare and enjoy your Poodle, whatever his or her size, whether you buy a ten-week-old pup from a breeder or adopt a three-year-old adult from a rescue organization. We want you to be fully aware of who your Poodle is, how you can be the best owner possible, and what fun, joy, and rewards await you.

For an in-depth look at what a Poodle is, from the breed's personality to her exercise requirements, and for information on acquiring one, see Chapter 1. Getting your home ready for a Poodle puppy or adult dog is covered in Chapter 2. The basics of good nutrition, or what to feed your Poodle and when, is covered in Chapter 3. Every Poodle needs medical care, including routine exams and vaccinations. See Chapter 4 for general medical information and Chapter 5 for the Poodle's unique health concerns. Basic training and lifetime schooling for Poodles is covered in Chapter 6. Grooming, a must for Poodles, is covered in Chapter 7; and activities and family life are the topics of Chapter 8. Chapter 9 looks at what you can expect as your Poodle ages and discusses the difficult decision of euthanasia. Appendix A provides a listing of resources, breed clubs, purebred registries, activity clubs, trainers, associations, publications, and books that will be helpful to you. Finally, Appendix B offers information about the official breed standard for the Poodle and is a must-read for anyone who appreciates the Poodle's beauty.

After finishing this book, you will undoubtedly understand why the Poodle is one of God's finest creations. Enjoy!

So, You Want a Poodle

> **In This Chapter**
> ○ What Makes a Poodle Special?
> ○ Keys to Your Poodle's Happiness
> ○ Where to Find the Perfect Poodle for You

There's no denying the impact a Poodle makes when he enters a room, strolls through a park, or passes by in a convertible, especially if he is freshly groomed. This breed is a showstopper. You can't help but stop, look, admire, and smile.

No wonder you're set on having a Poodle of your very own. But first, you owe it to this best of breeds, and yourself, to take time to understand the Poodle better. Do you know what makes a Poodle a Poodle? What does your Poodle need to be a happy camper? What should you never, never do to a Poodle? And where can you find a fabulous Poodle of your very own?

What Makes a Poodle Special?

You know the Poodle is a unique breed. But how did it come to be? As the story goes, wolf ancestors to the domestic breeds of dog we know today made contact with humans about 10,000 years ago. No one knows exactly how these wolf-dogs became domesticated, but it's likely that our human ancestors saw potential hunting partners, protectors, and companions in the wild canines that roamed around their campfires. Eventually they sought to capture and raise the puppies in captivity. From there the relationship between people and dogs began. In time, these wolf-dogs became domesticated, socialized, and were bred to fulfill specific functions, including guarding, herding, hunting, and toting. Of course, this didn't happen overnight but over thousands of years.

A Bit of History

From whence does the popular, intelligent, and gorgeous Poodle breed come? Though the Poodle's history is far-reaching, it's uncertain. Some breed historians believe today's Poodle is descended from a water retriever in Germany known as the *pudel* or *canis familiaris aquatius.* The English word *poodle* most likely derived from the German *pudel* or *pudelin,* which means to splash in the water. You've probably heard the term, "French Poodle." That moniker is derived from the Poodle's great popularity in France. Known in France as the *Caniche,* a name derived from the phrase, *chien canard* or duck dog, the Poodle gained national recognition as a hunting dog and later, a circus dog. A troupe of Poodles from France is said to have performed in London for King George III. The dogs jumped through hoops, skipped rope, tumbled, and pushed a wheelbarrow.

In sixteenth-century Europe, a dog known as the Rough-Haired Water Dog of England was popular with hunters because of its strength, water-resistant coat, and ability to swim. Some historians theorize that the modern Poodle is a direct descendent of the Water Dog of England. Another breed similar to the Poodle, the Irish Water Spaniel, is believed to be from similar lineage. The Standard Poodle is believed to be the oldest of the three varieties—Toy, Miniature, and Standard—and initially the most popular. As knowledge and interest in the breed grew, so did the number of Toys and Miniatures.

> Some breed historians believe today's Poodle is descended from a water retriever in Germany.

While it's difficult to map out a precise history of the breed, we do know that the Poodle's ancestors were hardworking water dogs, retrieving and accompanying their hunter-masters in the field, and were very good at what they did. Unfortunately, the Poodle's ability and heritage as a capable working dog isn't well known to the public. Many people today know the breed only as a companion.

Throughout the years, the Poodle has developed a reputation for its distinct coat and hairstyles. Early dogs had heavy, water-repellent coats that helped keep them warm while dashing in and out of water. But those dense coats proved impractical for working dogs going in and out of water all day. Once the thick coat was wet, it was difficult for the dog to move about. Hunters began trimming the dogs' coats short on the hindquarters, leaving it long on the chest and joints for warmth. The long hair on top of the head was also tied back with a brightly colored ribbon. This kept the hair out of the eyes and made the working dog more visible to the hunter.

Eventually, practicality turned into fashion. Utility cuts for the working Poodle developed into the ornamental styles we know today. Not surprisingly, the French took styling the Poodle's coat to extremes with poms, puffs, and fluffs. The Poodle-grooming business took off in nineteenth-century France, with Poodle barbers creating trims and clips on dogs that belonged to stylish Parisians.

> Not surprisingly, the French took styling the Poodle's coat to extremes with poms, puffs, and fluffs.

Also popular at that time was the corded Poodle (a modern term might be dreadlocks!). A corded coat is one that naturally rolls and twists into long ringlets; it isn't brushed. Each ringlet is left to grow until it reaches the ground. The cords were treated with oil, paraffin, and petroleum jelly to keep them in shape. Corded Poodles fell out of favor before World War I. However, it is an acceptable style to the American Kennel Club (AKC), and there is a hint of renewed interest in the corded-coat style.

Breed Standard

Describing the Poodle as an individual breed is best articulated by what's called a "breed standard." This specific standard is compared with what genetics determine—a dog's physical characteristics, such as height, weight, body type, color, or coat. Breed standards also spell out the breed's desired temperament, personality, and faults. Breed standards assigned by a kennel or dog club may vary slightly from nation to nation, and can change over time.

What's the American Kennel Club?

Founded in 1884, the American Kennel Club (AKC) is a non-profit organization dedicated to the protection and advancement of purebred dogs. Composed of over 500 dog clubs from across the nation, the AKC's objectives include maintaining a registry of purebred dogs, promoting responsible dog ownership, and sponsoring events, such as breed shows and field trials, that promote interest in and appreciation of the purebred dog.

To be eligible for AKC registration, a puppy must be the offspring of individually registered AKC parents, and the breeder must obtain the proper paperwork before the puppy's sale. Once registered, a dog is eligible to compete in AKC-sanctioned events and, if bred with another AKC-registered dog, to have his/her offspring registered.

The AKC approves an official breed standard for each of the 147 breeds currently eligible for registration. The standard is written and maintained by each individual breed club. An attempt to describe the "perfect" dog of each breed, the breed standard is the model responsible breeders use in their efforts to produce better dogs. Judges of AKC-sponsored events and competitions use the breed standards as the basis of their evaluations.

Because of the AKC's emphasis on excellence and high standards, it is a common misconception that "AKC registered" or "AKC registrable" is synonymous with quality. While a registration certificate identifies a dog and its progenitors as purebreds, it does not necessarily guarantee the health or quality of a dog. Some breeders breed for show quality, but others breed for profit, with little concern for breed standards. Thus, a potential buyer should not view AKC registration as an indication of a dog's quality.

In a nutshell, the breed standard paints a picture of what the ideal Poodle should look like and how it should act, making it distinct and special from other breeds. Only those dogs that most closely meet the standard (just as nobody's perfect, no dog is either!) receive championship status or are elected to be bred, at least in theory. The first American Kennel Club official standard for the Poodle was approved in 1901. It has seen many revisions over the years, with the current standard approved in 1990.

The very first AKC breed standard for the Poodle was similar to the standard for The Kennel Club (English), which was written in 1886. Three distinct varieties of the Poodle—Toy, Miniature, and Standard—existed then, but they were distinguished by weight rather than height as they are now. The following description summarizes the current breed standard, as set by the Poodle Club of America in 1990.

General Appearance

The Poodle is intelligent and elegant in appearance. Known for his alert expression, the Poodle is well proportioned and moves gracefully. The Poodle has what enthusiasts call "an air of distinction." Its poise and dignity are unique to this majestic breed.

Size

There are three sizes or varieties of Poodles: Standard, Miniature, and Toy. They are all the same breed. Toy Poodles are 10 inches tall or less at the shoulder, Miniatures are 15 inches or less, and Standards are 15 inches or taller.

These three are the only sizes recognized by the American Kennel Club, though prospective Poodle buyers may find "teacup" (very small Toys) or "royal" (very large Standards) Poodles as one of their choices. However, these are not AKC-accepted sizes.

Coat

No matter which size of Poodle you choose, the Poodle's curly coat is her crowning glory. White, black, brown, cream, blue, gray, and apricot are the colors accepted by the AKC. A well-bred Poodle's coat texture is one-of-a-kind: harsh, dense, and curly.

There are four AKC-accepted clips. Poodles under 12 months must be shown in a Puppy clip. Poodles 12 months or older in all regular classes must be shown in either the English Saddle or Continental clip. In the Stud Dog and Brood Bitch classes, and in a noncompetitive parade of champions, Poodles may wear the Sporting clip. Chapter 7 covers these in detail.

Personality

> Poodles are highly intelligent, good-natured, sensitive, and adaptable.

The Poodle's other greatest asset is his personality. Poodles are highly intelligent, good-natured, sensitive, and adaptable. Poodles are people lovers, and aim to please, generally following through on any request their owner may ask. Poodles are suited to show careers, field work, therapy dog work, or life as a pleasing companion. Being the adaptable animals they are, Poodles can live happily in a city apartment or take to life on the farm.

Mere Mortals

No Poodle is perfect, but what about Poodles who fail miserably to live up to the breed standard? Such dogs would not be good show or breeding candidates, but would be considered by

The Poodle and Bad Press

If the Poodle is your breed of choice, be prepared for some flak. Surprisingly, some people can't stand the breed, considering them good-for-nothing, spoiled, yappy, sissy dogs with big hair. According to these Poodle haters, anyone who has one is, well, of questionable character and competence.

Such negative perceptions of the Poodle aren't new. But they might take some getting used to for you, as a new Poodle owner. After all, you've just acquired a fabulous companion and certainly won't appreciate friends or family members snickering and joking about your Poodle, especially when you know how wrong they are about the breed.

Which begs this question: To what does the Poodle owe its negative, inaccurate stereotypes? One primary stumbling block is hair. Some people just can't get past the unusual and sometimes outrageous hairstyles, especially on show Poodles. Consider Susan Sloane's husband. Years ago, Sloane wanted a Poodle, while her husband was set on the Old English Sheepdog. "He was totally against me buying a Poodle," she says. "Nevertheless, I saved my own money and purchased Liza. After two weeks, he was astonished at her intelligence and was more than coming around to a Poodle way of thinking. But then the next objection came up. He would not walk any dog in that 'silly show cut.' Eventually, though, he began to see the beauty of the show trim," says Sloane. "He proudly strutted alongside Liza, bragging about his 'daughter' and was more than happy to explain to people why she was trimmed this way."

Ignorance is another reason the Poodle is plagued with image problems. The public doesn't really know and understand the breed. Poodle enthusiast

breeders as "pet quality." Such a Poodle is not to be bred or shown in conformation. Hardly a second-class citizen, though, a pet Poodle can make a fine companion for owners interested in owning and loving a wonderful pet.

Deb Johnson encountered this when chatting with a neighbor and co-worker. "I told her I was getting a Standard Poodle puppy," says Johnson, "and asked if I could use her as a person to help socialize him. She said, 'No offense, but I don't like Poodles.' I didn't push the issue. When she saw him, though, she liked him right off the bat. She didn't know Poodles came in a bigger size. She thought all Poodles were little dogs and she really just prefers bigger dogs."

Men in particular seem to have an aversion to the breed. Claudette Vatore experienced this phenomenon firsthand. "I'm a first-time dog owner so I needed to decide on a breed," she says. "High on my list were intelligence, liveliness, versatility, loyalty, bravery, and finally, a non-shedding coat. My search, surprisingly, ended with the Poodle. Here's a breed that comes in three sizes and a rainbow of coat colors. Really, there's a size and color of Poodle for every household in America! Nevertheless, my husband and sons did not want a Poodle. A silly, sissy, prissy dog—never!"

Vatore got her Poodle, a black Standard named Luc. Two years later, a black Standard named Kip joined the family. "It didn't take long for the men in my life to realize what makes the Poodle popular: intelligence, athletic ability, bravery, loyalty, strength, companionship, energy, affection, and heart."

The moral of the story? Don't be put off by Poodle putdowns. Just remember that in spite of some bad press, the Poodle is a very popular companion dog for good reason!

Is a Poodle Right for You?

"The Poodle is loving, loyal, extremely intelligent, mischievous, playful and a great companion while also being quite protective," says Poodle enthusiast Winona Schelat Kuhl, who lives with three Poodles: Puff, a Standard, and Frosty and Beau, who are both Miniatures.

Kuhl's description of a Poodle personality—intelligent, loving, loyal, mischievous—is common among those who know Poodles. Additionally, Poodles have something you can't quite put your finger on, something difficult to describe to those not familiar with the breed. It's what the official breed standard articulates as "an air of distinction and dignity peculiar to himself." No, the Poodle is not a snob. The breed is, however, sophisticated. "The correct Poodle temperament is outgoing but a bit haughty at times," says Poodle enthusiast Caroline Hair, "trainable, but not fawning, dignified with a clownish streak."

Though dignified, a well-bred Poodle is a "people" dog, thrilled to please her owner. She is docile, obedient, friendly, sensitive, steady, never shy or disagreeable. That's not to say a Poodle isn't a good watchdog. She can be protective and will bark at strangers in her home until taught or directed otherwise. On one occasion, Kuhl's Standard Poodle, Puff, did more than that. Kuhl's now-deceased husband was very ill at the time, but still living at home. Health-care workers—a visiting nurse, aides, physical therapist, and an oxygen-delivery person—were coming in and out of the house every day. "As each new person began duties in our home," says Kuhl, "I introduced them to Puff individually and explained to her, 'This is a friend who will be coming to help take care of Daddy.' After that, they would just open the door without knocking and call out who they were so I wouldn't have to go to admit them. Puff readily allowed this.

> Though dignified, a well-bred Poodle is a "people" dog, thrilled to please her owner.

"However, one day after the nurse and aide left and the van had picked up Al to take him to dialysis, I saw the oxygen man backing up his truck. I hit the button to open the garage door and went about my chores. When I suddenly heard yelling, growling, and a ruckus, I ran to the door where I found Puff standing guard. As I took her by the collar and opened the door, the oxygen man said, 'Your dog tried to bite me. My instructions say to just walk in.'"

But it was not the usual oxygen-delivery person. Puff did her job as watch-Poodle by keeping the "stranger" at bay. Kuhl introduced the new driver to Puff, and from that day on he was able to walk into the house without incident.

An outstanding trait of the Poodle personality is how smart, seemingly human-like, these dogs are. "Sometimes they are so clever, they almost can read your mind," says Poodle owner Michelle Mace.

Lisa Haidle, owner of the first Toy Poodle to earn a Versatility In Poodles (VIP) certificate, agrees, but adds a warning: "Smart dogs can be difficult to live with. They learn things, good and bad, in one try, and they remember everything!"

Poodle enthusiast Irma Shanahan shares a story about a Miniature Poodle that typifies the intelligence and determination of the breed. "When we first brought Cassidy home at eight weeks," says Shanahan, "we did not yet have a crate for her. So the first night we penned her in the sunroom of our one-story

Did You Know?

The United States and France have the highest rates of dog ownership in the world (for countries in which such statistics are available), with almost one dog for every three families. Germany and Switzerland have the lowest rates, with just one dog for every ten families.

house and retreated to the bedrooms to sleep. Of course, we got very little sleep. She cried and carried on all night. The second night she started to cry and whine, but other noises were coming from the sunroom as well. Finally silence, followed by a loud bang.

"I sat up in bed and saw, silhouetted by a night light, this eight-week-old puppy trotting down the hall! She had pulled herself up into a wing chair, walked across a candlestick stand, then launched herself over the three-foot table we'd put across the doorway as a barrier. The bang was the table hitting the floor. Needless to say, from that point on she slept in our bedroom and still does."

The flip side of the Poodle's sophistication and intellect is his love for play, what many familiar with the breed describe as having a sense of humor or being a clown. Consider the story of Pogo, a Standard owned by Grace Blair, M.D., co-founder of Versatility In Poodles, a non-profit organization dedicated to improving the Poodle's health. Dr. Blair routinely plays a hide-the-toys game with her Standard Poodles. She asks the dogs to sit, goes to the toy box, and pulls out a toy. Then she walks around the house pretending to hide the toy here or there, and eventually does hide it. Then she walks back to the dogs and says, "Okay, go find it," and the dogs gallop off looking for the hidden toy. One day a few years ago, Pogo, a black Standard, decided he was in the mood for play.

Says Dr. Blair, "This shows you how they think, and how they can put two and two together and play jokes on you. I was showing my five dogs at a dog show match, two in obedience and three in conformation. I was by myself, it was a horribly hot day, and I felt like a one-armed paper hanger.

> The flip side of the Poodle's sophistication and intellect is his love for play, what many familiar with the breed describe as having a sense of humor or being a clown.

"At the end of the day, I put all the dogs back in the motor home, turned on the air-conditioner, opened the outside compartments, and put the key ring holding the engine and the outside compartment keys in the sink so I could just reach in and get the key rather than lose it on the lawn.

"Once I finally got everything hauled back from the show site and stored, I went into the motor home, ready to head home. All the dogs except Pogo were in their crates, but there was no key in my sink, and I had no other keys with me. This was Sunday evening and I was the last person at the fairgrounds; this was during the days before cell phones. I was horribly hot, totally exhausted, and had a two-hour drive ahead.

"So, I started looking for my keys—between the dog crates, between the cushions on the sofa, under the chairs. I looked every place I could possibly think of. Pogo was bouncing around with this sparkle in his eye while I was near the point of sitting down and crying. I said, 'I can't find my keys. Pogo, where did you put my keys?'"

"He looked at me and cocked his head like, 'Well, you can't find your toys? I always find mine!' And he went bouncing back into the bedroom, put his head under my pillow, pulled out my keys, and brought them to me. He was playing the same hide-the-toys game I play with the dogs!"

Keeping one step ahead of the keen, witty, curious, and creative Poodle isn't always easy as Mace, who owns a 15-month-old Standard Poodle, can attest. "It was a little past dinnertime," she says, "and Jo-Jo had not yet been fed. Relying on her own skill and resolve, she decided to go hunting. There was a duck floating gently on the surface of the water, ducking and bobbing every so often, feigning ignorance of the presence of Jo-Jo watching ever so intently. The mighty brown hunter inched ever closer to the edge of the water, waiting for the right moment . . . closer . . . closer . . . *kersplash!*

"Jo-Jo grabbed the duck with strong white teeth and bit down hard, causing the duck to emit a high-pitched squeal. This excited Jo-Jo even more and she bit down again and again. All the commotion brought the three other Standard Poodles and one Toy Poodle in residence running to see what all the fuss was about. Fearing her prize might be stolen, Jo-Jo grabbed the duck and ran for the safety of her private den. With the frenzied pack in hot pursuit, the soaking-wet, suds-covered duck-stealer burst into my bedroom and made a beeline for my desk, where I sat catching up on e-mail in the 'relative' quiet of the evening.

> The Poodle's biddable nature is fairly consistent throughout the breed.

"Meanwhile, I heard my five-year-old daughter crying from the bathroom, 'Mommeee! Jo-Jo got in the bathtub again.'"

The Poodle's biddable nature is fairly consistent throughout the breed, though some dogs are less good-natured or more high-strung due to poor breeding, abuse or neglect, or lack of socialization and training. The personality of each individual Poodle, the likes and dislikes that distinguish him from others, varies. Some Poodles are active, some are more laid-back. "Over the 35 years we have had Miniature Poodles, their personalities have ranged from quiet, low-key Poodles to hyperactive balls of energy," says Shanahan. The bottom line on the Poodle temperament? According to Poodle enthusiast and groomer Tracey Kaul, "The Poodle personality is generally loving, and is striving to please. They have wonderful temperaments, are usually good with just about anything, and are wonderful dogs to be around in general."

Life Expectancy

The breed's life expectancy is always too short, according to Poodle enthusiasts. But how long you can expect your Poodle to live depends on the variety. Standards live 10 to 14 years on average, and Miniatures or Toys average 12 years to late teens. Of course, life span varies, depending on genetic makeup, health care, nutrition, and maintaining proper weight.

Keys to Your Poodle's Happiness

Do you know what it takes to make your Poodle a happy camper? You might be surprised. It's you!

To be truly happy, Poodles need people. You could say that a Poodle's primary "happiness requirement" is to be loved and wanted by a human. "They want nothing more than to please their owners and be with them as much as possible," says Mace.

It's quite simple. What's best for a Poodle, what will make her heart sing, is a loving, attentive owner who can lavish her with attention and include her in daily activities.

Daily activities are a biggie for your Poodle. She wants to be with her owner constantly, so much that she will usually follow you around the house. "All of my Poodles," says owner Belinda Hankins, "especially the Standards, follow every move I make in this house—from the living room to the kitchen, from kitchen to bedroom, from bedroom to bathroom, even in the middle of the night when everyone is comfortably sleeping. They even give me disgruntled looks and groans of disapproval that I'm 'making' them get up! I can't tell you how many times I've groggily stepped out of the shower right into a tangled pile of Poodle flesh that's huddled against the tub, nearly killing myself!"

Snip-Snip, Clip-Clip

If you're serious about acquiring a Poodle, then you must know regular grooming is a *must* to keep the coat in good condition. Poodles are high-maintenance dogs. Owners must be willing to pay $25 to $100 for grooming every four to eight weeks, or be handy enough to do the bathing, brushing, clipping, and trimming themselves. Otherwise, you are sure to have a matted, dirty, depressed Poodle on your hands.

"Poodles need grooming," says Kaul. "Neglect in this area will surely make your Poodle very unhappy. If her coat is not taken care of and is allowed to get matted, the dog will reflect that she knows how she looks and feels."

What About Lifestyle, Space, and Exercise?

What lifestyle is best for a Poodle? How much space and exercise is required for this breed? According to Poodle enthusiasts, the breed is extremely adaptable. Poodles can live happily in almost any circumstance, as long as they are living with a beloved owner. The environment is less important than the person. As long as the Poodle has you, she will adjust to your lifestyle.

"Poodles thrive in homes ranging from RVs to one-bedroom apartments to mansions," says Linda Smith, owner of a black Standard named Rally. "The loved Poodle can thrive in a one-person family, a group home, or anything in-between."

Kaul agrees: "Poodles adapt very easily to any lifestyle, whether it's an apartment with daily walks or a

What Will It Be—Puppy or Adult?

Do you want a puppy Poodle or an adult Poodle? They're all so cute! But depending on your lifestyle, one might be a better choice than the other.

Let's face it. Pups are adorable, especially Poodle pups. Have you ever seen such a face? But the flip side of the cuteness factor is puppies are a lot of work. It takes time to teach a puppy the ropes—housetraining, manners, socializing. If you're home a lot—maybe you work from a home office or you're a stay-at-home parent—a puppy could be a good bet. Of course, you also have to be willing to put in time, and not just a few weeks. We're talking years. Poodles are extremely intelligent, but certainly need to be trained.

Why not consider adopting an older Poodle? There are plenty of rescue organizations who can place a wonderful Poodle in your home. With an older, adult dog, you're past housetraining, crying, jumping (maybe), and chewing.

Don't rule out a puppy or an adult dog. Figure out which might best suit your lifestyle. Then decide.

ranch with 20 acres to play on. Poodles can be couch potatoes, content to watch TV with their masters, or they can race around a horse pasture chasing barn cats. It all depends on what a Poodle gets used to."

What about the size differences? Space requirements do vary somewhat among the Toy, Miniature, and Standard sizes. Although Toys and Minis obviously need less space and exercise than Standards, Poodle enthusiasts say that Standards can get by with less exercise than other breeds of similar size. Of course, all Poodles will be healthier and happier with plenty of exercise.

"Standards, originally bred as a hunting dog, are fairly active and love a good romp in open spaces; yet they are equally happy in an urban setting as long as they receive proper daily exercise," says Mace. "Toys and Minis are equally at home in rural or urban settings, with daily walks adequate for their size and activity levels. Poodles are a wonderfully versatile and adaptable breed, with a size to suit every lifestyle. As long as you give your Poodle enough love, training, and exercise, your dog will adapt to most any lifestyle you can provide."

However, space is less important than is getting a moderate amount of daily exercise. "The advantage of the breed's three different sizes gives everyone, from apartment dwellers to country homeowners, a chance to have all the qualities a Poodle offers in a size that fits their surroundings," says Shanahan. "I know of many Standards living in homes smaller than the one our three Minis dominate, who are just as happy and healthy. This is more a result of the 'people interaction factor' than of the size of the dog or the space it occupies," says Shanahan.

Don't Forget Basic Training

A Poodle's keen wit makes it a good student. But like all bright students, if not taught to direct her energies in a *positive* fashion, she will direct them elsewhere, usually into something mischievous. "Just as you train children the lines of acceptable behavior, you must also train a Poodle or any other breed," says Kuhl. "The difference is the Poodle learns readily. Left to their own devices, I imagine they would be holy terrors, just like any other spoiled brat you might encounter, human or otherwise."

At the very least, a Poodle should know the five basic obedience commands: heel, sit, down, stay, and come. A Poodle that obeys these commands is a trustworthy, livable, happy companion—and will probably stay out of trouble! Additionally, advanced and ongoing training is a good idea, too, because it gives this bright dog challenges to keep it busy mentally and physically. "Because they are so smart, Poodles do well in obedience class," says Smith. "All dogs should complete puppy obedience and basic obedience. This helps a Poodle know the rules and deepens the bond between Poodle and owner. Children should take turns training the dog, too. Poodles love their children so much that they and their children benefit from learning what to expect from each other and how to have fun." See Chapter 6 for an in-depth look at training your Poodle.

Surefire Ways to Make Your Poodle Miserable

Here are a few surefire ways to make a Poodle miserable, offered not to encourage, but to discourage such treatment.

Solitary Confinement If you really want to make a Poodle miserable, isolate it from daily human contact. As you just learned, the Poodle's primary "happiness requirement" is to be loved and wanted by a human. "As for happiness and misery," says Irma Shanahan, "they are different sides of the same coin. I tell people who ask about getting a Poodle that they better be prepared to pay quality attention to their dog in some form or another."

A Poodle separated from his owner is a sad Poodle indeed. "When I leave my Poodle for long periods of time, he is anxious at first," says Poodle enthusiast Tracy Raby, "then he suffers through a bout of depression." Even minor separations, such as putting your Poodle in the bedroom for the evening while

Did You Know?

The Saluki, a hunting dog raised by ancient Egyptians, is the oldest known breed.

you're hosting a dinner party, is downright upsetting. Your Poodle will want and need to be part of the event—and is usually the life of the party!

Bad Hair Day   Never let your Poodle's coat go to the dogs. If you do, your Poodle is sure to be depressed, even physically uncomfortable. Regular grooming is essential!

Harsh Words   The highly intelligent Poodle is very sensitive and willing to please. Kind words and a soft voice work best with this breed. Harsh or tough corrections are not necessary—and not recommended. "Poodles are easily corrected when training," says Kaul, "and usually don't need harsh correction, which will make them unhappy. My Poodles shake if I raise my voice at them."

School's Out   You have just read about the benefits of training your Poodle. But do you realize how miserable a Poodle is if you don't train her? Socialize, train, and keep your Poodle busy with fun activities. No matter how wondrous the breed, all dogs need proper socialization and training. If you neglect this, you are sure to have a Poodle you can't live with.

Where to Find the Perfect Poodle for You

"The perfect Poodle is the one that you love," says Mace. "Whether your Poodle comes from champion bloodlines or the local shelter, when dog and owner love each other, it is a perfect match."

But how do you find that perfect Poodle for you and your family? It mostly depends on what you intend to do with a Poodle. For example, if you're planning to enter

What to Ask a Breeder

○ What are common health problems found in Poodles?

○ Are your dogs routinely screened for heritable diseases?

○ What health certifications can you show me for parents and grandparents?

○ What are the most positive and negative characteristics of the breed?

○ What kind of temperament should I expect from a Poodle?

○ How long have you been breeding dogs?

○ Can you name five other breeders in this breed you'd recommend?

○ What do you expect of potential puppy owners?

○ What type of guarantee do you provide?

○ Will you take back this puppy at any age, for any reason?

○ Do you require limited registration and/or spay/neuter contracts on pet-quality puppies?

the breed show ring, contact a reputable, experienced Poodle breeder. Finding the "right" Poodle is not difficult if you have good information. Read the following carefully and you're on your way toward finding a match made in Poodle heaven!

Reputable Breeder

The Poodle lover's number one source for locating the pup of his or her dreams is a reputable breeder—one who knows, understands, and loves the breed. This person breeds with a specific purpose and plan—to improve the line, eliminate a fault, create a champion—not just to produce more pups.

Any breeder can claim to be reputable, but his or her actions are positive proof. For example, reputable breeders are very particular to whom they sell pups. Not just anyone who wants a puppy will get one. If you're dealing with a reputable breeder, chances are you'll have to pass *her* inspection before you take a pup home. Expect to be grilled!

You'll also know that a breeder has integrity if she requires that "pet-quality" animals (dogs who don't meet show standards but make perfectly wonderful pets) be spayed or neutered, and requires a contract. Contracts vary from breeder to breeder, but usually spell out the rights of seller and buyer, health information, altering, and buy-back/return policy. Another good sign of a reputable breeder is that she shows genuine love for and knowledge about the breed, and is actively involved in the breed fancy—clubs, competitions, or rescue groups. Additionally, you will find the kennel or home environment sparkling clean and well maintained.

> Like animal shelters and humane societies, rescue groups are nonprofit agencies, dependent upon donations to care for animals.

A reputable Poodle breeder is willing to answer questions, even about the breed's genetic faults. She is willing to provide names of others who have purchased pups, and will allow you to meet your puppy's parents if they're available and, if they're not available, will be willing to show you pictures.

Poodle Rescue Groups

"While it is always best to find a reputable breeder committed to improving the breed, educating new owners about everything Poodle, many wonderful Poodles can be obtained from a rescue organization or shelters," says Mace.

Poodle rescue groups are another great way to find your Poodle, and you can find many throughout the United States. Many clubs, including the Poodle Club of America, have ongoing rescue efforts. Like animal shelters and humane societies, rescue groups are non-profit agencies, dependent upon donations to care for animals. Most do not have funds to operate a shelter and rely on foster-care volunteers to house and care for puppies and dogs until they are matched with a good home. Poodle rescue volunteers are an extremely devoted bunch, often paying for the dogs' care out of their own pockets, and know a lot about the individual pups and dogs they foster.

Animal Shelters

Humane societies are a good place to find assorted pups and dogs, but seldom offer purebred Poodles. Breed rescue organizations frequently monitor incoming dogs at shelters and pick up purebreds for placement through individual breed rescue. Shelters sometimes do have purebreds with all types of backgrounds and temperaments available for adoption.

The wonderful part of adopting a Poodle from a shelter is you'll be giving a Poodle a chance at life. But keep in mind that you might learn less about a shelter Poodle than you would about a breed rescue Poodle who has lived with families in a home environment. Volunteer foster families are able to observe the dog closely to see how it interacts with kids, cats, and other dogs. Dogs in animal shelters typically live in kennels and, because of the number of incoming and outgoing animals, cannot be observed as closely. Also, though most shelters are extremely careful to adopt only healthy animals, there's a chance you'd be taking home an ill Poodle.

Newspaper Ads

Whatever the town, whatever the newspaper, you will always find classified ads that read something like, "Adorable Poodle Pups for Sale." Do such ads provide a good source for finding a Poodle? Most Poodle enthusiasts and reputable breeders say no. In most cases, these are advertisements from "backyard breeders." Although some reputable breeders do advertise in this manner, it's not common.

What's a backyard breeder and why should you avoid one? Basically, a backyard breeder is someone who owns a Poodle and decides that breeding her dog with the neighbor's Poodle would be a great idea. The result will be a fabulous litter of pups that could be registered and they will both make money! Any dog can be registered by a breed registry, but that doesn't mean the dog is of sound mind and temperament. There's little consideration for conformation, health, or temperament in backyard breeding.

> Any dog can be registered by a breed registry, but that doesn't mean the dog is of sound mind and temperament.

Reputable breeders rarely advertise in local newspapers—they don't have to. They usually sell pups by word of mouth, and pups often have homes well before they're born.

The best advice about buying a Poodle through newspaper ads is this: *Buyer Beware.* If you're set on buying a newspaper-ad Poodle, investigate the background of the advertiser and be prepared to ask a lot of questions about the pup's medical history. Find out what hereditary diseases are common in Poodles (see Chapter 5) and insist on seeing proof of health clearances.

What about ads for Poodles in dog or Poodle magazines? Serious, reputable breeders are more likely to advertise pups in well-respected magazines, but anyone, reputable or not, can buy an ad. In fact, many magazines have disclaimers, advising potential buyers to investigate puppy advertisers. Approach sellers in magazines the same way you approach newspaper advertisers—skeptically—and be sure to investigate the source.

Pet Stores

There's seldom a shortage of Poodle puppies at pet stores. But are pet stores a *good* place to acquire a Poodle? No, say most reputable breeders, rescue volunteers, and humane society workers. In fact, the American Humane Society is absolutely opposed to anyone purchasing pups at pet stores.

Why? Because reputable breeders don't wholesale pups to pet stores; puppy mills do. Puppy mills are large breeding operations that produce numerous breeds in volume with little regard for health, temperament, or conformation. While puppy mills are not illegal, many dog lovers consider them immoral. Puppy-mill pups are frequently ill, unsocialized, and poor examples of a breed. "Poodles are widely abused and misused by mass breeders," says Lisa Haidle.

Pet store buyers often purchase pets on impulse. They walk into a pet store, see an adorable puppy, and buy it with little thought. Impulse buying and pups are not a good combination. Too often, the owner deeply regrets the purchase later and ends up dumping the dog at a shelter.

If you absolutely must buy from a pet store, some states have laws to protect you from the inevitable. Called puppy "lemon laws" (modeled after laws enacted to give car buyers a way to get a refund), these laws give owners recourse if a pet-store animal proves ill or unsound (which is the case of many puppy-mill pups). Laws vary state to state, but usually cover illness or disease that exists at or before the time of sale. Buyers have a limited time to have the animal checked by a veterinarian, usually 7 to 15 days after the sale. State warranties for congenital or hereditary conditions vary from 10 days to one year. And state statutes may require sellers to disclose to buyers the history of the animal, including medical, parentage, and location of breeding.

Several U.S. pet superstores have teamed up with local shelters to offer pets for adoption.

On a positive, progressive note (and perhaps to get away from a well-earned negative image in the industry), several U.S. pet superstores have teamed up with local shelters to offer pets for adoption. Instead of selling puppy-mill pups, stores offer healthy dogs and cats, puppies and kittens, for adoption. Do some research and be sure you are acquiring a dog from one of these more reliable sources.

Giveaways

What if your co-worker tells you she has a dog—a Poodle!—that she wants to give away? Should you immediately say "I'll take it!"?

The American Humane Association recommends that potential owners be wary of "hand-me-down" pets. There's usually a reason someone wants to rid themselves of a dog, and it's usually not a good reason. The dog may be sick, ill-tempered, or an incessant chewer. Be careful that someone else's problem isn't pawned off on you. Of course, there's a chance, however slight, that this dog might be a good companion once given a loving home, training, and veterinary care, and occasionally there are great pets that need to find a home. However, in such situations, proceed with extreme caution. It's risky, but some people are lucky gamblers.

Internet

Countless animal-related organizations, agencies, breeders, individuals, and shelters have made the leap into cyberspace. That includes those wishing to sell puppies and dogs. If you choose to shop the Internet for Poodles, use the same caution you'd use with newspaper advertisers. Check references. Ask questions. Stick with well-known Poodle clubs. And if at all possible, visit the breeder. Puppy mills do business on the Internet, too.

Puppy or Adult? Male or Female?

Do you want a Poodle puppy or adult? Male or female? Depending upon your lifestyle, one might be a better choice than the other.

Pups are certainly adorable, but they are a lot of work. Repeat: They are a lot of work! It will take time and effort to teach your puppy the ropes: housetraining, manners, grooming, and socializing. If you're home a lot—perhaps you work from a home office or you are a stay-at-home parent—a puppy could be a good bet since you may be able to supervise and acclimate your new friend better. As well, puppies almost invariably are a bit more playful, and you can develop his personality to your liking. Remember, too, that the first year of a dog's life is an expensive one! However, if you're not up to the tireless effort puppyhood requires, consider adopting an adult Poodle. You can find many available at rescue organizations and sometimes at animal shelters. With an adult dog, you're past housetraining, crying, jumping, and chewing—hopefully. Adult Poodles also come with a developed personality, which can be wonderful.

When it comes to the choice between a male or female Poodle, you'll encounter proponents of each sex. Some believe female Poodles bond more closely to men and vice versa. In general, enthusiasts say a female Poodle has the attitude of "what can you do for me?" while the male Poodle has the attitude of "what can I do for you?"

Small, Medium, or Large?

The Poodle is a one-breed-fits-all in terms of size. What's so cool about the Poodle is that there's a size to fit anyone or any household!

The Toy variety is popular among individuals with limited space. Though small in size, the Toy is hardy in stature and has all the heart and spirit of a big dog. Toys can be trained to do just about anything except play the retrieving game. Because of its small size, Toys are sometimes overly spoiled and babied by their owners. Like all dogs, Toys need training and proper socialization.

> What's so cool about the Poodle is that there's a size to fit anyone or any household!

Because of its tiny size, the Toy may not be a good choice for a family with young children. Larger Poodles are better able to handle the normal roughhousing that goes along with kids. If properly supervised, though, a Toy can fit nicely into a family home.

The Miniature Poodle, larger and sturdier than the Toy but not a big dog, is also popular among individuals with limited space, and travels well, too.

For those who love big dogs and Poodles, the Standard variety is an excellent choice. Exercise and activity requirements are greater than for smaller varieties, but a 100-acre ranch is not a necessity. A Standard can live comfortably in the city with daily romps in the park.

Maintenance costs go up with each variety, Toy, Miniature, or Standard. Obviously, it costs more to feed and groom a Standard than it does to groom a Toy or Mini.

Pick of the Litter

It's difficult to choose the right pup from a litter. There are no hard-and-fast rules established by dog experts. Every Poodle puppy is different, and you won't find one perfect pup in any litter. They all have potential; they just need the right owners to bring out their best. Additionally, every breeder, behaviorist, and veterinarian will tell you something different about how to pick a pup. And, in many cases, reputable breeders do not allow you to choose your own puppy. They make the choice for you, based on what they know about their pups and what they learn about you.

Generally, though, if you ask yourself these questions, you can learn enough about what you want in a Poodle to share with a knowledgeable breeder or adoption counselor who can help you make a pick.

○ *What do you want to do with your Poodle?* Do you primarily want a companion or are you planning to compete in hunt tests or conformation shows? Do you want to try obedience or agility? What exactly do you have in mind?

○ *What type of lifestyle do you have?* Are you home a lot or do you travel frequently? Are you active or do you enjoy sipping tea in the shade? Or do you need to consider how your Poodle will travel with you? How and where does a Poodle fit in your life?

○ *What is your temperament?* Are you strong-willed or laid-back?

Armed with the answers to these questions, visit with several Poodle breeders and adoption counselors. Share the information with the breeder, and ask for her help in choosing an appropriate pup. After all, the breeder knows best when it comes to her pups. If you're fairly laid-back, for example, and wish only for a companion, a sharp breeder will know whether she has an equally laid-back dog to match your needs.

Puppy Tests

Dog breeders and behaviorists may use what's called "puppy tests" or "temperament tests" to predict what a puppy will act like when it grows up. Technically, temperament testing assesses puppies for motor ability, sensory and emotional states, sociability, problem-solving ability, interaction with other dogs, and interaction with people. Puppies are tested at specific ages for their responses to stimuli or situations; they are then assessed as having temperaments such as outgoing, aggressive, passive or timid, dominant or dependent. Unfortunately, there is no consensus among dog breeders, trainers, behaviorists, or veterinarians regarding what temperament testing is or should be, whether or not it's accurate and useful, and who should test the pups (the breeder or prospective buyer?). There is no standard test, and there isn't even a standard name for testing. Besides temperament testing, it's also called puppy testing, puppy evaluation testing, or puppy aptitude testing—which can make the task of deciphering terms and meanings breeders and other canine professionals use difficult for prospective puppy buyers. However, you can determine some characteristics through puppy tests, such as:

○ Level of dominance
○ Whether the pup is receptive to training
○ Whether the pup will retrieve
○ Whether the pup is outgoing or introverted
○ Whether the pup is people oriented or antisocial

The Healthy Poodle

For the most part, determining whether a Poodle puppy is healthy is much easier than trying to predict her temperament and personality. When you visit a breeder, look for these signs of good health in his puppies:

○ Proper weight; not too chubby or thin
○ Clean, odor-free, and kept in clean surroundings
○ Clear eyes and nose
○ Clean, odor-free ears
○ Full hair coat, with no balding patches
○ Friendly, happy, playful appearance

Not all conditions can be determined by a visual exam. Be aware of inheritable diseases (more on this in Chapter 5) such as hip dysplasia, genetic eye disease, von Willebrand's disease, thyroid malfunction, epilepsy, sebaceous adenitis, Addison's disease, juvenile renal disease and patellar luxation that affect the breed. Routine screening for these conditions is the best assurance (there are no guarantees) that you'll acquire a healthy Poodle.

After All This, What If?

It won't happen. Or if it does, it's a one-in-a-million chance. You've acquired your Poodle after researching the breed, but after living with the dog for a while, you realize the Poodle is not the dog you wanted. Don't panic. And don't immediately assume that getting rid of the Poodle is the solution to your problem.

> Like diamonds, the best dogs may lie hidden under a rough exterior, waiting for a little help and guidance to shine.

Realize that disappointment can happen no matter what breed you bring home. It's rare that anyone immediately has the "perfect" canine companion. Like diamonds, the best dogs may lie hidden under a rough exterior, waiting for a little help and guidance to shine. Good companions are partly created; they're the result of your efforts. If you put some time and energy into your puppy or dog, chances are you will gain a suitable companion.

It is likely that you might not have exactly what you wanted. (Who does have everything they want all the time?) For example, perhaps your Poodle is acting "naughty," chewing things she shouldn't. Rather than dump the dog at a shelter, seek guidance from a professional trainer. Make a list of behaviors you dislike in the dog that you can take to someone who can help you work through them. The solution to the problem requires your willingness to work on any problems, not getting rid of the Poodle.

Welcome Home!

2

In This Chapter

○ Preparing for Your Poodle's Arrival
○ Poodle-Proofing Your House
○ Which Supplies Do You Really Need?
○ Homecoming Day for Your Poodle

Ready, set, bring that Poodle home! You've done your research, searched high and low for the perfect Poodle for you, and it's time to throw a welcome home party for the newcomer. Right?

Not so fast. Before you race off, some important prep work has to be done. Bringing home a Poodle puppy or adult is similar to bringing home a newborn baby. You have to get ready so you can be ready! There are supplies to buy, arrangements to make, details to consider. You're not the planner type? That's okay, but you must know that planning will make life easier for all involved—you, the Poodle, the family. It's less stressful if you're prepared; promise!

Here's how to plan for your Poodle's homecoming—and his first days in his new home.

Preparing for Your Poodle's Arrival

Have you given any thought as to what decisions your family must make before bringing your Poodle home? If not, please do. These decisions are the cornerstone of homecoming plans for your Poodle.

Can really you afford a dog?   Let's face it. It takes money to own and care for a pet. And, the purchase or adoption price of a Poodle puppy or adult is nothing compared to the ongoing costs of owning a pet. You must also consider grooming (lots of grooming!), veterinary fees, equipment and supplies, training costs, and food. If you don't have enough money in your budget for all of these necessities, you won't be able to properly care for your Poodle.

So before you purchase or adopt a Poodle, review your budget. Be honest with yourself. Do you have a good handle on how much you make and spend? Do you pay bills on time and put a little away each month for emergencies? Or are you barely able to pay minimum payments on your high-balance credit cards? If you're struggling to keep your head above financial water, then it's best to delay acquiring a pet until you're on stable ground.

While you may really want a Poodle, you must realize Poodle care isn't cheap. For example, feeding a dog can cost $115 to $400 a year, according to the Humane Society of the United States, and training classes can cost $50 to $120 for eight sessions. Grooming can cost $600 to $1,200 a year.

Take a realistic look at your budget. Then evaluate whether you can afford a dog. If you don't have the funds right now, don't despair. Start a Poodle savings fund. You may have to wait to bring home a Poodle, but it's worth the wait!

Are you prepared to give a Poodle your undivided attention? As you learned in Chapter 1, the Poodle is a breed that needs and relies upon human companionship. Do you have time in your life to give to your new Poodle puppy or dog? If you're rarely home, you should probably give up the idea of a Poodle. Consider a few goldfish instead. A Poodle requires some undivided attention and needs to follow you room to room in the house. Be honest with yourself. Perhaps you love the breed, but don't think you can provide a Poodle with the attention, training, and care he needs. If that's the case, you'll both be miserable. Preventing such difficulties is quite simple. Take inventory of your life. Do you really want to make time for a Poodle? If you work, can you drive home at lunch to take your dog out? How about training classes every Saturday morning and grooming every few weeks? You get the picture. It's all about time. Will you make time for the Poodle in your life?

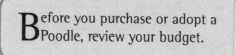

Before you purchase or adopt a Poodle, review your budget.

Who will groom your Poodle? You might learn to groom your Poodle at home. It isn't easy, but many dedicated Poodle enthusiasts do just that. Otherwise, you will need to hire a professional groomer to snip, clip, and clean your Poodle on a regular basis. Word of mouth is the best way to find a reputable groomer, so ask the breeder or another Poodle owner for the name of a groomer or salon. Poodles take grooming very seriously, so you must choose this person carefully to make the experience pleasant for your Poodle.

Who will train your Poodle?   Training is a must for all companion dogs, and the Poodle is no exception. Before you bring home a Poodle, decide how you're going to go about schooling the dog, which means learning about training techniques, interviewing trainers, signing up for classes, and how you will help your dog with his "homework." In other words, you must do your homework, first.

> Training is a must for all companion dogs, and the Poodle is no exception.

What veterinarian/clinic are you planning on using?   Regular veterinary care by a skilled practitioner is essential to your Poodle's good health. A puppy will need frequent checkups, dewormings, immunizations, and spaying or neutering unless you've purchased a breeding prospect. Adult dogs need regular checkups once or twice a year, immunization boosters, and/or treatment for various ailments. Geriatric Poodles require more frequent checks, boosters, and possibly additional medical attention if suffering from a chronic condition such as arthritis. Regardless of age, the Poodle needs regular veterinary care. Who will provide that for your dog?

Are you prepared to honor your breeder's contract?   Reputable breeders provide buyers with a contract, as do some Poodle rescue organizations. While they vary, contracts usually spell out items such as spaying or neutering requirements, the return policy, health certifications, and any guarantees. Be sure to read any contract you sign carefully, and be willing to abide by it. For example, some breeders require that if for some reason you decide to give up the Poodle, you must contact the breeder first. He or she will usually take back the dog rather than risk the dog going to a bad home. Others require that "pet-quality" Poodles (those the breeder decides are not of breeding quality) be spayed or neutered. You must be willing to honor that.

Carefully read any contract you sign, and understand that reputable breeders ask buyers to sign in order to protect the Poodle, not to stick buyers with unreasonable demands. If you're working with an experienced, trustworthy breeder, rest assured that her number one concern is what's best for the Poodle.

Poodle-Proofing Your House

Nope, you're not ready to bring home your Poodle yet. But now that you've made these important decisions, you're closer. Your next tasks are setting boundaries, preparing the house, and preparing the yard.

Setting Boundaries and House Rules

Your next step is deciding on boundaries. Boundary-setting is a popular topic in the human psychology world today—there are entire books on the subject. It's not surprising that people have a difficult time understanding and setting boundaries with their pets as well. The primary problem is that when behavioral and physical boundaries aren't set, the owner-pet relationship sours, usually very quickly. You can avoid this, and it's really quite simple. Just as you set limits for children (no playing in the street because it's dangerous, for example), you must set limits for the Poodle in your life, for your own good as well as his. Those limits might include:

○ No sleeping on people beds
○ Free running only in the fenced backyard
○ No jumping up on furniture
○ Wear a seatbelt in the car or ride in a crate
○ No begging at the dinner table
○ Chew only doggie toys, not the kids' toys

Obviously, this list could go on and on, but you get the point. You must think through behavioral and physical boundaries before bringing home your Poodle. What are your house rules? Decide what is acceptable and what isn't, keeping your Poodle's safety and health (and your sanity!) in mind.

Some house rules are inflexible and must be enforced for the safety and well-being of the Poodle. No running free in the neighborhood, for example. Other rules depend more on the individual. One Poodle owner allows her Mini to sleep with her, while another prefers placing a doggie bed at the foot of the people bed. When it comes to house rules, the Poodle is a quick learner. Your job is simply to decide what your rules are, teach the Poodle what's expected, and be consistent in enforcing established boundaries. Advises Michelle Mace, "Most Poodles prefer the comfort of your couch or favorite armchair for lounging, so decide from the start whether or not your Poodle will be allowed on the furniture, and be consistent!"

> When behavioral and physical boundaries aren't set, the owner-pet relationship sours, usually very quickly.

What Do You Mean It's My Turn?

Divvying Up Dog-Care Responsibilities

Often, parents buy a dog "for the kids" and end up taking on all the responsibilities of caring for the pet themselves. Even couples have been known to purchase a puppy with the understanding that they'll share dog-care duties, only to find one spouse doing the majority of the work once the pup arrives. When family members shirk their responsibilities, it not only can cause resentment, it can also prove detrimental to the puppy's care. To avoid these problems, call a family meeting before bringing your new dog home and divide all dog-care duties among family members. Keep in mind that, although children should be given some responsibilities related to puppy care, you may want certain jobs, such as obedience-training an adolescent or adult Poodle or food and water responsibilities, to be handled by an adult. Games such as Fetch and Hide-and-Seek are two excellent ideas for children. Also, clearly spell out during the meeting the boundaries you expect the dog to follow, so all family members will be consistent in their dealings with your new pet.

Questions you should answer include:

○ Who will feed the dog?

○ Who will walk the dog?

○ Who will clean up after the dog?

○ Who will groom the dog?

○ Who will housetrain the dog?

○ Who will obedience-train the dog?

○ Who will play with the dog to ensure he gets to release his energy and doesn't become bored?

○ What kind of games are okay to play with the new dog and what kind of games should you avoid?

○ Who will take the dog to the veterinarian for his regular checkups and shots, as well as if he becomes sick?

○ Where will the dog sleep at night?

○ Where will the dog stay during the day when people are home? Once he has learned the rules of the household, will he have free run of the house or be confined to a crate or certain rooms?

○ Where will the dog stay during the day when no one is at home?

○ Will the dog be allowed on the furniture?

○ How will the dog be contained in the yard?

○ What kind of treats will you give to the dog? Will you give people food to the dog occasionally, or never?

○ How will you correct the dog when he makes a mistake?

The good news, according to Poodle enthusiasts, is that preparing your home and yard for this breed is easier than for some other breeds. The Poodle tends to be a *little* less naughty. Even so, before bringing home the Poodle, you must "Poodle-proof" your home and yard. Just as parents of toddlers put away breakables, remove potentially dangerous items, and block off areas in the home and yard to protect the youngster, as a Poodle owner you must carefully inspect your home and yard for potential hazards. An unsupervised Poodle puppy or adult may chew, explore, or taste what he shouldn't—and cause damage or experience harm. "Poodles tend to be very inquisitive," says Shanahan, "and unless they are very shy, will get into everything. The house and yard should be gone over with an eye to what would either damage the Poodle or be irreplaceable if it were chewed."

Preparing the House

The best way to keep your Poodle safe inside the house is to supervise him, especially if he's a puppy. As mothers of young children can attest, the disappearance of a youngster followed by several moments of silence is a good indication that something naughty is going on. Run, don't walk, to the scene of the crime! The same is true with Poodles, especially pups. If there's trouble to be found, a puppy can find it. If you can't oversee the dog's activities, confine him in a crate (more on crates later).

Following that, get down on your knees (not to pray, though prayer may help!) and look at your home from the Poodle's eye level. It may seem silly, but looking at the world from your Poodle's perspective might enable you to see what "toys" are within reach, such as dangling

Ooops!

If you have a puppy, or even an adult dog, there's a good chance you'll be faced with cleaning up a doggie mess at some point, whether feces, urine, or vomit. While certainly not a pleasant topic, it must be addressed.

First, realize that messes do happen with even the best-trained dogs—a sick Poodle with diarrhea, for example, or a puppy learning the housebreaking ropes.

Next, what are you going to use to not only clean up the mess, but eliminate the odor and remove the stain? The best advice is to purchase a product made especially for pet stain and odor removal. Do not use an ammonia-based product. Because ammonia is present in urine, it will only enhance the unpleasant odor of the carpet, especially to your keen-nosed Poodle.

Clean up the solid mess first and mop up what's wet. Then apply an enzyme-based stain-and-odor remover. Make sure you follow directions to the letter for best results.

Following cleaning, get to the root of the mistake. Did your Poodle have an accident because you neglected housebreaking lessons? Could your dog have a bladder infection or other illness? If that's the case, be sure to consult your veterinarian.

electrical cords. The best approach is a systematic, room-by-room investigation. Use common sense. If it seems dangerous, it probably is.

"Poodle-proofing the home depends on the age and size of the Poodle in question," says Poodle enthusiast Winona Kuhl. What tempts a Toy may not tempt your Standard. Keep your Poodle's size in mind while giving your house a look-see.

For example, Standard Poodles are known "counter-surfers," though all Poodles have been known to search a counter for goodies. Kuhl warns: "Never, never, never leave a Standard Poodle alone in the kitchen with your dinner on the countertop, not even for a minute!"

Holiday Hazards

Dangers are present any time of year, but extra hazards face your Poodle during holiday seasons. For example, the cookies, cakes, and other sweets that are a big part of Thanksgiving and Christmas dinners can be a hazard to your Poodle. Don't be tempted to share these goodies with your pet. Chocolate is especially dangerous because it contains the chemical theobromine. While an overdose of chocolate may sound great to you, your Poodle could suffer from chocolate toxicosis if she eats the stuff. At its worst this condition can be fatal or cause severe digestive upset. Candy and sweets are popular at Easter and Halloween, too, so keep goodies out of sight and out of reach. (Remember, Standard Poodles are especially skilled counter-surfers!)

Rich foods are a favorite part of holidays: turkey, ham, lamb, dressing, mashed potatoes, and gravy are all delicious, but way too rich for your Poodle. Don't be tempted to share your dinner!

If digestive upset isn't enough, you have to worry about all those holiday decorations, such as Christmas tree decorations and candles, Easter baskets, and Halloween costumes. Your Poodle, especially pups, may try to eat those, too—or at least nibble them. Supervise your Poodle carefully during holiday times to prevent mishaps.

Noise and confusion associated with holidays—houseguests, parties, and constant doorbell ringing—can upset your Poodle. If she is upset by such commotion, confine her to a quiet area in the house.

On July Fourth, you'll be wise to keep your Poodle close to you. Some dogs are frightened by the noise of fireworks and will bolt out the door, never to be seen again.

And if you think kitchen countertops are out of reach for the Mini and Toy varieties, think again. Some describe Poodles as having springs in their feet. A jump onto a countertop is a breeze.

Poodles also have a penchant for paper of any kind—paper towels, tissue, toilet paper. "All three of ours will dump bathroom trash to get at the paper," says Irma Shanahan, "but they never

Common Hazards for Dogs

- Household cleaners, laundry detergents, bleach, furniture polish
- Medication
- Suntan lotion
- Poisons (such as ant poison, snail bait, and rat poison)
- Mousetraps
- Human trash (poultry bones, spoiled food)
- Pins, needles, buttons, other sewing accessories
- Ribbons, fabric, or string that can get lodged in the throat or intestine
- Plastic
- Rubber bands, paper clips, twist ties, thumbtacks
- Shoe polish
- Alcohol
- Cigarettes and other tobacco products
- Matches
- Antifreeze, motor oil, brake fluid, windshield-washer fluid
- Paint and paint remover
- Nails, screws, saws

touch the kitchen trash with garbage in it. Many Poodle owners I have talked with have the same problem so we think it's a breed-oriented thing."

To combat the Poodle's paper obsession, Poodle enthusiasts recommend heavy-duty, doggie-proof trashcans. Empty trash frequently and block off rooms with trashcans. As you inspect your house room by room, watch particularly for hazards in these areas:

Kitchen Mmmm. What an enticing room. Oh, those countertops! Not only does it smell good (from cooking and garbage), but there's a lot of family activity in this room. Your Poodle will undoubtedly want to join in. Take a good look around. Are there breakable items on counters that could be easily knocked off?

How about dangling electrical cords that could be chewed? Are cleaning supplies within reach? If so, put them away in cabinets with child-proof latches. How about the trashcan? Look at your kitchen carefully to determine potential dangers. Then take steps to make it a safer place.

Bathroom   This is another room that's filled with potential dangers. Keep all medications locked away in child-proof cabinets to prevent accidental poisoning. Keep the toilet lid down to discourage the Poodle from drinking from the bowl and possibly ingesting toilet-bowl cleaner. Puppies seem especially fond of licking those flush-activated cleaners that hook under the rim. Last, but not least, keep the bathroom wastebasket out of reach, perhaps in a cabinet.

Living Room and Family Room   These rooms are like a treasure chest, filled with furniture, electrical cords, houseplants, books, and magazines—all waiting to be nibbled. Eating any of this stuff is dangerous. Then there are lamps and beautiful glassware carefully arranged on end tables, which could be knocked off when your Poodle investigates. Do your best to eliminate such dangers, and supervise your dog closely.

Bedroom   Poodles know a good thing when they see it, so don't be surprised to find your dog napping on your bed. Shut the door to the room if you wish to stop this. Don't leave out toiletries, makeup, brushes, hair clips— anything that the inquisitive Poodle might wish to sniff and taste. To protect your personal items as well as your Poodle's health, store such items away in dresser drawers. If you enjoy reading before you doze off, take care to put your books away in the morning so your Poodle doesn't "finish" them for good. Don't forget to hide the trashcan and don't leave tissue boxes in open sight. Be especially careful in children's rooms, which are usually filled with all kinds of fun toys. Have your children put away toys or keep their bedroom doors shut (the latter suggestion is probably more realistic!). It's easy for a Poodle to choke on a small toy.

Garage and Basement The family garage is frequently the storehouse for antifreeze, poisons, paint, insecticides, gasoline, and, of course, the car. If possible, store all these potentially deadly items in locked cabinets or on tall shelves. Probably the best advice is to prohibit your Poodle from entering your garage. There are far too many risks, and accidents take only a second. Antifreeze, for example, is deadly. Just a few licks and that's it. Its extreme toxicity is compounded by the fact that pets apparently find its taste attractive.

If your basement is a storage disaster, it's probably best to keep your Poodle out by means of a closed door or doggie gate. Otherwise, keep all hazards in locked cabinets or on high shelves, and keep storage boxes up high. Better yet, invest in durable plastic tubs for storing holiday decorations, old photos, and important papers.

Dogs have an instinctual need to investigate their surroundings. While you can't barricade your pet from everything in your home unless she is in her crate, you can use some simple precautions.

Preparing the Yard

Though not essential, a fenced yard is a great asset for Poodle owners. Once you've made sure it's safe, a yard is the

Did You Know?

The smallest dog ever documented was a Yorkshire Terrier, measuring 2.5 inches tall by 3.75 inches long fully grown and weighing only 4 ounces.

Peach of a Poodle

Susan Sloane of Isis Standard Poodles likes to share a peachy story about one of her Standards. Several summers ago Sloane noticed that Liza, her 12-year-old black Standard, kept gazing up into a peach tree on the property. "Every time I went out to sit with my dogs, I would find her right under the tree," says Sloane.

The fruit on the tree soon ripened, and the peaches were ready to be picked. "I had planned on making a peach pie, my favorite," says Sloane. But one afternoon, Liza took fruity matters into her own paws. "I watched in amazement as she stood upon her hindlegs," says Sloane, "with her front paws on the trunk of the tree. Then she eased herself out on a branch, positioned herself, and pulled down another branch with one of her front paws. Liza then proceeded to pick the peach of her choice.

"Now keep in mind the others were watching her the whole time. Next thing I knew, all five Poodles were picking peaches using Liza's method. The ones that had fallen to the ground weren't good enough! Only fresh from the vine, so to speak."

Needless to say, "No peach pie for me that year," says Sloane.

perfect place to allow your Poodle free rein. "No matter what size Poodle you get, a fenced yard is recommended," says Michelle Mace. "The size, spacing, and height of the fence should suit the size of the dog. No Poodle should ever be tied or staked to a post or doghouse. Poodles are people dogs, happiest when they are with humans for companionship. Make sure the fence is secure, with doggie-proof latches or locks. A determined Poodle can figure out how to open basic latches."

While a yard can certainly be a great play area for your Poodle, it's also chock-full of potential dangers. Before you send the Poodle out to play, make sure the area is safe. Remove

Common Poisonous Plants

This list contains some, but not all, common plants that can harm your dog. Consult a plant book or a nursery if you have any doubts about a plant in your home or yard.

Alfalfa

Amaryllis

Asparagus (Sperengeri) fern

Azalea

Beech tree

Belladonna

Bird of paradise

Black locust tree

Caladium

Castor bean

Chinaberry

Coriaria

Crown of thorns

Daffodil

Daphne

Datura

Dieffenbachia

Elephant's ear

Euonymus

Foxglove

Henbane

Honeysuckle

Hydrangea

Iris

Ivy (especially English, heart, needlepoint, and ripple)

Jack-in-the-pulpit

Jerusalem cherry

Jessamine

Jimsonweed

Larkspur

Lily-of-the-valley

Mistletoe berries

Monkshood

Moonseed

Morning glory

Mums (spider and pot)

Nightshades

Oak trees (acorns)

Oleander

Periwinkle

Philodendron

Plant bulbs (most)

Poinsettia

Potato (green parts and eyes)

Precatory bean (rosary pea)

Rhododendron

Rhubarb (leaves, upper stem)

Skunk cabbage

Tobacco

Tomato vines

Tulip

Umbrella plant

Water hemlock

Wisteria

Yew tree (Japanese, English, Western, American)

potentially dangerous items from the yard. Avoid using lawn and garden chemicals in the Poodle's play area since they are potential dangers. Remove decorative plants that are poisonous if ingested.

Which Supplies Do You Really Need?

Of course, you'll want to treat your Poodle to the lifestyle to which he will become accustomed. We're talking pet supplies, including food, dishes, collar, leash, crate, grooming supplies, and toys. As long as you have the funds and like to shop, stocking your cupboards with dog supplies will be fun!

But first, a word about your buying budget. You probably realize you'll need to make many purchases before you bring home a Poodle. Those purchases add up fast if you buy them all at once, and the total cost might shock you! If you're like most working people and not an heir to an unlimited trust fund, buying everything you need for your Poodle might be tough. If so, you'll have to budget money carefully and may even start making purchases a year or six months ahead. (If you're waiting for a puppy from a good breeder, you may have to wait this long anyway.) Check pet-supply stores frequently and buy supplies on sale (ex-

cept food, which is perishable). Or, put away money every month toward supply purchases so buying them doesn't pinch your budget.

Don't be fooled into thinking you have to buy the most expensive products, or that you have to buy them all! Shop carefully for *quality* products you really need. Never before have pet owners been faced with so many pet foods, services, and products from

Supply Checklist

Food and water bowls (ceramic or stainless steel)

Crate (plastic, wire, or both)

Dog bed or crate cushion, if you are sure he won't chew it

Doggie/baby gates

Outdoor kennel or secure perimeter fencing

Doghouse

Collar

Leash

ID tag

Enzyme cleaner

Grooming supplies (pin brush, slicker brush, greyhound comb, shampoo, dental and ear-cleaning supplies)

Safe toys

which to choose. In fact, the U.S. pet industry is a billion-dollar business. It's easy to get caught up in the fun of buying and then find you've spent your budget or have bought items you really don't need. So, take your time and choose your purchases carefully. Ask other dog owners for advice, read reviews from a trusted magazine or Web site. Simply put, be a wise consumer.

If you've bought essential supplies, and still have cash burning a hole in your pocket, you can find plenty of fun ways to spend your hard-earned money—Poodle motif stationery, collector plates, T-shirts, tote bags, coffee mugs, photo frames, clocks, key chains, flags, welcome mats, books, magazines, switch-plate covers, collectibles, stuffed animals, and the list goes on and on. All may seem irresistible, especially to new Poodle owners, but "first things first" is a sound approach: Budget and buy essentials first, then if you have a little left over, buy a bit of fluff if you like! The following sections list what experienced Poodle owners consider necessary.

Crate, Bedding, and Gates   Experienced Poodle owners recommend crate-training, especially for pups. "I always recommend a crate, for any dog," says Kuhl. "Crate-training is essential if you plan to show the dog, but even if you don't attend shows, a crate is the best method for housebreaking."

Ask the breeder the best crate size for your Poodle. Generally, the crate should be large enough to house an adult Poodle comfortably. There are two types: enclosed plastic and wire. Preferences vary among enthusiasts, and both types have advantages. The hard plastic crate is great if you live in a cold climate because it's more warm and snug than the drafty wire cages. On the other hand, it can be extremely hot in warm climates.

> Although you may be tempted to line the crate with something fuzzy or fluffy, don't. A Poodle pup might pull or nibble on loose threads or fuzz.

Open wire crates aren't as snug, but can be covered with a blanket in chilly weather. Whatever type you choose, be sure it's well-made, with a sturdy door and latch.

You'll need washable or disposable bedding for the crate floor, too. You can buy special dog bedding at a pet-supply store, but that's not really necessary. An old sheet is fine. Although you may be tempted to line the crate with something fuzzy or fluffy, don't. A Poodle pup might pull or nibble on loose threads or fuzz. Make sure whatever fabric you choose is tightly woven. And never provide bedding for a puppy who likes to chew. It can be extremely dangerous. Wait until your puppy will leave it alone before providing it.

A dog bed or large pillow is another option, as is allowing the Poodle in bed with you (as many Poodle owners do!).

High-Tech Identification Protection

Identification tags are your dog's first line of defense if she ever gets lost. Many a dog has been quickly reunited with her family because she was wearing a tag with the owner's phone number. However, what if your dog's collar comes off or is removed? How will your Poodle find her way back home? Two other forms of identification can supplement the ID tag: tattooing and microchip implants.

With tattooing, a series of numbers or letters, or a combination of numbers and letters, is imprinted onto your pet's body, and the code is then recorded in a database. If someone finds your Poodle, they can call the toll-free number to a tattoo registry, which maintains a database record with your name and phone number, corresponding to your dog's tattoo ID code. The toll-free number usually is provided on a tag that attaches to your dog's collar. An advantage to the tattoo is that it is a permanent and visible means of identification. One disadvantage is that, if your dog loses her collar, whoever finds your pet may not know who to call. If your dog won't let a stranger near her, the person who finds her may not be able to get close enough to read the tattoo. Also, horror stories exist of stolen dogs who have had a tattooed ear removed to keep them from being identified. To prevent this, it is safer to tattoo your dog's inner thigh.

Like tattoos, microchips contain a unique code, which can be read by a hand-held scanner that is passed over the skin of the animal where the chip was inserted. The code corresponds to information in a database, such as the owner's name and phone number. An advantage to microchips is that they, too, are permanent. The microchip itself is composed of non-toxic components sealed in biocompatible glass. The chip, about the size of the lead tip of a pencil or a grain of rice, is fitted into a hypodermic needle and injected under the skin of a dog between her shoulder blades. A disadvantage is that not all scanners read all microchips. Humane societies usually have only enough money to invest in one scanner, at best, and if that scanner can't read the chip in your dog, it's useless. Again, if your dog is uncomfortable with being handled by strangers, she may be hard to scan.

Tattoos and microchips are gaining popularity as permanent means of identifying your pet. However, the standard ID tag that dangles from the collar of your pup remains an invaluable tool for helping to return your lost pet to you.

Another handy way of confining or limiting access for the Poodle pup or adult is to use doggie gates or puppy pens. As parents of toddlers block off a room, you can lock the Poodle out of your office, for example. You can buy specially made doggie gates and pens, but those made for children work just as well (and are sometimes less expensive!).

Meals and Treats   Have plenty of food on hand before you bring home your new canine friend. It's a good idea to ask the breeder or rescue volunteer what the Poodle has been eating and continue with that diet, at least for a while. Switching foods quickly can cause digestive upset and diarrhea—something you won't want to deal with the first week you have your Poodle. (For more information on what food to buy, see Chapter 3.)

You may also want to have a few treats on hand. Buy snacks made of wholesome, quality ingredients, with no sugar and additives. Fresh vegetables are good snacks, too.

Feeding Bowls   Your Poodle needs his own bowls, one for food and one for water. Choose bowls big enough for a full-grown Poodle or ask your breeder to recommend a good size. Poodle enthusiasts recommend stainless steel or ceramic bowls, rather than plastic. "Plastic bowls can give some dogs an acne-like rash on their lips and chin," says Mace, "and also cause some dogs—especially whites, creams, and apricots—to lose the black pigment of their noses. I would also recommend a raised eating and drinking station for a Mini or Standard due to their propensity to bloat, which can be caused by ingesting excessive air with food or water."

Collars and Leads   You'll need to "dress" your Poodle with a well-fitting collar and leash. With an endless number of styles and types of leashes, collars, and harnesses on the market—in leather, nylon, and prints—the sky is the limit. Ask your breeder or veterinarian to recommend her favorite collar and lead and give them a try. An adjustable nylon collar with a quick-release buckle is great for pups because you can adjust it as your puppy grows. A training collar may be in order, but wait to buy that when you begin training classes. Trainers usually have a specific collar in mind for students. Be sure you buy an identification tag to attach to the Poodle's collar that includes the dog's name, your name, current address, and telephone number. Be aware that if you plan on showing your Poodle in the breed ring, you may not want to keep a collar on the dog at all times because it can wear or tear the coat, a no-no for a Poodle in show coat. Follow the advice of your show mentor if this is the case.

> Ask your breeder or veterinarian to recommend her favorite collar and lead and give them a try.

Toys   Every Poodle must have toys. According to enthusiasts, Poodles (no matter what size) prefer soft, stuffed toys, especially those that play music or make some kind of sound. However, be sure to supervise your Poodle when he has squeaker toys. If they break, the noise instrument can be dangerous if swallowed. Poodles also like tennis balls, though the harsh covering can wear down the teeth of an active chewer. Thin latex toys are not recommended because they are easily chewed up and swallowed. Rawhide toys are a Poodle favorite, but not necessarily a Poodle owner favorite. Rawhide toys leave a sticky, smelly residue on the Poodle's hairy legs that is less than attractive. As well, overindulgence or rapid eating can cause tummy upset, resulting in vomiting, diarrhea, and, though rare, serious intestinal problems.

How Much Is This Going to Cost Me?

The basic supplies for your new dog can come with a hefty price tag depending on size and quality, and often it's a price you'll be paying more than once. Remember to factor in these costs when making the decision to get a dog. Prices likely will vary depending on where you live, but the following should give you a good idea of what to expect.

Item	Low Price	High Price
Crate	$20.00	$200.00
Food and Water Bowls	3.00	60.00
Collar	4.00	40.00
Leash	4.00	50.00
ID Tag	3.00	15.00
Pet Stain/Odor Remover	4.00	10.00
Brush	4.00	20.00
Toys	1.00	40.00
Food (8 lb. bag)	4.00	9.00
Bed	10.00	200.00
TOTAL	$57.00	$644.00

Grooming Supplies   When it comes to grooming and grooming supplies, the Poodle is high-maintenance. Even if you plan on hiring a professional groomer to clip your Poodle, you'll need tools at home to keep the coat in good shape between trims. Figure on buying a comb, slicker brush, pin brush, toenail clippers and styptic powder, cotton balls and ear cleaner or powder, quality shampoo, doggie toothbrush and toothpaste, and your choice of flea-control products.

Cleanup Tools Don't forget the delicate matter of cleaning up and disposing of the Poodle's waste. Whether this is a big job or a relatively small job depends upon your Poodle's size. Generally, you'll need a poop scoop and a place to dispose of fecal matter. If you have a yard, consider installing an in-ground, mini septic tank made especially for animal waste. For waste pickup at the park or on walks in the neighborhood, carry along plastic bags. You can purchase bags made especially for this or recycle plastic grocery bags.

First-Aid Kit Be prepared! All Poodle owners should have a first-aid kit on hand for their dogs. Hopefully, you'll never have to use it, but it's best to be prepared for emergencies that require first aid. Following is a list of suggested items. Add or subtract as needed, and ask your vet for suggestions and instructions for using it. Store the kit in an easy-to-find location, and check it frequently to make sure liquids have not spilled, dried up, or expired. Replace medications and materials after they are used.

○ Activated charcoal tablets or liquid
○ Adhesive tape
○ Antibacterial ointment
○ Eye ointment
○ Sterile gauze bandages and dressing pads
○ Hydrogen peroxide (3% solution)
○ Petroleum jelly
○ Dosing syringe
○ Diarrhea medicine
○ Rectal thermometer
○ Rubber gloves

Did You Know?

Researchers are almost positive that dogs dream. If you look at a sleeping dog, sometimes you'll notice its eyes move beneath its eyelids. Because this is what humans do when they dream, researchers believe it is an indication of dreams in dogs, too. No word yet on what they dream about.

○ Rubbing alcohol

○ Scissors

○ Tourniquet

○ Towel

○ Tweezers

○ First-aid book (You need to know what to do with this stuff!)

Homecoming Day for Your Poodle

Warm, genuine hospitality is truly delightful—and rare. Being a welcome guest makes you feel important, appreciated, even loved. So before you bring home your Poodle, make it your aim to extend your warmest wishes to your new family member.

Puppy's First Night

Puppyhood has a number of firsts: first look at the world through opened eyes, first bark, first tumble with littermates, and of course, first night away from mom. A first night home with a new owner can be a little stressful for puppy and owner. Some puppies miss their mom and littermates and whine through the night. First-time puppy owners often feel anxious.

Reduce the stress of bringing home your puppy by purchasing all your supplies beforehand. Don't wait until the day you plan to pick up the pup from the breeder to stop by the pet-supply store.

Plan puppy's eating and sleeping arrangements. Where will puppy eat and drink? Where will you place the crate? Think through these arrangements carefully and make a plan before bringing puppy home. Perhaps a call to your puppy's breeder will give you some suggestions.

Ask the breeder for a list of do's and don'ts, and get the list prior to puppy's first night. Many breeders provide buyers with a list, which may include suggested food, vet referral, toys, and other details. The responsible breeder wants to make sure puppy's first and subsequent nights away from his first home are happy and safe.

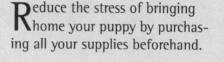

Reduce the stress of bringing home your puppy by purchasing all your supplies beforehand.

Puppy may be a little homesick at first, and may whimper and cry at night. This isn't unusual, but can be upsetting. Try comforting the puppy by placing his crate next to your bed. That way puppy can smell you, hear you, and feel less alone. At bedtime, place your puppy in his crate and shut the door.

First nights can be trying, says Linda Hargett. "If your puppy begins to cry, an 'arghh' may suffice. If he continues, turn a deaf ear for a few minutes. If he does not stop after five or ten minutes, give a sharp rap on the top of the crate and say 'quiet.' I spent the first few nights that my pup was with me with my hand hanging off the bed in front of the crate. If he could see my hand, he was quiet!"

Ask the breeder what environment the puppy is used to sleeping in and try to recreate it. For example, use a similar blanket. Also, tire your puppy out before bedtime so he's sleepy and ready for rest.

Making an Adult Poodle Feel Welcome

It's unlikely that an adult Poodle is missing her mom when she comes to live with you, but the move from one home (or foster care) to another can be stressful. The Poodle doesn't know you and you don't know her. However, your job in this case won't be terribly difficult. Adult Poodles adjust very well to new homes. "I have acquired over a dozen dogs as adults," says Mace, "and barring psychological problems, they all seemed to adjust very well and bond quickly. That's the nice thing about Poodles. They love everybody!"

> Adult Poodles adjust very well to new homes.

To encourage bonding and help an adult Poodle adjust, try these suggestions:

○ Learn as much as you can about the dog—her likes and dislikes, favorite toys—before you bring her home.
○ Try to follow the routine the dog is used to.
○ Give bunches of TLC by stroking the dog, talking to her, and praising her.
○ Allow your new Poodle to sleep near you—for example, place her crate next to your bed.
○ Give her treats!
○ Play ball or take walks with your Poodle if that's what she loves to do.
○ Feed her the same food, out of the same type of bowls she's used to.
○ Introduce new family members, other pets, and activities slowly.
○ Be consistent with your obedience commands.

Food for Thought

Do you like to eat? Of course you do! So does your Poodle. What are you going to feed her to help her grow up healthy, feel great, and remain in good condition? Nutritious food, obviously. Next we'll discuss why good nutrition matters and which dog foods are the most healthful for your Poodle.

Why Nutrition Matters

"We are what we eat," says Poodle enthusiast Lisa Haidle. "Dogs are no different than people in that way."

59

Good nutrition matters. What you feed your Poodle, in most cases, determines her health. Feed your dog a healthful diet and you're likely to have a pet who feels good and acts well.

Conversely, poor nutrition, says Grace Blair, M.D., an experienced Poodle breeder, can result in poor or unbalanced growth, temperament changes, bone and joint problems, vitamin deficiency, premature aging, and decreased ability to resist disease.

Food is the fuel required to nourish the Poodle's body. Your Poodle needs a special balance of nutrients in his food to create energy and maintain good health.

> Feed your dog a healthful diet and you're likely to have a pet who feels good and acts well.

If that balance is upset, either from a lack of food or the wrong foods, health problems can arise. Dogs need at least 43 different nutrients. A deficiency, or excess, of any one of those nutrients can lead to illness. Many nutrients must be present in your Poodle's diet and in the appropriate ratios for the best health.

The nutrients found in food are the body's building blocks. A Poodle's body uses these nutrients to build good health, including strong bones, an effective immune system, and a healthy coat of hair. When the body lacks nutrients, it cannot work effectively.

Protein is one nutrient required by your Poodle. Proteins, which are composed of the amino acids found in meat, eggs, fish, and soybeans, supply your Poodle with the nutrients she needs to grow, repair tissue, and maintain health. They also form antibodies to fight infection. Your Poodle's body produces some amino acids, but she must obtain others directly from food sources. Meat, eggs, and dairy products are considered complete proteins which means they supply all the essential amino acids. Grains and vegetables are incomplete proteins. Both are essential to your Poodle's health. A Poodle suffering a protein deficiency has a decreased appetite, poor growth, weight loss, a rough or dull coat, and lower reproductive performance.

Fats are an important nutrient, too, and provide your Poodle with the most concentrated source of energy. Per unit of weight, fats contain two and one-fourths as much energy as an equivalent weight of protein or carbohydrates. Fats carry fat-soluble vitamins D, E, A, and K, and supply linoleic acid, a fatty acid essential for skin and hair. Additionally, fats help the body keep warm, move nutrients, and send nerve impulses. A diet that is too low in fat may result in a dry, coarse coat and dry, flaky skin.

Carbohydrates provide your Poodle with quick energy. Your Poodle needs a fresh, ongoing supply of carbohydrates to help spare protein for body growth and repair. Cellulose, an indigestible carbohydrate, provides bulk for proper digestion. Corn, rice, wheat, and oats are common sources of carbohydrates.

Vitamins and minerals are essential for a Poodle's normal body functions, bone development, and certain chemical reactions. Vitamins aid in resistance to disease and are an essential part of the enzyme structure. They help convert mineral elements into structural components of bones and teeth, play a part in red blood cell formation and reproduction, and help to maintain a healthy appetite and healthy skin.

Vitamins are classified into fat-soluble and water-soluble groups. The fat-soluble vitamins—A, D, E, and K—are stored in the body, which means over-supplementing can be toxic.

Water-soluble vitamins include the B-complex and C vitamins. These are not stored in any sufficient amount in the body since those not metabolized are excreted in urine. Water-soluble vitamins must be replaced daily.

Minerals are essential for bone and tissue development, and for proper body function.

The total mineral content in dog food is called its "ash content." Ash contains calcium, phosphorus, sodium chloride, potassium, and other minerals that are essential nutrients.

> Water constitutes up to 84 percent of the weight of newborn pups, and 50 to 60 percent of the weight of adult dogs.

Water is essential to proper cell and organ function. Without it, the body cannot eliminate waste products, keep a constant temperature, circulate blood, or transport nutrients. Because the body has a limited capacity to store water, life may continue for weeks in the absence of food, but only for days if water is not available. Water constitutes up to 84 percent of the weight of newborn pups, and 50 to 60 percent of the weight of adult dogs. A healthy Poodle is properly hydrated.

Good nutrition will help your Poodle in the following ways:

- Develop normally from puppy to adult
- Maintain a thick and luxurious coat
- Have strong teeth and healthy gums
- Have plenty of energy for play and fun
- Develop a strong immune system able to resist disease and the ability to recover and heal quickly in case of illness or injury
- Feel good and act happy
- Be strong with good muscle tone
- Maintain good digestive health

Choosing the Best Food for Your Poodle

Good nutrition is essential. But what food is best?

Realize that every person you ask about dog foods—Poodle owners, breeders, veterinarians, pet-food company representatives, pet-store clerks—has an opinion, all differing, on what diet is "best" for your Poodle. According to veterinarians and Poodle experts, no one commercially prepared food is best for all Poodles. Each dog is an individual, even when it comes to her kibbles. "The best food for your dog is whichever food she thrives on," says Poodle owner Michelle Mace.

A good way to tell whether a food is "best" is to see how your Poodle responds to the diet. Study the dog for six to eight weeks on a particular diet. Look for a shiny coat, high energy level, good nature, healthy teeth, well-formed stools—all signs that your Poodle is receiving the nutrients she needs from her diet.

Types of Pet Foods

Thanks to pet food companies, feeding your Poodle can be as simple as opening a bag, can, or box. You can choose from hundreds of commercially prepared diets available in three main types: dry, canned, and soft-moist. These food types vary in moisture content, texture, cost, palatability, and nutritional content.

Generally, most dry dog food diets contain 18 to 27 percent protein, 7 to 15 percent fat, and 35 to 50 percent carbohydrate. Dry kibble is the most economical way to feed a dog, and it's easy and convenient for owners. Dry diets have the added benefit of helping reduce plaque and tartar on a pet's teeth.

Soft-moist diets contain approximately 16 to 25 percent protein, 5 to 10 percent fat, 25 to 35 percent carbohydrate, and 30 percent water. Soft-moist diets are favored over dry by many dogs, but are more expensive to feed.

Canned dog foods usually contain 8 to 15 percent protein, 2 to 15 percent fat, and moisture

What's on the Label?

The wide variety of cans, bags, and boxes of pet food shelved in shops throughout the nation has at least one thing in common: labeling. True, the colors, pictures, and words used on individual foods vary, as do the diets within. But all labels must, by law, contain specific information.

Pet food labels give basic information about the diet's ingredient content, nutrient guaranteed analysis, feeding instructions, net weight, the name and address of the manufacturer or distributor, and additional facts about the product. No, pet food labels don't tell everything about a product. But they do give a savvy consumer a good way to begin comparing foods.

At the federal level, pet food labeling and advertising claims are regulated by the Food and Drug Administration, the U.S. Department of Agriculture, and the Federal Trade Commission. State feed control officials determine regulations to which pet food manufacturers in individual states must adhere. Another organization with an important role in labeling pet foods is the Association of American Feed Control Officials (AAFCO). The association is made up of officials from all the states, Canada, and Puerto Rico. Although the AAFCO has no regulatory authority (state and federal officials do), it does set forth guidelines, or "models," for feed and pet food regulations that individual states are encouraged to adopt. A large number of states comply with the suggested laws and guidelines. The AAFCO also provides nutritional guidelines for dog and cat foods called nutrient profiles and guidelines for testing foods.

Pet food companies that sell diets that don't meet the label guarantee are subject to a warning, a fine, removal of the product, or cancellation of the product's registration.

Pet food labels contain several elements:

The product name must be placed on the principal display panel, that part of the label most likely to be seen by consumers.

content of approximately 75 percent. Canned diets seem tastiest to dogs, but they are also the most expensive to feed per serving.

Certain nutrient guarantees—guaranteed analysis—are required on all pet food labels: crude protein (minimum percentage), crude fat (minimum percentage), crude fiber (maximum percentage), and moisture (maximum percentage).

The package must include an ingredient listing of all the ingredients used to make the food; they must be listed on the label in descending order of predominance by weight.

Additives must be noted. That includes nutritional additives such as vitamins and minerals, antioxidants such as BHA or BHT, chemical preservatives, flavoring agents, and coloring.

The net weight must be placed on the principal display panel.

Manufacturer information, the name and address of the manufacturer, packer, or distributor, must be included on the label.

The label must state in the nutritional adequacy statement whether or not the product provides complete and balanced nutrition and if it is appropriate for all life stages or one particular life stage.

The amount of food required, or feeding directions, must be printed on the label.

The caloric statement, which is the calorie content of the product, must appear away from the guaranteed analysis and be under the heading "calorie content."

Last but not least many pet food packages include a toll-free consumer information number. This isn't mandatory, but it's a good resource for owners wanting to learn more about the product they're feeding their pet.

Pet Food Categories

A pet food shopping spree can take you across town and back—literally. In addition to the several types of diets, pet foods are further distinguished within the pet industry by where you buy them and a few other factors.

Super-premium pet foods are generally sold in pet specialty stores and veterinary clinics. Prices are highest, but diets are usually energy dense or have more calories per pound of food. Because dogs need less, it may be cheaper over the long run.

Premium foods are traditionally sold at grocery stores but are also available at pet-supply stores. Premium diets are moderately priced.

Grocery store brands are those pet foods sold under the individual store's name as opposed to a national brand name. Grocery store brands are advertised to offer the same quality as nationally advertised brands at a lower price, but rarely meet these standards.

Non-premium, or off brands, are usually stocked at feed stores and are inexpensive. Like generic foods, you get what you pay for—less expensive foods reflect less expensive ingredients. While some dogs do okay on these foods, both generic and non-premium foods are considered marginal diets at best.

Generic pet foods were extremely popular in the 1980s. These generic foods were low-priced compared to brand name products and were purported to be nutritionally equivalent to national brands. Generic pet foods have declined in popularity, in part because of nutritional inadequacies and the increase of quality store brands.

Each category of pet food has its proponents among veterinarians, breeders, and owners, though you will find few dog-care experts who support generic, store, or off-brand dog foods. Some believe only in feeding super-premium foods, while others believe premium and grocery store brands are sufficient. The primary difference is density per volume. A serving of premium food is likely to have more nutrients absorbed and digested than a serving of non-premium. The dog eats less but gets a higher percentage of nutrients.

In order to determine the best food for your Poodle, you need to understand her nutritional requirements. First, let's dispel a common myth about the dog—she is not a carnivore (strictly a meat eater). Instead, she is an omnivore, which means she needs a small amount of plant material as well as meat for a complete, balanced diet. This stems from the eating habits of her ancestors, who consumed plant matter as well as meat. Therefore, while your Poodle in most cases shouldn't have a purely vegetarian diet (there are vegetarian diets available, but they are very difficult for most dogs to digest), some plant material is important for proper nutritional balance. Once you have determined what your Poodle's specific dietary needs are, stick with a food that meets these needs and is palpable to your Poodle. Changing dog food randomly because a different brand is on sale or switching foods suddenly for any reason can give dogs diarrhea or other digestive problems.

A food that meets the Association of American Feed Control Officials (AAFCO) guidelines will contain a statement verifying that the food has undergone feeding trials by AAFCO and it provides complete and balanced nutrition. Foods not evaluated by AAFCO may not make a "complete and balanced" claim. If the label doesn't include this statement, do not buy the dog food, no matter how highly recommended it may be by your breeder or neighbor down the street.

Pet food companies that sell diets that do not meet the label guarantee are subject to warning, fine, removal of the product, or cancellation of product registration.

Did You Know?

Houston topped the 1998 list of cities with the highest number of postal workers bitten by dogs, with Chicago a close second.

In general, the ingredient list gives you a hint as to whether you are dealing with a premium or lower-quality food. Premium foods tend to list chicken, lamb, turkey, and meat by-products as their first ingredients, while lower-quality foods often have plant sources such as corn as their top ingredient. You must read closely to see if any ingredients were split in their listing, however. For example, a bag that lists several different types of corn scattered throughout its ingredient list may actually contain as high a portion of corn as the "honest" bag that lists corn first and only once. Corn is corn, no matter how you describe it.

> In general, the ingredient list gives you a hint as to whether you are dealing with a premium or lower-quality food.

Canned Versus Dry

Most brands of food come in two forms—dry and canned. Both types have their pros and cons.

Dry food is the more popular type, accounting for 80 to 90 percent of the dog-food market in the United States. Proponents argue that dry food aids in dental health by scraping away tartar during the chewing process and by helping maintain healthy gums. Chewing dry food, as opposed to gulping canned, also stimulates salivation and assists in digestion. Dry food also stays fresh longer when left out than canned food, which can turn rancid quickly. Finally, dry food usually is less expensive.

Canned food has the advantage of generally being more palatable. On the downside, canned food tends to be more expensive and can't be left out or it will go bad. If your dog doesn't finish his portion, refrigerate the leftovers. You can warm them for a few seconds in the microwave before the next meal to make them more enticing, but stir the food, carefully making sure there aren't any "hot pockets" before feeding them to your dog. Unfortunately, some dogs refuse to eat leftovers regardless of whether they are heated, adding to the expense of canned food.

A third category of dog food is semi-moist food. Semi-moist food usually comes in individual bags and is colored and shaped to look like real meat. While this food may look more appealing than dry or canned, this is for your benefit, not your dog's. These foods typically contain high amounts of corn syrup or other sweeteners that are unhealthy for your pet.

In general, dry food is easier to feed, better for your dog's teeth, and less expensive than canned products. If your dog likes his kibble, don't mess with a good thing!

Check the Stools

A good way to evaluate a Poodle's diet is to evaluate his feces. No, it's not a pleasant task, but it does tell a lot. The feces give clues as to what's going on in the pet's digestive system. Healthy pets on a good diet leave well-formed, firm droppings with little odor. Feces consistency indicates how well an animal absorbs nutrients from food, thus illustrating the balance of fiber, water, and all-around quality of the diet. Firm feces usually mean the animal is receiving a quality diet formulated to enable the system to absorb as many nutrients as possible.

High-quality pet food is usually digested more quickly than food of poorer quality. The quicker the food is digested, the less odor to the feces. Feces that are an unusual color (green or magenta, for example) can reflect coloring additives in the diet.

Food Allergies

It's not common, but some dogs develop food allergies. Digestive upset, itchy skin, or hair loss can be signs that something in the animal's diet is triggering an allergic reaction. What exactly is an allergic reaction? It's an exaggerated response of the immune system to something that's usually harmless; wheat, for example. What the pet is allergic to is called an allergen.

The way the body responds to that allergen is called a hypersensitivity reaction. There are two kinds of hypersensitivity reactions. The immediate type occurs within minutes of exposure and often produces hives, itching, and sometimes, trouble breathing or collapse; anaphylactic shock is an example of this. The delayed reaction produces itching hours or days afterward.

The most common food allergens are wheat, milk, soy, chicken, eggs, beef, fish, and corn. Dyes and preservatives may also trigger allergies.

Treating allergies usually begins with a diet trial supervised by a veterinarian. But not just any diet—preferably foods to which your Poodle hasn't been exposed. Changing from one pet food to another doesn't work because many foods contain similar ingredients. Dietary restriction is the only way to truly determine what food(s) the Poodle is allergic to. Once the offending agent is pinpointed, an appropriate diet can be started.

Feeding Stages

Within each pet food category, you will find diets formulated for a specific life stage or nutritional need. Puppy diets, for example, have higher levels of nutrients to meet a young dog's rapid growth and development. Other diets are formulated to have higher levels of protein and calories for working dogs. Still others are formulated to be lower in calories and fat to help less active or older dogs maintain normal body weight. Diets vary among manufacturers, but you can generally find foods formulated for the specific nutritional needs of the following dog categories:

❍ Pregnant and/or lactating bitches

❍ Puppies

❍ Mature dogs

❍ Working dogs (such as canine competitors, hunting dogs, sled dogs, herding dogs)

❍ Senior dogs

❍ Dogs with illnesses (such as heart disease, intestinal disorders, urinary tract problems, tooth decay, allergies, and cancer)

Cost Differences

If you're a savvy shopper, you are sure to notice the price differences in pet food. From high-end to low-end, there's a price to please everyone. Price differences are usually based on the quality and quantity of the various ingredients in the diet. Higher-end foods use more expensive ingredients. For example, you might find lamb or turkey in a super-premium diet, rather than less expensive chicken or beef. But be aware that price isn't everything when it comes to dog food. In fact, a low price can be deceiving. The lower-end diet may be less expensive, but it also contains less nutrients per volume when compared to higher quality. That means you have to feed your dog more to obtain the same nutrients. You may pay less initially, but you'll end up buying more food per year.

Complete and Balanced

When it comes to choosing a commercial diet for your Poodle, remember this phrase: *complete and balanced.* A complete and balanced diet is designed to provide your Poodle with all the nutrients he needs to thrive at a particular life stage. Additional supplements are not necessary. A food purporting to be nutritionally complete and balanced on the package must, by law, meet specific standards set by the National Research Council or pass performance tests designed by the Association of American Feed Control Officials. Many complete and balanced diets meet both requirements. The ideal dog food will have on its label that it has been AAFCO tested by feeding trial and is certified complete and balanced. Be sure the diet you choose is for the appropriate life stage. If your Poodle is an adult, be sure the package states the diet is complete and balanced for an adult dog.

Good Taste

A commercially prepared diet may be nutritionally jam-packed, but it's no good if the Poodle won't eat it. Dogs, like people, do have eating preferences, therefore palatability, or good taste, is essential.

Research shows that when given a choice, dogs typically prefer high-fat type foods. Dogs can detect subtle differences in the quality of ingredients used in foods. The way the diet feels in the dog's mouth—texture, density, size, and shape—all affect whether or not the dog will eat it.

> Dogs, like people, do have eating preferences, therefore palatability, or good taste, is essential.

The bottom line? While your Poodle has to like eating what he's eating, don't judge nutrition based on taste alone. Kids love candy, but that doesn't always mean it's good for them.

Feeding Directions

Commercially prepared diets are labeled with feeding directions, which are average portions for different weights and ages of dogs.

Recommendations vary among diet types, categories, and life stages. Read the feeding directions on the diet you buy, but remember that's only a starting point. Actual feeding amounts will depend on your Poodle's age, activity level, size, environment, and body metabolism. (For specific information on how much to feed your Poodle, see page 80 in this chapter.)

Storing Your Poodle's Food

How do you keep dog food fresh once it's purchased? Canned foods have a long shelf-life and are easily stored. Simply place the cans in a pantry or kitchen cupboard where you store all other canned goods. Once you open a can, it must be covered and refrigerated until you use it again, and you must use it within three days of opening.

Store dry food in a cool, dark area. If you live in a hot, humid climate, keep the food in an air-conditioned room, if possible. To prevent insects and rodents from sharing your Poodle's meals, once you open the bag place it in a large plastic garbage can with a tight-fitting lid. Keep the food in its original bag to keep it fresh. Wash and dry the can after each bag is finished.

It may be tempting, especially if your brand of food is on sale, but don't over-buy. Purchase only as much as your Poodle can eat while the food is still fresh. The longer the food sits, the more chance of spoilage or bug infestation. This is especially true with natural pet foods that do not contain chemical preservatives and have a shorter shelf-life.

Did You Know?

Dogs and cats in the United States consume almost $7 billion worth of pet food a year.

Au Natural

A growing number of owners are choosing more natural ways to care for their pets, including what they feed them. Concerned that commercially prepared pet foods are not as healthful as they should be, owners are feeding "natural" diets—raw diets of meat, vegetables, and grains—cooking for their dogs at home, or ordering pre-made meals from natural-oriented companies. Holistic-oriented veterinarians (currently the American Holistic Veterinary Medical Association, or AHVMA, has 800 members) routinely advocate fresh diets or natural commercial diets as the best means of offering nutrients.

Why all the fuss about commercially prepared pet food? According to holistic advocates, the best way to prevent disease and maintain good health is proper nutrition. The cornerstone of holistic medicine is prevention and early detection of disease. Nutrition is essential for preventing illness. According to holistic advocates, commercially prepared foods cannot provide an adequate amount of nutrition due to the high level of processing, the use of questionable ingredients (by-products, for example, which can include diseased chicken, beef, or pork), the use of inferior ingredients such as low-quality grains, and the addition of artificial colors, preservatives, flavors, sugar, or corn syrup. Fresh, organic foods (raw and cooked meat, grains, vegetables), say holistic advocates, are the best way to provide the body (whether dog or person) with sufficient nutrition. Commercially prepared foods, though thoroughly researched and tested, are anything but fresh and are rarely organic.

> According to holistic advocates, the best way to prevent disease and maintain good health is proper nutrition.

The holistic perspective on feeding pets is not without critics. In fact, many holistic vets are considered "flakes" by their traditional colleagues. However, there's nothing flaky about the positive results holistic advocates see in dogs who are fed fresh diets.

What's in a Fresh Diet?

Recipes, amounts, and techniques vary, but fresh diets for dogs often include lean and fatty raw meats, dairy products, grains such as rice or oats (these should be cooked), legumes, vegetables, and supplements. Such a diet may also be called a raw diet, a BARF diet (biologically appropriate raw food), or a natural diet.

Fresh-diet enthusiasts recommend preparing raw diets with the finest quality ingredients available: organic. Organic foods have the least amount of chemical residue and the highest nutritional value because they are grown or raised by natural means, with every effort not to use materials (such as chemical fertilizers or growth hormones) believed to be harmful to people, pets, and the environment.

While difficult to find and buy 25 years ago, organic foods are easy to obtain today. Look in the yellow pages for natural or health-food stores in your area. Or locate a farm co-operative or individual with a naturally cultivated backyard garden.

Hand in hand with fresh diets are dietary supplements. Bonemeal, nutritional yeast, kelp, vegetable oil, and vitamins are usually recommended to fortify the diet. It's essential to have a vet's guidance on which supplements, if any, are necessary for your individual Poodle, though. It can be a tricky business, and requires expert help.

What Poodle Owners Say About Fresh Diets

Fresh diets have a dedicated following in the Poodle world, for good reason: results. "The benefits [of a fresh diet] are staggering," says Poodle enthusiast Belinda Hankins, who has been feeding her Poodles a raw diet for three years. "I have noticed so many improvements in the health of my dogs, who were never really unhealthy to begin with. They are more alert and vigorous, their coats are better, their skin is wonderful, their energy levels are higher, their eyes are brighter, and their breath is better."

Kadelia Hamilton reports positive results in her Poodles. She says, "I find it amusing that in our 'high-tech' age, returning to the basics has worked better for my dogs than any of the 'new and improved,' 'complete and balanced' commercial dog foods I've fed. For years I fed 'premium' kibble, switching from one to another when my brand was no longer available or a formula change caused a problem with my dogs, and I thought my dogs were in optimum condition. After sorting through reading material and attending seminars, I decided to make a commitment, on a trial basis only, to feed a diet of fresh food for several months. The results were truly amazing, most notably with my arthritic dog who had been given numerous drugs, herbs, and food supplements with little or no improvement, and euthanasia was in his near future. After switching to a fresh diet, he greatly improved and seems to enjoy life again."

Julie Borst, Poodle breeder and professional groomer, has been feeding her Poodles a combination kibble and raw diet since 1985. She is especially pleased with the good health of her pregnant bitches— she feeds them an entirely raw diet the last two weeks of gestation and the first two weeks of nursing. "I am thrilled with the benefits of feeding this diet," she says, "especially with how well the mother dogs do. In my past experience, I found bitches did not adjust as well hormonally after the birth, and they'd be lethargic and have diarrhea for days. Not so on this diet. Milk production is unequaled," says Borst, "as is the pups' weight gain."

In addition, notes Borst, "The other obvious difference is the clear, bright eyes of my dogs. They are beaming with good health."

However, a raw diet should be thoughtfully approached. It is much more than throwing your dog a raw steak for dinner. Raw diets do carry risk, especially if great care is not taken. Raw meat can cause many diseases, including E. coli, salmonella, and parasites. If not properly administered, your dog can become very ill and even die from the effects of a raw diet. If you are considering this option, discuss it in-depth with your veterinary nutritionist. She can give you necessary guidelines, and direct you to other experts in the field.

Get to the Kitchen!

If you're interested in feeding your Poodle a fresh-food diet of any kind, start by consulting with a holistic-oriented veterinarian (contact the AHVMA for a referral using contact information provided in Appendix A). He or she is knowledgeable on all things holistic, and is qualified to help you plan a menu. Since balance is essential to good health, it's best not to try making meals on your own—at least not at first. You can also consult a veterinary nutritionist. They make diets to suit individual dogs' needs.

There are several good sources for learning more about feeding natural

Did You Know?
Veterinarians estimate that between 30 percent and 50 percent of today's dog population is overweight.

diets. For a comprehensive look at natural health for pets, and specific fresh diet recipes, check out Appendix A.

Don't expect your allopathic veterinarian to get on board with this idea. Most are opposed to owners cooking for their dogs, due to concerns about nutrient balance and handling of raw meats. Both are realistic concerns. But if you're working with a holistic practitioner and take proper care, there is little need to avoid trying this method. Safe handling will not prevent many food-borne illnesses, although it will decrease risk. You can learn to prepare a balanced diet and handle foods safely.

> Realize that if you really want to feed your dog a fresh-food diet, you have to prepare it.

Following a consultation with a holistic vet, get to the kitchen! Realize that if you really want to feed your dog a fresh-food diet, you have to prepare it. That means you'll be buying, mixing, fixing, chopping, freezing, and serving—a lot. It's definitely much more work than opening a bag, can, or box. But to those with a dedicated holistic mindset, the extra work is worthwhile.

If you rarely cook for yourself now, or disdain the idea of more cooking, perhaps a fresh-food diet isn't the best idea for you. Consider a pre-made fresh diet or commercial natural diet instead.

Pre-Made Fresh Diets

If you're interested in feeding your Poodle a fresh diet, but are turned off by all the fixing and mixing, consider ordering pre-made foods. Many holistic-oriented individuals and companies will do all the prep for you and, for a price, ship to you a frozen batch of fresh food (usually meat and supplements). All you need to do is thaw the meal before feeding and add veggies and grains as recommended by your holistic vet.

Commercial Natural Diets

Keeping step with consumer interest in natural foods, pet food companies have developed diets for those who wish to buy natural but prefer to keep it simple.

How is "natural" defined? Good question. There are no regulations in the pet industry as to how the term can be used, so it can mean a variety of things. For those with a holistic mindset, a natural diet generally means:

○ The diet is made with minimal processing and low heat.
○ The diet has a high bioavailability—it's made with whole foods and contains chelated and esterized vitamins and minerals (chelation and esterification are chemical processes by which manufacturers increase bioavailability).
○ Ingredients are high quality, such as human-grade meats, grains, organic veggies, and dairy products.
○ The diet contains no artificial anything—including colors, preservatives, or flavors, and no growth hormones or antibiotics.
○ The diet is preserved naturally, with vitamin E and C. No ethoxiquin, a chemical preservative.
○ The diet is protein-based, with turkey, beef, chicken, lamb, or rabbit.

Natural diets vary in quality, so check them carefully. Read the label and, if in doubt, call the company. Be wary of diets with highly processed ingredients or by-products because it's difficult to determine precisely what these comprise. You can purchase these diets at health-food stores, some pet-supply stores, by mail order, and via the Internet. Again, your best bet is with AAFCO tested as complete and balanced foods.

Vegetarian Delight

For vegetarian owners who wish to share their philosophy with the family Poodle, the best advice is to consult with a board certified veterinary nutritionist. Dogs like eating meat, but they are considered omnivores—animals who can meet nutritional needs from a wide variety of sources. Wild coyotes and wolves, for example, eat grasses, berries, and other vegetable matter. That means dogs can subsist on a vegetarian diet, or a diet low in meat. However, dogs are individuals. Some can thrive on a meatless diet, some can't. It's essential that you work with a veterinary nutritionist as well as a holistic veterinarian who together can help you plan a vegetarian menu and chart your dog's health. Be aware that most holistic veterinarians and nutritionists do not recommend a vegan diet for dogs, one that excludes all animal foods such as meat products or eggs.

> Dogs like eating meat, but they are considered omnivores—animals who can meet nutritional needs from a wide variety of sources.

How Often and How Much Do I Feed My Poodle?

How much should you feed your Poodle and how often? There's no exact answer to that because this depends on the size, age, and activity level of each individual Poodle. Feeding amount and schedule also depend on which diet you're using and how cold it is outside. (Dogs who spend a lot of time outdoors in cold temperatures require more food.)

Feed and Observe

Begin by following the feeding instructions spelled out on the dog food package. Realize that these instructions are a starting point, and apply to all breeds of a certain weight. Your Poodle is an individual and every dog is different.

Following that, observe your Poodle's body condition.

○ **Too thin.** An overly thin Poodle will have visible or easily felt ribs and hip bones may be visible. The waist and belly are obviously tucked up when viewed from the side. *Increase food.*

○ **Just right.** The ribs should have just a little fat over them; you should be able to easily feel them with slight pressure. Your Poodle should have a waist when viewed from above, and the belly should be tucked up when viewed from the side. *Continue as is.*

○ **Too heavy.** If you can't easily feel your Poodle's ribs and can easily see fat covering them, he is too heavy. His waist is absent or barely visible when viewed from above, or his belly may hang. *Decrease food.*

How Often?

How often you feed your Poodle depends on how old he is and his (or your) personal preference. Pups must be fed several times a day, usually three. The average adult Poodle can be fed once or twice a day, in the morning, evening, or both. Many owners like the idea of feeding twice a day, while others find it inconvenient and opt to feed once a day. Toy puppies have a very rapid metabolism and may require four to six meals a day to avoid hypoglycemia, a life-threatening drop in blood sugar levels. By six months of age, most Toy pups can cut back to three or four meals a day.

> Toy puppies have a very rapid metabolism and may require four to six meals a day to avoid hypoglycemia, a life-threatening drop in blood sugar levels.

Free-feeding, leaving food out for the Poodle at all times, is not recommended because it can lead to excess weight gain.

Establish a Routine

Dogs are creatures of habit, and seem to enjoy eating at the same time every day. Feeding your Poodle pup at the same time every day helps establish eating habits and makes housebreaking easier. Pups usually need to urinate or defecate after eating. If you feed him at the same time every day, you can predict when nature calls.

Feeding Puppies

Poodle pups have special feeding requirements. A puppy's stomach is not large enough to hold sufficient food in one feeding to provide his daily nutritional needs. When a puppy graduates from mother's milk to solid food at about six weeks of age, he will require three to four meals a day, with the exception of Toys, who may need four to six meals. When he reaches about four to five months old, twice-a-day feedings may be sufficient. He can graduate to once-a-day meals at eight to nine months of age.

A pup's nutritional requirements for growth and development are greater than those for an adult dog. If you opt to feed your Poodle pup a commercially prepared diet, feed one formulated especially for pups to ensure that your Poodle gets the nutrients he needs. A Poodle pup who eats a complete and balanced commercial puppy diet doesn't need additional supplements. Adding supplements can cause nutritional imbalance. However, if you are supplying your dog with a home-cooked or fresh-diet meal plan, supplements may be necessary. Consult with a veterinary nutritionist.

Dry food can be moistened with warm water to encourage pups to eat. Milk can be used, too, but only in extremely small amounts. Cow's milk causes digestive upset in some puppies and dogs. A tablespoon of canned food can be added to increase interest, as well.

These are general guidelines for feeding your Poodle pup; consult with your veterinarian for more specific advice.

Adult Meals

The adult Poodle is a mature dog, usually age one year or older. Healthy adult dogs who are not pregnant, nursing, or hardworking have somewhat low nutritional requirements. Feeding is fairly straightforward if you're feeding commercially prepared kibble. Buy a complete and balanced diet made for the adult dog and give your dog the recommended amount once or twice a day. Add a tablespoon of canned food for taste if you wish. Adjust the amount according to the Poodle's activity level and body condition.

The Importance of Water

Water is important to every living creature, and your Poodle is no exception.

Water makes up around 60 percent of your adult dog's body and even more of your puppy's constitution. Dogs need water to help their cells function properly and to aid in proper digestion. Basically, dogs need water to live. Without water, a dog will die within only a few days.

The water in your dog's body needs to be replenished on a regular basis, since it is routinely lost through respiration, digestion, and urination. On hot days or when exercising heavily, your dog needs even more water to keep his body running smoothly.

To keep your Poodle at optimum health, provide him with constant access to plenty of cool, fresh water.

Feeding Hardworking Poodles

Highly active Poodles—those who work in the field or compete in agility trials or flyball competition—use a lot of energy. The hard-working dog can require two to three time more kilocalories per pound of body weight than what is required for normal activity. To maintain good body condition and keep up his stamina, the hardworking Poodle must eat a high-energy diet.

Many veterinarians recommend commercially prepared "performance" diets for highly active dogs. (These are not "weekend warriors," but are dogs that are *consistently* active.) Higher-fat, higher-protein diets supply the working dog with needed calories. Because performance diets are higher in protein than maintenance diets, there's a misconception that the active dog just needs extra protein. However, all nutrients are required in greater amounts. Additionally, research indicates that moderately high-protein diets are unlikely to cause kidney damage—in spite of some breeders' and owners' beliefs that it does.

Multiple, small meals are best for highly active Poodles to keep up their blood sugar level. Snacks throughout the day may be necessary, too, as is appropriate hydration. However, active dogs should not be fed or watered immediately before or after a work session. Feeding meals too close to working can decrease performance or cause digestive discomfort.

> To maintain good body condition and keep up his stamina, the hardworking Poodle must eat a high-energy diet.

Feeding Your Elderly Poodle

Older Poodles—those who have reached the last 25 percent of their expected life span—are usually less active than adult dogs and pups. Thus, their energy requirements are reduced and they can gain weight easily if fed too much or fed a high-calorie diet. Some veterinarians recommend "senior" diets; foods high in nutrients but reduced in calories to keep senior Poodles at a healthy weight.

The Fat Fight

Too much food, too much of the wrong kind of food, lack of activity—all can lead to obesity, the excess accumulation of body fat. An animal weighing 20 percent or more above her ideal weight can be considered obese. The risk of obesity increases with age. As your Poodle grows older, keeping her weight on target can become more difficult.

So what's so terrible about a little extra weight? Well, it's unhealthy! Your overweight Poodle may be susceptible to these problems:

○ Impaired heart and breathing functions
○ Reduced life span
○ Heat stress
○ Stress on skeletal system
○ Increased surgical risk

What causes obesity? Several factors contribute, including diet, genetics, and hormonal disorders. Hormone imbalances such as thyroid or pituitary gland dysfunction, as well as diabetes mellitus, can lead to obesity. Additionally, spaying and neutering can be associated with obesity due to possible metabolic changes.

However, diet is the most common cause of obesity in dogs. When your Poodle eats more than she should, she consumes more calories than she can use. Too much food, too many treats, and table scraps cause obesity!

Here's how you can prevent obesity:

○ Feed only what your Poodle needs.
○ Do not free-feed. Serve the meal and if it's not eaten in 15 minutes, pick it up.
○ Refrain from feeding fatty table scraps and high-calorie treats.
○ Guard kitchen countertops! Poodles are known to swipe food that's left out.
○ Keep your Poodle active. Play, walk to the park, get involved in a canine sport.
○ Make sure everyone in the family agrees not to overfeed the Poodle.
○ Consult with a veterinarian before starting your dog on a weight-loss program.

Is It Okay to Share My Food?

Is it okay to share your meals with your Poodle? The answer to that depends on who you ask. Some Poodle enthusiasts say no—no table scraps at all. Adding "people food" to the Poodle's diet upsets her balanced canine diet. Others say, why not? A few tidbits here and there won't hurt.

Before you share meals with your Poodle, realize that table scraps are often rich and high in fat, which can cause digestive upset. And, extra tidbits can cause a Poodle to gain excessive weight.

It's probably best to avoid giving scraps. However, if you are tempted to share (and most owners are), limit it to a few morsels now and then. Never give table scraps to an overweight Poodle.

A better idea than giving table scraps is offering your Poodle wholesome, nutritious treats. Treats should be lowfat, low-sodium, and preservative-free, and should comprise no more than 5 to 10 percent of your Poodle's diet, depending upon the type of treats you're giving.

Here are a few healthful ideas:

○ Hard biscuits (store-bought or homemade)
○ Raw veggies (such as carrots or broccoli)
○ Cooked liver or chicken tidbits
○ Cheese tidbits

Appendix A contains a list of Web sites full of healthful and delicious treats you can make and bake for your precious Poodle.

Do not feed your Poodle sugary treats, candies, cake, or anything that contains chocolate. While considered the perfect food by some people, chocolate contains a chemical, theobromine, that is potentially toxic to dogs. At the very least, it causes digestive upset.

Toxic Treats—
Dangerous Foods for Dogs

Certain treats, while they are all right for human consumption, can be dangerous, or even lethal, to your pet.

Certain high-fat meats such as pork are difficult for dogs to digest and can trigger pancreatitis, a potentially dangerous inflammation of the pancreas. Also, meats doused in rich sauces, rich gravy, or spices can wreak havoc on your dog's digestive system.

Bones pose a serious danger to your dog. Never feed your dog bones left over from your meal, especially poultry, fish, and pork bones. Pieces can break off and cause constipation, intestinal punctures, or blockage of your dog's digestive tract.

Never be tempted to ease your dog's thirst with anything other than water. Soda contains sugar or artificial sweeteners and unhealthy additives, and alcohol can be harmful or even fatal if consumed in large quantities.

Avoid salty, calorie-laden snacks, such as potato chips. Excessive salt can dehydrate your pet, and extra fat calories will only translate into extra pounds.

Sugary snacks, such as candy and cookies, are also bad for your Poodle. At the least, they fill him up with empty calories and leave him less interested in his own food, which can result in poor nutrition. At the worst, they can make your dog sick, causing diarrhea and/or vomiting.

Chocolate is especially dangerous for dogs; it can even be deadly. Different types of chocolate pose varying risks. While milk chocolate will probably make your Poodle ill, baking chocolate could possibly kill him. Be safe and never feed your dog chocolate of any kind.

What's All the Fuss About Supplements?

When is it necessary to give your Poodle food supplements? "Never, if the dog is fed a balanced diet," says Dr. Blair. "If supplements are given," she says, "it can and often does lead to an unbalanced diet, and other needed minerals and vitamins may not be absorbed properly."

So, if you feed your normal, healthy Poodle a commercially prepared, complete and balanced diet, no additional supplements are necessary. Don't add anything. (If you're cooking for your dog and feeding a fresh-food diet, supplements are necessary as directed by a holistic veterinarian.)

At times supplements—given only under veterinary supervision—are necessary. For example, lactating bitches may require added nutrients, especially if they're nursing a large litter. Or a sled dog racing the Iditarod needs her diet supplemented with meats and fats in order to consume the 10,000 to 15,000 calories a day to keep warm and maintain body weight while running 100 miles a day.

If you're feeding your Poodle a commercially prepared diet that is complete and balanced, and your Poodle looks great, forget about supplements.

Medical Care
Every Poodle Needs

In This Chapter

○ Your Poodle's Veterinary Care
○ Preventive Medicine
○ Sick Calls and Emergencies
○ The Cost of Veterinary Care

G ood health is a blessing. But as you know, good health also requires effort, which includes medical care. And that's just what your Poodle will need—medical care—to maintain her good health for years to come.

Your Poodle's Veterinary Care

Regular veterinary visits are the best way to ensure your Poodle's good health. You, as well as the veterinarian, are important members of your Poodle's health-care team, whether you're preventing diseases through vaccination or identifying illnesses as they pop up.

Since most breeder and adoption contracts stipulate that new owners have the dog checked by a veterinarian of their choice within a few days of purchase or adoption, you'll need to locate a vet before you pick up your Poodle. That way, you can have your new pet examined promptly.

Your Poodle is healthiest when you take an active role in managing and overseeing her health, and that means partnering with a skilled veterinarian. As a caring owner, you are responsible for the overall well-being and health of your Poodle, from puppyhood through her elderly years.

Veterinarians agree that owners are crucial in managing the health of their pets. The ideal situation is a partnership with your veterinarian based on trust, listening, and determining needs. The ultimate goal is to have a healthy Poodle.

> The ideal situation is a partnership with your veterinarian based on trust, listening, and determining needs.

Owners being partners with their veterinarians is a somewhat new idea to owners and to the veterinary community. Ten to 15 years ago, most owners left the worries of health care to their veterinarians. Now the team approach is growing in popularity. Today, owners are more aware, more educated, and more concerned about their dogs' health.

What are your responsibilities as a member of your Poodle's health-care team? You won't have to don a mask and gown and perform surgery (though that's what some owners envision when they hear talk about managing their dogs' health). Taking an active role in your dog's health care is much simpler than that.

Learn as much as you can about your Poodle, breed particulars, proper grooming, natural temperament, and appropriate training techniques. Learn about dogs in general: normal canine behavior, roles as companions and workers, the variety of breeds, common illnesses and diseases. Read books and magazines, surf the Internet, chat with other Poodle owners, and consult with trainers and veterinarians.

If you put in some effort, you will be a better owner. An educated owner is more likely to be a good owner.

Whatever efforts you put toward becoming actively involved in your Poodle's health care and partnering with your vet, your Poodle will enjoy many health benefits. The firm commitment to your Poodle is something to feel good about, and you'll sleep soundly at night, knowing you've attended to all your Poodle's needs with care.

Selecting the Right Partner

"You should choose a vet who is genuinely concerned for the health and well-being of your pet," suggests Poodle owner Michelle Mace, "and one who is open-minded to your concerns for the health care of your pet."

Veterinarians vary in personality, approach to treatment, and medical perspective. The usual academic degree for a veterinarian in the United States is D.V.M. or V.M.D., both of which stand for doctor of veterinary medicine. Veterinarians usually operate a small-animal or large-animal practice. Small-animal veterinarians offer care for dogs, cats, birds, rabbits, and the like. Large-animal vets care for such animals as horses, cows, pigs, and goats. You'll want a

Oh, So Special

What's a veterinary specialist? That term can be confusing to owners. A glance under the heading "Veterinarian" in the yellow pages reveals a wide variety of listings under the vets' names: general medicine, specializing in surgery, cancer treatments, cardiology, vaccinations, dentistry, internal medicine. But a veterinary specialist isn't a practitioner who limits her practice to dogs or is interested in a particular area of medicine, such as dentistry. A veterinary specialist is a veterinarian who is board certified by a specialty board approved by the American Veterinary Medical Association (AVMA).

To earn the title of veterinary specialist, the veterinarian must complete a veterinary school program approved by the AVMA, and usually extends her education by completing a one-year internship and a two- or three-year residency program in a particular discipline. She must be licensed to practice veterinary medicine in at least one state.

Once the educational requirements are finished, the vet then has to pass a battery of rigorous examinations in her field. Only then can she receive official certification by a specialty board, such as the American College of Veterinary Behaviorists or the American College of Zoological Medicine. Certification requirements vary but are governed by the American Board of Veterinary Specialists (ABVS).

The Board has specific guidelines on how specialists may list names or practices. Veterinarians may not imply or infer that they're specialists when they aren't. The terms an owner should look for when seeking out a true specialist are board certified (board eligible or board qualified aren't the same and are considered misleading by the ABVS), diplomate, ACVIM (American College of Veterinary Internal Medicine), and ABVP. The board-certified veterinary specialist's name and title are usually listed like this: Mary Veterinarian, D.V.M., Diplomate American Board of Veterinary Practitioners, Board Certified in Surgery.

If your Poodle requires the services of a veterinary specialist, your general practitioner will usually give you a referral. If you want to contact a specialist on your own, contact your local or state veterinary association for a name or call the American Veterinary Medical Association at (800) 248-2862 for a listing of board-certified vets in your area. If you live near a school of veterinary medicine, contact the college. Many specialists work at veterinary colleges.

veterinarian who operates a small-animal practice for your Poodle's general practitioner.

Small-animal veterinarians can limit their practice to a certain species—a dog-only or cat-only practice, for example. Or some veterinarians have taken an interest in exotic pets, offering medical care to rabbits, birds, ferrets, and reptiles. Additionally, veterinarians are trained in medical specialties. There are currently 20 specialties recognized by the American Veterinary Medical Association (AVMA). Specialty disciplines include behavior, emergency care, dermatology, ophthalmology, nutrition, and surgery. While you don't want to start with a specialist, you can rest assured that one is available should you need expertise for your Poodle's specific health problem.

Make a list of the things you feel are important in a veterinarian and a veterinary hospital. What are the doctor's credentials? Are the veterinarian and the facility members of the AAHA? Although this isn't necessarily a requirement in choosing a doctor, AAHA members must adhere to certain standards for medical procedures and hospital management, so membership means these requirements have been met.

Does the veterinarian seem to genuinely like animals? And, just as important, does she genuinely like people? While there are many wonderful veterinarians out there who have a special way with animals, the one you choose must be able to communicate with people. It is important that you feel comfortable with your Poodle's veterinarian and that she is able to explain complex medical information in layperson's terms.

Is the facility small, with just one or two veterinarians, or is it a large multi-doctor practice or even a teaching hospital? Many people want a veterinarian who will get to know them and their dog personally.

Seeing the same veterinarian each visit allows her to know the dog's medical history intimately, which can be advantageous when diagnosing ailments. A negative of smaller facilities is that they may lack some of the high-tech equipment found in different establishments. This may mean you'll be referred to a different hospital for certain procedures during your dog's lifetime. Large practices, on the other hand, often have doctors specializing in certain areas of veterinary medicine and modern equipment and laboratories on-site to conduct tests and interpret the results. You may end up seeing a different doctor each time you visit a larger facility, however, making it difficult to establish an ongoing relationship.

Is someone on call 24 hours a day? If not, does the hospital recommend an after-hours facility for emergencies? If so, you need to check out that facility as well.

Where is the hospital located? If you live in a busy household, you may need to choose a hospital close to home. You'll also want a veterinarian who is convenient to get to during an emergency. At the same time, it may be worthwhile to choose one located a few miles away rather than settle for a closer hospital that doesn't meet your other requirements.

> While there are many wonderful veterinarians out there who have a special way with animals, the one you choose must be able to communicate with people.

For most owners, a hospital's hours are also an important factor. Choose a facility whose hours of operation coincide with your schedule. Most hospitals have evening hours at least one night a week, and/or are open on Saturdays. Although rare, some veterinarians still make house calls; such a doctor may offer the convenience you're seeking.

Perhaps you prefer a veterinarian with a holistic approach to medicine. In addition to veterinary training, a licensed veterinarian can be certified in three alternative modalities: acupuncture, chiropractic, and homeopathy, with certified veterinary acupuncturists the most numerous. Certification and accreditation for acupuncture is available to licensed vets through the International Veterinary Acupuncture Society, and through a few state accreditation boards and veterinary courses. Chiropractic certification is available to licensed vets through the American Veterinary Chiropractic Association. Homeopathy certification is available to licensed vets through the Academy of Veterinary Homeopathy. Certification doesn't guarantee expertise in alternative therapies, but it does indicate a strong interest. The AVMA does not list or recognize these specialty certifications.

Search Clues

How can you locate the right veterinarian for your Poodle?

Word of mouth is always the best first step. Start by asking the Poodle's breeder for a referral. Most breeders have a favorite vet who treats all their dogs and pups.

Ask a Poodle rescue volunteer or dog-owning friend for a name. Contact the local Poodle club and ask for a referral or ask your Poodle's trainer to recommend a vet.

Look in the yellow pages of your local telephone book or search the Internet. Stick with national, well-recognized Poodle clubs and organizations.

Once you've acquired a few names, visit the office. Look for a clean, well-lit, up-to-date, friendly environment. Chat with the staff and let them know you're

Did You Know?

Shelters in the United States take in nearly 11 million cats and dogs each year. Nearly 75 percent of those animals have to be euthanized.

searching for a vet. Don't be afraid to ask waiting clients what they think of the vet and staff. Ask for a tour (be aware this might be difficult at busy times) and a listing of fees and services offered—grooming or emergency services, for example. Or does the vet sell pet-supply products? Other considerations include suitable location, convenient hours, and helpful staff. Give the clinic a good look-see, make mental notes of what you like or dislike, and visit another clinic. Then make your decision.

With "busy" being everyone's key word today, you may not have time to visit several clinics. While it's the best way to research, it does take time. If you trust your Poodle's breeder, chances are her veterinarian is a good starting point.

The First Visit

The first visit with a veterinarian is an important one. If you're pleased with the practitioner, it will be the beginning of a partnership. If you aren't pleased, it will be the end of your relationship. Either way, you have to be prepared to make this decision.

> Whether your new Poodle is a puppy or adult, you must have the dog examined within a few days of purchase or adoption to ensure its health status.

Whether your new Poodle is a puppy or adult, you must have the dog examined within a few days of purchase or adoption to ensure its health status. To make the most of this first visit, it's wise to bring along the following:

○ All health records, including vaccine history, deworming schedule, genetic tests/certification, surgeries, treatments. Be sure to obtain these from your breeder, the dog's previous owner, or rescue group
○ Breeder or adoption contracts
○ Medications your Poodle is currently taking

○ Know what your Poodle has been eating, including specific ingredients in the diet

○ Stool sample (if requested by clinic staff)

○ A list of questions/concerns you may have

Getting to the clinic is often a concern for owners. Puppies especially may not be accustomed to car rides, though the same is true for some adult dogs. To make the journey as safe as possible, fit your Poodle with a collar and leash, and place her in a crate in the car. It's better that you confine your dog during the ride, especially if this is her first ride. You certainly don't want to risk her jumping about in the car, distracting you and potentially causing an accident. Later on, you may wish to teach your Poodle to sit in the backseat with a safety restraint. But for this all-important first visit, plan on putting your Poodle in her crate.

What to Expect

What can you expect at your first visit to your veterinarian? For you, it's an opportunity to meet the vet up close and personal, and learn more about proper health care for your Poodle. It's a time to ask questions, and chat with the vet to determine whether he or she is the person you want caring for your Poodle. For your Poodle, it's a time to determine her health status.

Upon your arrival at the clinic, the veterinary staff will ask you to fill out forms stating basic information to start a file: your name, address, telephone number, your Poodle's name, age, breeder, health history, and so on. Be sure you inform the staff that this is a first visit with a new dog, as recommended by the breeder or rescue agency. After you've finished with the paperwork,

Questions to Ask Your Veterinarian

Ask questions such as those listed below to evaluate whether a veterinarian is right for you and your dog.

○ What are the credentials of the veterinarian(s)? Is the hospital affiliated with the AAHA?

○ How many veterinarians work at the hospital? Can I request to see the same doctor each time I visit or will I see whoever is available?

○ What type of equipment do you have on-hand at the hospital? If you do not have certain equipment, where would you send my dog to receive treatment? What is that facility's reputation?

○ Do you have an on-site lab or do you send out for test results? How quickly are results available?

○ What are your hospital's hours and where are you located?

○ Do you offer any add-on services such as boarding or grooming?

○ What are the average fees for checkups, spaying/neutering, vaccinations, etc.? Do you offer a wellness program or a multi-pet discount?

○ Do you treat any other Poodles in your practice? (While most canine medicine applies to all breeds, certain diseases and health concerns apply specifically to Poodles. You should make sure your veterinarian is knowledgeable about genetic problems that run in the breed.)

you and your dog may have to wait a few minutes. If so, be sure to keep your Poodle on-leash, or if she's a small pup, in the crate or on your lap. That way, your dog won't come in contact with other pets that might be ill or less than friendly.

Next, you and your Poodle will be ushered into an examining room to wait for your consultation with the vet. A veterinary assistant may come in to prepare, ask a few questions, or take the Poodle's pulse, respiratory rate, and temperature.

When the veterinarian arrives, he or she will greet you and your Poodle, then get down to the serious business of investigat-

Questions Your Veterinarian May Ask You

○ Is this your first dog? Is this your first Poodle?

○ What are your feelings on spaying/neutering? (Dogs who are pet quality and are not going to be bred should be spayed or neutered. This helps prevent overpopulation and also is healthier for your dog.)

○ Have you located a training school for your new dog? (Your veterinarian may offer recommendations, or the hospital itself may hold training classes.)

○ What type of food are you feeding?

○ What types of toys does your dog play with? (Some toys should only be played with under supervision, such as toys with squeakers, or toys that are easily chewed apart.)

○ Are you crate-training your dog?

○ Do you have any questions concerning housetraining, obedience training, nutrition, etc.?

ing your Poodle's health status. Most likely, the first exam will include these elements:

○ A review of the Poodle's health, vaccination, and certification history

○ Specific questions and a discussion about the Poodle's health history, diet, and lifestyle

○ A careful check of the Poodle from head to toe for signs of illness or infectious diseases such as cloudy eyes, runny nose, infected ears, irritated skin, or hair loss. Your vet will include a look in your Poodle's eyes, ears, and mouth, and listen to her heart and lungs via stethoscope. The vet may manipulate her legs and knees for soundness, and feel your Poodle's abdomen for lumps that could indicate a hernia or tumor; a distended belly can be a sign of internal parasites

○ A check for congenital defects

❍ Planning for a spay or neuter

❍ Planning for a vaccination schedule

❍ An exam of your Poodle's stool sample under the microscope for the presence of internal parasites, followed by deworming if necessary

❍ Heartworm testing and preventive

❍ Discussion of behavior and training issues

❍ Grooming suggestions and toenail trim

While your Poodle's appearance doesn't tell all, the veterinarian can learn a lot about your pet's health during this comprehensive physical exam. It's like checking a watermelon for ripeness. A watermelon that's ripe, juicy, and ready to eat feels and looks right. A Poodle who's healthy feels and looks right, too.

> A watermelon that's ripe, juicy, and ready to eat feels and looks right. A Poodle who's healthy feels and looks right, too.

A veterinarian is trained to see and notice subtle signs of good or bad health.

Some illnesses cannot be detected by a physical exam or may not be noticeably present in your Poodle. Inheritable diseases such as hip and elbow dysplasia cannot be determined by a visual exam. Your veterinarian may recommend tests to screen for these conditions. She may also advise testing for heartworms, which is essential before placing a dog on heartworm preventive medication. Additionally, your vet may ask for specific tests if she suspects a problem.

Once the vet completes the exam, it's time for you to ask questions. Perhaps you're unsure of how often to vaccinate or how to keep your Poodle's ears clean. Query your vet to make the most of your visit, especially if you're a new puppy owner. Remember, you must be able to communicate with this important member of your Poodle's health-care team. "Most important is having a vet who will take time to talk with you and listen to your concerns," says Poodle owner Linda Hargett. "Communication is paramount in the vet-client relationship."

Following are a few questions you might want to ask the veterinarian:

○ Is my Poodle healthy? What brings you to this conclusion?
○ What vaccination schedule do you recommend?
○ Does the office send out vaccination reminders to clients?
○ When can the puppy be spayed or neutered?
○ Will heartworm testing and preventive medication be necessary?
○ What is your recommendation for flea control?
○ What diet and feeding schedule do you think is best for my Poodle pup (or adult)?
○ Can you offer a groomer and trainer referral?
○ Do you suggest routine teeth brushing for my Poodle?
○ How often do you want to see my Poodle for checkups?

Preventive Medicine

An ounce of prevention is worth a pound of cure. This saying rings especially true when it comes to preventing poor health and illness in your Poodle. Preventive medicine—providing your Poodle care *before* something goes wrong—is another important aspect of medical care every Poodle needs.

Regular Visits

The cornerstone of preventive care is regular veterinary visits. This may seem obvious, especially if you're a new owner of a Poodle pup or adult and have just had your pet checked or have an appointment scheduled for next week. Later on, when the newness of owning a Poodle wears off, these visits may diminish in importance in your mind. However, the importance of having your vet check your Poodle routinely *never* diminishes.

Once or twice a year, the vet updates vaccinations; listens to the Poodle's heart and lungs; checks the eyes, nose, and mouth; feels for suspicious lumps and bumps; takes the Poodle's temperature; checks joints and internal organs; orders tests; checks for internal parasites; and so on. These exams are invaluable opportunities for your vet to evaluate your Poodle's overall health and catch potential health problems early, when they can be most easily corrected.

Make it a priority to take your Poodle to the veterinary clinic every year, or more often if your practitioner advises that.

Vaccinations

Vaccinations are an essential part of preventive medicine for your Poodle. Vaccines prevent dogs from getting a host of nasty diseases such as rabies, parvovirus, or distemper. Vaccinations are given to boost an animal's immunity—or ability to fight a particular disease.

There are two types of vaccines: modified live virus and killed virus vaccine. Some veterinarians believe that modified live vaccines are the most effective and last longer. At times, vaccines fail and dogs suffer disease even though they've been vaccinated. This is usually because the vaccines weren't given correctly, were outdated, mishandled, or were ineffective because the dog was sick or immature when the vaccine was given and failed to develop immunity. These risks can be minimized by allowing a veterinarian to vaccinate, rather than buying mail-order vaccinations and doing it yourself. Your vet is trained in proper vaccine handling and administration.

Beginning at six to eight weeks, pups need to start a series of vaccinations to build immunity. Even after beginning vaccinations, though, young pups are vulnerable to disease. Many vets recommend limiting your puppy's exposure to other dogs until her first series of shots is complete. Traditionally, boosters are given yearly. This tradition is based on manufacturers' recommendations and labeling. However, few studies actually prove how long vaccines are effective.

To remain effective, vaccinations must be current. That means following your Poodle pup's initial shots with boosters as directed by the veterinarian. Some vaccines are required by law. In addition, rabies vaccinations and boosters are ruled by local laws designed to prevent spread of this deadly disease from pets to people. Many states require annual rabies vaccinations; others every three years. Your veterinarian knows these laws—make sure you understand the vaccination intervals in your state.

According to the American Animal Hospital Association, growing evidence indicates that protection from vaccination is longer lasting than previously believed. In addition, holistic-oriented practitioners especially are concerned that vaccination is not as harmless as once thought. This awareness has led many infectious disease experts, researchers, and veterinarians to recommend a reduced frequency of vaccinations. What this means is yearly boosters may or may not be recommended by the vet for your Poodle, depending on her specific risk situation.

Did You Know?

Tests conducted at the Institute for the Study of Animal Problems in Washington, D.C., revealed that dogs and cats, like humans, are either right- or left-handed.

Sample Vaccination Schedule

Following is a sample vaccination schedule for pups and dogs. Your vet may recommend other vaccines—coronavirus or Lyme disease, for instance—or a slightly different schedule, such as eliminating leptospirosis.

Eight Weeks: Distemper, hepatitis, leptospirosis, parainfluenza, and
    parvo (DHLPP), usually combined in one injection
Twelve Weeks: DHLPP, possibly Lyme disease, and bordetella
Sixteen Weeks: DHLPP, rabies, Lyme disease (if begun at 12 weeks)
Twenty Weeks: Parvo booster for pups considered at high risk
One Year, after last vaccination, or as directed by veterinarian: DHLPP,
    rabies, bordetella, and Lyme (if previously given)

Spaying and Neutering

"Spaying or neutering is the best option for owners who want happy, healthy, hassle-free pets," says Poodle owner Michelle Mace.

Altering a young puppy before it has a chance to breed ensures it will not grow up to add to the overpopulated world of homeless animals.

Not surprisingly, spaying or neutering is an important part of preventive medicine. Surgically altering your Poodle so she cannot breed has many health benefits. For example, female dogs spayed before the first heat cycle are less likely to develop breast cancer, and spaying eliminates the chance of pyometra, a potentially fatal uterine infection. There is no truth to the myth that there are behavioral or health benefits if you allow your female Poodle to first have a litter, then have her spayed.

Breeding Myths: Common Misconceptions About Breeding Dogs

○ Females need to birth one litter to calm down.

○ "Mother" dogs are sweeter and gentler than females who never have puppies.

○ Children should experience the miracle of birth close up.

○ By breeding my dog, I'll produce a puppy just like him/her.

○ By selling puppies, I'll offset some of the money I've spent on my dog.

Neutered male dogs are at lower risk of developing prostate infections and they won't roam about looking for a mate, which can lead to their getting hit by a car or getting into fights. A spayed or neutered pet is a more content pet than one left intact. Altering before puberty can prevent some aggressive behavior.

But that's not all. Spaying or neutering your Poodle will prevent unwanted litters that will add to the already overpopulated world of homeless animals, including purebreds. Approximately 30 percent of the 8 to 12 million animals entering humane shelters in the United States are purebred, according to the American Humane Association. There simply aren't enough good homes for all the purebreds and mixed breeds alike. *Do your part to stop pet overpopulation. Spay or neuter your Poodle!*

Dogs are usually altered at five to eight months of age; and they tolerate anesthesia well at this age and heal quickly. However, some veterinarians alter much younger pups, at 8 to 12 weeks of age. Although early spay and neuter surgeries are not widespread, they do have a following, especially among Humane

Myths About Spaying and Neutering

If you hear any of the following myths regarding spaying and neutering your Poodle, don't believe them. They're old wives' tales, not statements of fact.

- ○ Female dogs should have one litter before being spayed.
- ○ Altered dogs get fat.
- ○ Neutered male dogs lack machismo.
- ○ Children should experience the birth of a litter.
- ○ Wait until the dog goes through puberty before spaying or neutering.
- ○ It's cruel to take away a dog's ability to mate naturally.
- ○ A dog's personality will change if altered.

Society workers concerned about pet overpopulation. Altering a young puppy before it has a chance to breed ensures it will not grow up to add to the overpopulated world of homeless animals.

Consult with your individual veterinarian to learn what is the best time to spay or neuter your Poodle. If you're adopting an adult from a shelter or rescue organization, the procedure has probably already been done, but check to make sure.

Good Food

As discussed in the previous chapter, good food acts as preventive medicine for your Poodle. Since food is the fuel required to nourish your Poodle's body, the body needs a special balance of nutrients to create energy and good health. If that balance is upset by either lack of food or the wrong foods, health problems can arise. A deficiency, or excess, of any nutrients can lead to illness.

Your Poodle needs good food, a proper diet that supplies all the nutrients appropriate to its life stage, to be in top health. If you feed your Poodle properly, he will probably be healthy. If you don't feed him properly, or overfeed, his health will suffer.

Get Up and Go!

Adequate exercise goes hand in hand with a proper diet for your Poodle. If your Poodle doesn't get enough exercise, he may become overweight, bored, difficult to manage, and develop destructive and annoying behaviors.

You can prevent health problems associated with obesity by encouraging your Poodle to get up and go. For activity suggestions, see Chapter 8. Pick something you both enjoy and get busy.

Heartworm Prevention and Dewormings

It's fairly common for dogs to have internal parasites such as hookworms, tapeworms, whipworms, roundworms, or heartworms. All survive by living off their host, your Poodle. If your dog is infected with any internal parasites, his health will suffer. Internal parasites literally suck the life out of their host. Deworming medicine may be necessary to prevent ill health due to hookworms, tapeworms, whipworms, and roundworms.

Heartworms, which are spread via mosquitoes, are long worms that live in the heart and pulmonary arteries of a dog and eventually cause heart failure and death. Fortunately, medications are available to prevent heartworm infestation. Heartworm preventive medicine makes good sense, especially in areas with a heavy mosquito population. Ask your vet if heartworm preventive is necessary for your Poodle. A test is required before giving the dog medication to make sure he isn't already infected.

Flea Control

There's no doubt about it: Fleas are extremely irritating, annoying pests. But did you know that if left uncontrolled, a flea infestation on your Poodle can actually cause poor health? A heavily infested Poodle can become anemic from all the biting and blood-sucking. And, should your Poodle ingest a flea while biting and scratching, he could become infected with tapeworms. Fleas frequently harbor immature tapeworms, which they acquire by eating tapeworm eggs, in their intestines. Once the dog swallows an infested flea, he too becomes infested.

If that isn't bad enough, fleas also are the cause of flea-bite dermatitis. Some animals are highly allergic to the flea's bite— and it takes only one chomp. The result is an itching-scratching-chewing cycle that is hard to break. The pet is miserable, and looks bad, too. The coat thins from all the chewing and scratching, and the skin is red and irritated, ripe for a secondary bacterial infection.

> Ask your vet to recommend a flea-control program for your Poodle.

The best way to prevent these maladies is to keep fleas under control on your Poodle. This is not easy, but is the best way to prevent severe problems later on. Ask your vet to recommend a flea-control program for your Poodle.

Grooming and Dental Care

Why do you brush your teeth? To prevent dental problems, of course! You can do the same for your Poodle. Many vets recommend regular toothbrushing for pets, beginning at about eight weeks of age. Use a child-size, soft-bristle toothbrush and doggie toothpaste to discourage plaque buildup and avoid periodontal disease. Daily brushing is best, but several times a week is better than never.

Grooming is a necessary part of your Poodle's preventive care program. That includes regular trimming, bathing, brushing, ear cleaning, and toenail trimming. The time you or a professional groomer spend brushing and fussing over the Poodle is an opportunity to check the dog for signs of ill health, as well as improve your Poodle's looks.

Safety

Just as the parents of young children must be on "red alert" to dangers surrounding their little ones, so must you be aware of potential dangers to your Poodle in your home, yard, and neighborhood. You can't foresee the future, but being on your toes can prevent injuries and accidents that will cause you heartache and your Poodle pain.

Pet-proof your Poodle's environment as suggested in Chapter 2. Take the advice given there seriously. You really can prevent tragedy by thinking ahead. Store all toxins (medicine, household cleaners, paint, antifreeze) up and away from your Poodle, and teach him not to chew anything but safe, doggie toys.

When you're out, keep your Poodle on-leash. A curious and wandering Poodle could be bitten by a wild animal, stung by an insect, poisoned by a toxic plant, or cut by walking on a piece of glass.

Sick Calls and Emergencies

Trauma or injury can befall your beloved Poodle in the wink of an eye. Though it's certainly not something you wish to think about, you must. What will you do if your Poodle suddenly becomes ill?

When to Call Your Veterinarian

Generally, call the veterinary clinic or the local emergency hospital *immediately* if you notice:

- Wounds that expose bone or are actively bleeding
- Bleeding from the mouth, which could indicate internal bleeding
- Difficulty breathing
- A temperature higher than 104 degrees Fahrenheit
- Paralysis
- Eye injuries, or unequal pupil size or irregular eye movements
- Straining to urinate, but not passing urine
- Broken bones
- Sudden onset of severe diarrhea or vomiting
- Shock or convulsions
- Burns
- Collapse
- Your Poodle has been hit by a car, even if he seems okay
- Attempts to vomit but nothing comes up
- A suddenly swollen or painful belly

Call within 24 hours if you notice any of these signs:

- Minor wounds that are not actively bleeding
- Depression or loss of appetite, but otherwise appears okay
- Slightly elevated temperature
- Moderate lameness
- Runny eyes or nose
- Frequent urination attempts, with urine passing each time

First Aid

In the event of trauma or the sudden onset of illness, it may be necessary for you to practice first aid. This is a common term, but what exactly does it mean? First aid is the initial help following illness or accident that can save a dog's life, though it is not a substitute for professional care. The objectives of first aid are to:

○ Preserve life
○ Relieve suffering
○ Prevent the illness or injury from becoming worse until the animal can be treated by a veterinarian

To decide whether you must administer first aid, first assess your Poodle's illness or injury. Conditions such as the following require immediate attention to ensure the dog's safety:

○ Bleeding
○ Difficulty breathing
○ Shock
○ Poisoning
○ Heatstroke
○ Burns and frostbite
○ Convulsions

Emergencies happen without warning, so wise dog owners prepare for the unexpected. Study first-aid basics. Make sure you keep a canine medical book on hand to reference as needed and keep your vet's phone number (day and night)

Did You Know?

A dog's heart beats between 70 and 120 times per minute, compared with 70 to 80 times per minute for humans.

Signs Your Poodle
Is Feeling Under the Weather

- ○ Acts tired, sluggish, and would rather stay in bed
- ○ Isn't hungry, refuses several meals in a row
- ○ Drinks an excessive amount of water
- ○ Throws up several times
- ○ Has diarrhea or blood in stools
- ○ Whimpers when touched
- ○ Drools excessively

- ○ Loses weight, but isn't on a weight-loss program
- ○ Has very pale or very red gums
- ○ Has bloated-looking tummy
- ○ Has runny eyes or nose
- ○ Scoots or bites or chews at rear end
- ○ Coughs and sneezes a lot
- ○ Shakes head excessively

by the telephone. And don't forget to prepare a first-aid kit as suggested in Chapter 2. (See Chapter 5 for more information on first aid and emergency care.)

Exactly what your vet will do to restore your Poodle's health following a crisis depends on the dog's illness or injury, and will vary according to each individual veterinarian. You can expect the veterinarian to examine the ill or injured animal, run tests if necessary, then develop a plan of treatment. The practitioner may treat, hospitalize, administer, operate, or medicate. A hospital stay may be required, or you may be asked to treat or medicate the Poodle at home. Follow-up visits may be in order.

Emergency Instructions for the Boarding Kennel/Pet Sitter

What if your dog becomes sick or gets hurt while you are away? Before you leave your dog at a boarding kennel, ask if they have a veterinarian on staff or if they use one in the area for emergencies. In either case, it's a good idea to give them the name and number of your dog's veterinarian, especially if your Poodle has a specific medical condition. If you have hired a dog sitter, leave an emergency list with your veterinarian's phone number, the phone number of the local emergency hospital, and the phone number for the National Animal Poison Control Center (888-548-2423). Also leave information on any medications your dog needs or any special medical conditions to watch out for. Prepare for the unexpected to ensure that your dog gets the care she needs should an emergency occur.

Down the Hatch

Owners often cringe at the thought of giving the family pet medicine. But it's not as difficult as you might think if you know a few tricks of the trade.

○ *Pills, tablets, and capsules.* Don't be tempted to crunch up medication and serve it with breakfast. Medications often taste bitter, and chances are both breakfast and the medicine will go uneaten. Instead, tip your Poodle's muzzle upward, place the pill at the very back of his throat in the center, then close his mouth and hold it shut. Stroke your dog gently until he swallows. Be sure to place the pill in the center of the back of his throat. If you place it too far on either side, your Poodle can work the tablet forward and spit it out.

○ *Liquids.* A large-size sterile plastic syringe (without the needle) is ideal for administering liquid medications. Draw in the measured amount of medicine, tilt your Poodle's head back slightly, and place the syringe into his mouth between the cheek and molars. Hold his mouth shut and squirt the medicine in a little at a time. Give your Poodle time to swallow between squirts.

○ *Eye ointments.* Pull down the lower eyelid and squeeze a dab of ointment into the surface of the eye. Replace the lid, and use your fingers to close the eyelids together in order to distribute the medication. Eye drops can be applied by holding your dog's eye open (top and bottom) and dropping directly on the eyeball. Do not touch the eyelid or eyeball with ointment tubes or droppers.

○ *Ear medications.* Hold your Poodle's ear up vertically so you can see the ear canal. Squeeze the ear ointment deep into the ear canal, but be sure not to touch the inside of the ear with the tube so you don't accidentally injure the delicate ear canal skin. Keep holding the ear flap up with one hand, and with the other, gently massage the base of the ear to distribute the medicine. Once you let go, though, be prepared! Most dogs will shake dramatically after having their ears medicated. You could end up with ear medicine on you, as well as in your Poodle's ears.

The Cost of Veterinary Care

One reality is that owning a Poodle requires money. You will need to pay for veterinary care, along with everything else—food, grooming, supplies, training fees, and so on. The good news is that routine annual care for a healthy Poodle isn't terribly expensive. The Humane Society of the United States estimates the average dog owner spends $135 a year on medical care. Puppyhood can be more expensive with vaccines alone costing $200 the first year, $65 a year thereafter.

The bad news is emergency services, long-term treatment for a chronic condition, or care from a veterinary specialist can be quite costly, adding up to four digits very quickly. For example, one year of chemotherapy treatment for a dog suffering from cancer can cost as much as $3,000. Yikes! That's a lot of money!

According to the American Veterinary Medical Association *1997 US Pet Ownership and Demographic Source Book,* the total veterinary medical expenditures for dogs were estimated at approximately $7 billion in 1996, with some 95 million dogs visiting the veterinarian. The average cost of those office visits was $73.60, an increase of $23.64 from 1991. Seven billion dollars is not small change. Why does veterinary care cost so much?

While it's less costly than human medicine, veterinary medicine is no less sophisticated (for example, a canine CAT scan costs $300 to $700, human CAT scan costs $750 to $1,000). Expensive and technical procedures are available to animals, just as they are to people. For example, veterinary specialists perform hip replacements for dogs with dysplasia, MRIs (magnetic resonance imaging), kidney transplants, or eye surgery. All these sophisticated treatments require expensive high-tech equipment and highly trained individuals to perform them. These factors, along with economic inflation, contribute to the high cost of care.

Some consider it socially unacceptable to discuss veterinary fees, but the best advice is to talk openly. Ask the veterinary staff for a list of services and their fees. How much is an office visit, basic vaccinations, and spaying or neutering, for example?

Ten Questions to Ask Every Provider

Before choosing a pet insurance or membership plan, be sure to get straight-forward answers to all your questions. If it makes you more comfortable, get the answers in writing.

1. Does your policy follow fee/benefits schedules? If so, please send me your detailed coverage limits. In the meantime, please give me examples of coverage limits for three common canine procedures so I can compare them to my current veterinary charges.

2. Does your policy cover basic wellness care, or does it cover only accidents and illnesses? Do you offer a wellness care endorsement that I can purchase on top of my basic plan for an additional fee? What other endorsements do you offer, and how much do they cost?

3. Under your policy's rules, can I continue taking my dog to his current veterinarian, or do I need to switch to another veterinarian?

4. Does your policy cover hereditary conditions, congenital conditions, or pre-existing conditions? Please explain each coverage or exclusion as it pertains specifically to my dog. Is there a feature where pre-existing conditions will be covered if my dog's pre-existing condition requires no treatment after a specified period? What is that period?

5. What happens to my premium and to my dog's policy if your company goes out of business? What guarantees do I have that I won't be throwing my money away?

6. How quickly do you pay claims?

7. What is your policy's deductible? Does the deductible apply per incident or annually? How does the deductible differ per plan?

8. Does the policy have payment limits over a year's period or during my pet's lifetime? How do the payment limits differ per plan?

9. What is the A.M. Best Co. rating of your insurance underwriter, and what does that rating mean?

10. Is there a cancellation period after I receive my policy or membership? How long do I have to review all my materials once I receive them, and what is the cancellation procedure?

What will the vet charge to test your Poodle for heartworms, and how much is the monthly preventive? Know what your individual veterinarian will charge for his services and procedures so you won't be shocked when you receive the bill.

In addition to asking about customary fees, communicate with your veterinarian. Make an effort to develop a relationship with this important member of your Poodle's health-care team. If you're concerned about specific treatment costs, tell him. Perhaps the veterinarian can suggest less expensive treatment options, such as rest and medication for a short period before ordering more expensive tests. Or, some veterinary clinics offer three- and six-month, same-as-cash, payment plans or longer-term interest financing. Many accept major credit cards. And ask whether your veterinarian offers discounts on certain services for seniors or regular clients.

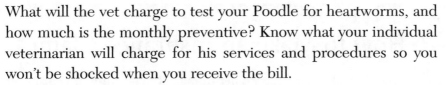

Ask whether your veterinarian offers discounts on certain services for seniors or regular clients.

There's no shame in discussing treatment costs with your veterinarian. Vets are very familiar with this fact of life. They know families have a limit to what they can and will pay for their pets, and they know the money comes out of pocket. (Unlike human health-care insurance, which covers most medical bills, only 1 percent of overall pet health care is paid by pet health insurers.) Most veterinarians are willing to work with owners concerned with costs.

Pet Insurance and Rainy Day Savings

With the increase in veterinary costs and the increase of owner commitment to top-of-the-line care for pets comes pet health

How to Make an Insurance Claim

It's your responsibility as a policyholder to make the best use of your insurance plan. Take these steps to get the most for your money:

1. Designate a file for pet insurance forms.

2. Always take a claim form with you to the veterinarian's office. Many companies require a veterinarian's signature.

3. Make copies of receipts. A receipt must accompany every claim form. Some companies require only copies; others require originals. Keep a copy for your records.

4. Make copies of completed claim forms. If a question or payment issue arises, a copy to review on your end of the phone line will be reassuring.

5. Note an acceptable payment period on your calendar. Reimbursement may slip your mind, and it may be delayed in cases where a problem is encountered and you forget to inquire about the payment's status.

6. Mark claims paid and date received. Leave a paper trail that's easy to understand. Looking back a year later, you'll be glad for the notations.

© 1999 Solveig Fredrickson

insurance, such as medical plans designed to defray the costs of hip replacement surgery, which could run $3,500 out of pocket. While only 1 percent of U.S. pets are covered by such plans, consumer interest is growing, especially among owners who will do anything to save a pet. In Great Britain, ten percent of the nation's pets have health insurance and in Sweden, 17 percent of pets are covered.

Most plans only cover accidents or illness—no well-doggie checkups, immunization, parasites, genetic conditions—which is why interest in the United States is lukewarm.

Another plan is to buy some "self insurance." Simply set up a rainy day savings fund especially for your Poodle. Use it for routine care or unexpected treatment. According to the Humane Society of the United States, the average cost of owning a dog is $1,200 a year, including food. If you can squirrel away $100 or more a month, you'll have a nice nest egg should you need it.

Still, pet health insurance can be a lifesaver if the unforeseen should happen, such as your Poodle is diagnosed with cancer or needs extensive surgery. While most pet owners can afford the low cost of caring for a healthy animal, an ill pet is another story.

Shop carefully for pet insurance. Check out yearly costs and deductibles, know which treatments and exams are and aren't covered, and other rules and conditions. Appendix A contains contact information for more on pet insurance.

Common Health Concerns

A s a dedicated and responsible owner, you must be educated about health problems that could befall your Poodle. While this chapter does not provide a comprehensive discussion of canine health problems, it will give you a good introduction to the problems the average Poodle owner may face during the dog's lifetime. Read on to find out more.

Parasites, Inside and Out

Dogs are susceptible to internal and external parasites, and most dogs are infested with internal or external parasites at some time during their lifetime. It's essential to keep your Poodle free of all parasites because these buggers can make your pet very ill. Don't be alarmed, though. An infestation is not necessarily a sign that your Poodle is weak or diseased. Internal and external parasites are a fact of life with dogs (and cats). It's important that you learn what they are, how to recognize the signs, and when to get treatment promptly.

> Internal and external parasites are a fact of life with dogs (and cats).

Internal Parasites

Internal parasites are organisms that live inside your dog's body, usually in the intestines but also in the heart and other organs and tissues. If your Poodle exhibits any of the following, he may be infested with an internal parasite and should be examined by your veterinarian:

❍ Unexplained weight loss
❍ A shiny coat turns dull
❍ Overall poor condition
❍ Lethargy and weakness
❍ Coughing
❍ Diarrhea or dark, bloody stools
❍ What appears to be bits of rice in the dog's feces

Let's examine internal parasites one at a time.

Roundworms   One of the most common internal parasites found in dogs are roundworms or ascarids. Adult roundworms thrive in the dog's intestine, growing from one to seven inches in length. Dogs pick up roundworms by coming in contact with dirt or soil that contains roundworm eggs. For example, your Poodle is sniffing the yard, picks up eggs on his nose and mouth, licks, and ingests them. The eggs hatch in the intestine and the larvae make their way to the lungs via the bloodstream. The larvae return to the intestines and grow into adult roundworms.

Roundworms are especially common in puppies. Most pups are born with roundworm larvae acquired from the dam (mother) during gestation. Pups can also ingest roundworm larvae while nursing if the mother is infested.

Although the idea of larvae and adult worms inside your Poodle's body is certainly repulsive, it doesn't necessarily pose a severe health risk to the adult dog. Severe infestations in pups, however, can be more serious and can lead to death.

Puppies infested with roundworms usually have a dull coat and a characteristic pot belly. The dog may vomit, lose weight, have diarrhea, and there may be worms in the stool or vomit. Roundworms look like long, thin white earthworms, or like spaghetti that moves. Adult dogs usually show few signs.

Roundworms can affect people as well, usually children, often as a result of playing in soil that contains roundworm eggs. Because people are not the usual host for this parasite, the larvae do not grow into adults. Rather, they migrate throughout the body, causing fever, anemia, enlarged liver, or pneumonia. The condition is rare in the United States, but controlling roundworms in your Poodle can make the risk almost nonexistent.

A dog with roundworms must be treated by a veterinarian. The vet will determine whether the puppy or adult dog has roundworms by checking a stool sample for the parasite under the microscope, then prescribing medication, called a dewormer. Pups are usually dewormed several times to make sure larvae don't grow into adults. For an exact deworming schedule for your Poodle pup or adult, consult with your veterinarian.

Hookworms   Another creepy-crawlie that can affect your Poodle is the hookworm. A dog becomes infested with hookworms by coming in contact with soil or feces that contain hookworm larvae. The larvae migrate to the intestine where they grow into adults, which are small, thin worms one-quarter- to one-half-inch long. They attach to the wall of the small intestine and make a living by drawing blood from the host. A dog infested with hookworms passes eggs in its feces, thus continuing the possibility of infestations.

Hookworms can affect adult dogs, but are definitely more common in pups, who can acquire them through the mother's milk. A severe hookworm infestation causes bloody, dark stools and anemia, and can be deadly to small pups. In adult dogs, hookworms usually cause diarrhea, anemia, and weight loss.

Hookworm eggs can be detected in the feces, which is how the vet determines infestation. Deworming is essential, but fairly simple. Continued treatment may be necessary for small pups with severe infestations or for dogs living in contaminated environments. Once a dog's yard or kennel has been filled with hookworm eggs, reinfestation can occur for years.

Tapeworms   You've probably heard about tapeworms, those nasty parasites that can grow to several feet in length inside a dog's small intestine. The tapeworm head fastens to the intestine wall and makes its living off the host. The tapeworm body is made up of segments that contain egg packets. The segments, about one-quarter inch in length, are passed in the feces and look like rice.

The most common type of tapeworm that affects dogs is acquired when the dog ingests a flea that has immature tapeworms in its intestine. (Fleas become infected by eating tapeworm eggs.) The immature tapeworms travel to the intestine and grow into adults. Dogs can also become infected with tapeworms by eating uncooked meat, raw fish, or dead animals.

Surprisingly, tapeworms ordinarily do not cause severe effects. Even a heavy infestation only causes mild diarrhea, weight loss, or loss of appetite. Tapeworm segments are noticeable in the feces.

In spite of relatively mild ill effects, tapeworms do undermine a dog's general health, so they must be eradicated from your Poodle's body. Following a veterinary diagnosis of tapeworms, deworming is essential.

Whipworms Another internal parasite that can affect your Poodle are whipworms, which are two to three inches long, and have a whip-like appearance. Adult whipworms live in the large intestine, and survive by fastening to the intestine wall. Whipworm infestations are less noticeable than are those of other internal parasites, partly because the female whipworm lays fewer eggs and lays them erratically. This makes a whipworm infestation difficult to detect at times as the eggs are seen in the stool only occasionally. Heavy infestations do occur, though, and dogs with whipworms lose weight, have black, tarry diarrhea, and usually display poor condition. Treatment by a veterinarian is essential, though it can take several checks to accurately diagnose whipworms.

Heartworms Heartworm infection begins when the larvae from an infected

Did You Know?

An average of 800 dogs and cats are euthanized every hour in the United States.

mosquito are laid inside a dog as the mosquito feeds. The larvae burrow through connective tissue and migrate to a blood vessel and grow into adult worms. This takes three to four months. The worms make their way into a vein and are carried to the right side of the heart, where they remain. Adult heartworms are four to twelve inches in length and can live up to five years in the dog's heart. These adult worms reproduce, producing microfilaria; a female can produce up to 5,000 immature heartworms a day.

To complete the parasite cycle, the microfilaria go to a secondary host, the mosquito. Once ingested by a mosquito, they develop into infective larvae. The infective larvae then move to the mouth of the mosquito and are ready to infect the new host—your Poodle—when the mosquito comes calling for a blood meal.

> At first, a dog infected with heartworms has no symptoms. In fact, dogs can have heartworms for several years before showing signs.

At first, a dog infected with heartworms has no symptoms. In fact, dogs can have heartworms for several years before showing signs. A heartworm diagnosis is made when the vet finds microfilaria in the blood or runs a test that detects antibody to heartworm. Heartworms eventually take a toll, and the dog may begin to cough, be short of breath, and be unable to exercise. The dog then becomes tired, weak, in poor condition, and loses weight. As the number and size of heartworms increase, the dog's breathing is labored even when resting. Eventually, without treatment, the dog can suffer congestive heart failure or die suddenly.

Once an infected dog shows symptoms, treatment is difficult and potentially dangerous. The medications used to kill heartworms and larvae are toxic, and the dog must be strong enough to withstand the treatment. Occasionally, adult worms are surgically removed in dogs too ill to withstand the medication. Because of the risks associated with treatment, hospitalization is usually necessary.

The good news about heartworms is that preventive medications are available. Depending on where you live and the prevalence of heartworms, your vet may recommend heartworm preventive for your Poodle. These preventive drugs inhibit microfilaria from growing in the blood. Many vets recommend daily doses beginning several weeks before and after mosquito season. Or a preventive may be prescribed once a month to kill young worms that have accumulated. If you live in an area where mosquitoes are year-round pests, some veterinarians recommend starting pups on heartworm preventives at 9 to 12 weeks of age, for the remainder of the dog's life. Though effective, heartworm preventives can have side effects, so be sure to understand and discuss potential problems with the veterinarian.

Your Poodle must be tested for the presence of heartworms before starting on preventive medication, and tested once or twice a year thereafter. The test makes sure the dog is microfilaria-free, otherwise he could have a fatal reaction to the medicine, especially the daily form. While heartworm preventives are nearly 100 percent effective, the only absolute and surefire way to keep your Poodle from being infected by heartworms is to keep him from being bitten by a mosquito. That task, of course, is practically impossible. But you can minimize the opportunity for mosquito bites by keeping your Poodle indoors when the buggers come out to feed in the evening. Spray your yard and kennel areas for mosquitoes. Because mosquitoes thrive and breed in swamps or areas of brackish water and are more common in coastal areas, steer clear of these areas if possible. They can also reproduce in small areas of standing water such as old car tires, bird baths, and small fish ponds. Check your yard and kennel area for water traps and remove them.

Coccidia   This internal protozoan parasite is most common in puppies, though coccidia can affect adult dogs as well. Protozoans are one-celled organisms that are not visible to the naked eye, yet are responsible for several conditions in dogs including coccidiosis, giardiasis, toxoplasmosis, trichomoniasis, Nantucket disease, canine hepatozoonosis, and Chagas' disease. An infection from a protozoan parasite usually results when the dog ingests the cyst form, or oocyst, of the protozoan. These cysts then migrate to the bowel where they mature and eventually shed in the feces.

Coccidiosis usually occurs in young dogs housed in overcrowded, unsanitary, or cold, damp conditions. Pups can be infected by their mother or pick up the parasite in a contaminated environment, such as in a kennel, where it can spread quickly. Coccidia can lie dormant, causing the pup no ill health, but become active during a period of stress. Infected pups usually have mild diarrhea at first. As the infection progresses, the pup may have mucus-like, bloody diarrhea, become anemic and weak, and lose his appetite. Pups and dogs that are infected but recover can become carriers.

> Good hygiene helps prevent coccidiosis, so it's important that you keep your Poodle's kennel clean.

Veterinary treatment is essential for coccidiosis. A drug to kill the protozoan may be prescribed, as well as medication to stop the diarrhea.

Good hygiene helps prevent coccidiosis, so it's important that you keep your Poodle's kennel clean. If your dog is already infected, cleanliness is essential to keep it from spreading. Infected pups and dogs must be isolated, fecal matter picked up, and the area cleaned with boiling water or disinfectant to kill oocysts. Coccidian cysts can be extremely difficult to kill, so make sure you work with your veterinarian to formulate the best possible plan to avoid reinfection.

Giardia   Giardia is another protozoan parasite that affects dogs (it also affects people), causing giardiasis, a disease characterized by diarrhea. The giardia parasite is usually waterborne, found in lakes, streams, or rivers. The most common sign of giardiasis is diarrhea, mixed with mucus and blood.

Treatment is essential, and the veterinarian will prescribe medication to kill the giardia parasite. Because giardia can spread to people, families with infected pets must be very careful to treat the animal and clean up feces, though it is unlikely to spread from pet to human.

External Parasites

What goes inside also goes outside—sort of. Not only can your Poodle be infected with internal parasites, but she can also be infested with external parasites such as fleas, ticks, skin mites, and ringworm. Here's the scoop on what you might find crawling in, around, or under that curly Poodle coat.

Fleas   You may not see them, but surely you've felt them—especially if you live in a climate that's mild year-round. We're talking fleas, those biting bugs that just love to chew on pets.

Fleas have to make a living, and they do it by biting your Poodle and feeding on her blood. If you're nearby, you're likely to get bitten, too. Flea bites itch

Elizabethan Style

Hopefully, your Poodle won't suffer an injury, wound, or skin problem that mustn't be scratched, bitten, or pawed. If you must prevent him from bothering a sore area, a device called an Elizabethan collar will do the job. Named for the high neck ruff popular during the reign of Queen Elizabeth, this lampshade-like collar prevents your Poodle from turning his head to chew and makes scratching nearly impossible. The size of the collar is tailored to fit the size of the dog. The Elizabethan collar is effective, but is not particularly well received by wearers because it's bulky.

and are very irritating to your dog. A Poodle with fleas can be seen biting, scratching, biting, scratching, biting. In most cases, a flea infestation causes only mild discomfort, but some dogs are highly allergic to the saliva of the flea. The result is flea allergy dermatitis, a condition marked by red, irritated skin, hair loss, and misery. Secondary bacterial infections can occur.

Additionally, since the flea is the intermediate host of the tapeworm (these bad-guy parasites all have to work together, you know), most dogs with a lot of fleas also end up with tapeworms.

How can you tell your Poodle has fleas? Your Poodle's biting and scratching is a major clue, and flea dirt—small, sand-size black and white grains—is a big indicator. Flea dirt is flea feces and flea eggs. The fecal matter is actually digested blood, your Poodle's blood. When dampened on a white piece of paper, flea dirt turns reddish-brown.

You may also see the flea in person, a small, dark-brown bug that looks like a dot. Fleas don't fly, but jump. And how they can jump! Some sources say they leap more than 100 times their own body length. They can survive for months without a meal and will reproduce very rapidly if conditions are right.

Fleas thrive in a warm, humid environment, which is why they love living on dogs' bodies. And, the higher the temperature and humidity, the more they reproduce. Although 98 percent of all fleas live off the dog, only stopping for a bloody meal, it is possible for fleas to mate right there on your Poodle. A female can lay some 2,000 eggs in a lifetime. The eggs either hatch right on your dog, or fall off and hatch elsewhere—in your yard, the dog's crate, your carpeting. Once the eggs hatch into larvae, they feed and continue developing into a pupal stage. If conditions are right, adult fleas follow in two to three weeks, though they can remain in the pupal stage for several months. Once they are adults, the hungry fleas search for a host—your Poodle.

> You can select from many, many ways to control fleas on your dog and in your home and yard.

You can select from many, many ways to control fleas on your dog and in your home and yard. Pesticide-based flea dips, shampoos, topical treatments, flea collars, sprays, foggers, and powders are among the more popular control methods. You can also try pills or natural products such as herbal collars, flea traps, and flea combs. The selection of flea-control products is seemingly endless, which is a good clue that fleas are tough to eradicate. Ask your veterinarian for a flea-control program that's right for your Poodle.

Regardless of the types of products you use, though, remember this: It's a battle to get rid of fleas, and you've got to fight constantly, especially if you live in an area that is warm year-round. Plan a three-pronged attack, launched simultaneously:

○ Eliminate fleas on the Poodle
○ Eliminate fleas in the house
○ Eliminate fleas in the yard

For example, on the day you take your Poodle to the grooming shop for a haircut and flea bath, fog the house, spray the yard, and wash the Poodle's bedding. If you just de-flea your Poodle and fail to get rid of fleas in the house and yard, then as soon as the Poodle returns home the fleas hop right back on. You're right back where you started—and $50 poorer. Remember this above all else about flea control: The fight against fleas must include the dog, the house, and the yard, all at the same time.

You must know that getting rid of fleas is not a one-time battle consisting of a flea bath and a good spraying of the house and yard once a year in the spring. Ha! Fighting fleas is a consistent series of battles. For example, spray the yard once a month, vacuum the house every day (to pick up flea eggs and live fleas wandering about), fog the house every six weeks, wash bedding once a week, and flea comb every day. However, newer prescription topicals minimize the battles. You may only have to treat the dog once every month or so and scale back the environmental battles, but you can't let up otherwise—given the opportunity, fleas will return.

It's a constant struggle to keep the flea population to a minimum, but don't grow weary. What you'll find if you keep up the good fight and don't get behind is that the battle is easier and your Poodle is healthier and happier.

Ticks   Ticks are another external parasite you may someday find on your Poodle. Several species of ticks live on dogs, but the brown dog tick is the most common. Dogs usually pick up ticks while romping outside in wooded or grassy areas. You're most likely to find ticks on your Poodle's head, ears, neck, and between the toes. If you've heard that ticks are blood suckers, you're right. The female tick imbeds into the dog's skin, feeds, and becomes engorged with blood.

Ticks are carriers of several diseases, most notably Lyme disease and Rocky Mountain spotted fever. Lyme disease is spread by the bite of ticks infected with *Borrelia burgdorferi spirochete* bacteria. The deer tick and the western black-legged tick are the most common carriers of Lyme disease. This disease is most frequent May through August, but can occur anytime. A dog with Lyme disease appears to have arthritis—it is lame with swollen, tender joints. The dog may also be lethargic and feverish. Lyme disease is sometimes tricky to diagnose but when pinpointed, antibiotics are prescribed. If you live where ticks are common, ask your vet to recommend a tick-control program.

> Ticks are carriers of several diseases, most notably Lyme disease and Rocky Mountain spotted fever.

Rocky Mountain spotted fever is also carried by ticks, most commonly wood ticks and dog ticks. Ticks infected with the *rickettsia* bacteria that bite a dog can cause a condition that results in fever, loss of appetite, and sore joints. In people, Rocky Mountain spotted fever acts like the flu, with fever, vomiting, achiness, and chills as common symptoms. Antibiotics are prescribed to treat the condition in both dogs and people.

If you find a few ticks on your Poodle following a walk in the woods, it's best to remove them. Preferably with tweezers (not with your bare hand!), grab the tick by its head, near the dog's skin, and pull it out, head and all. Avoid injuring or annoying the tick, as this may allow it to inject disease-ridden saliva back into the dog!

If the Poodle is covered with ticks, give the vet a call. He or she can recommend a spray or dip to use at home, or will suggest taking the Poodle to the clinic for dipping.

Mites   If ticks aren't creepy enough, consider a tiny, microscopic bug called a mite. These parasites can hop onto your Poodle and cause a miserable condition known as mange. The two types are sarcoptic and demodetic. Mange is diagnosed by the veterinarian examining skin scrapings under the microscope and identifying the mange mite.

Sarcoptic mange causes *severe* itching in pets. The horrible itching is caused when the female mites bite and chew into the skin to lay eggs. Eggs hatch in about a week, and the baby mites grow into adults and begin to lay eggs themselves. Sarcoptic mange mites seem to prefer the skin on the dog's ears, elbows, hocks, and face. Hair falls out in these infested areas, and skin becomes crusty and red.

The signs of demodetic mange are similar, minus the itch. A dog infested with the *Demodex canis* mite can have either a localized or generalized form of this condition. Localized demodetic mange usually occurs in young dogs, up to a year. Hair thins around the eyelids, lips, mouth, or front legs, and usually affects only one or two spots, not several areas at once. In the generalized form, the hair thins in larger areas, on the head, legs, and body. Sores develop and can become infected.

> **D**ogs who develop demodetic mange should not be bred.

Treatment is essential for both types of mange. Dogs with sarcoptic mange are usually bathed in insecticides to kill the mites. Several baths may be necessary. Cortisone is often prescribed to soothe the itch.

Many cases of the localized form of demodetic mange heal by themselves in a few months, though topical medication may be prescribed. Dogs suffering with the generalized form aren't so fortunate. Treatment is necessary, but it takes time and a cure isn't always possible. The dog may be clipped and bathed in a strong dip to kill the mites. Antibiotics may be prescribed, but cortisone usually isn't because it can worsen the condition. Dogs with generalized demodetic mange—or even localized forms that don't heal quickly—are likely to have weak immune systems. In older dogs, this may be due to an underlying illness, such as Cushing's disease. In puppies and young dogs, the immune system is most likely weak due to inherited defects. Therefore, dogs who develop demodetic mange should not be bread.

There's another tiny mite that lives inside pets' ears, called the ear mite. These tiny bugs, much smaller than the head of pin, feed on skin debris in the ear canal. The symptoms of ear mites are unmistakable—intense scratching and head shaking due to severe itching. Inside the ear you'll see reddish-brown or black waxy debris. These signs also can accompany ear infections, so a veterinary visit is necessary to be certain of the cause.

The veterinarian makes a diagnosis of ear mites by finding them in during microscopic exams. Ear mites are highly contagious among dogs and cats, and the condition must be treated. The ears will need to be cleaned of debris and treated with medication that kills the bugs. The medication does not destroy eggs, so treatment must continue for several weeks until all eggs are hatched.

Ringworm   If you ever see a circular pattern of hair loss with a red ring on your Poodle's skin, your dog may have ringworm. No, it's not actually caused by a worm, like tapeworms or roundworms, but this skin disease is caused by a fungus, *Microsporum canis,* and other closely related fungi. Ringworm can be easily transmitted to dogs from other animals or people, or picked up from fungus pores in the environment, such as from dirt, bedding, or brushes that have touched an infected animal.

Ringworm most often grows in circular patches one-half inch to two inches across. It causes scaly skin, hair loss, and sores. The vet diagnoses ringworm by examining skin scrapings under the microscope or by culturing the fungus, which may take five to ten days. Treatment may include clipping the hair followed by bathing the dog in an antifungal solution, or administering oral medication.

Since ringworm is contagious between dogs and people, be very careful about handling a dog with the condition. Children are especially susceptible, so if your family Poodle does have ringworm, kids should avoid contact with him until the condition is treated. It is also important to clean the dog's bedding, vacuum, change the household air filters, and use other environmental controls frequently until the dog is declared cured. Otherwise, the fungus may grow in the house and cause re-infection.

Common Diseases

Most diseases are easily prevented, but in spite of the best preventive care, kennel hygiene, and current vaccinations, several infectious diseases can affect your Poodle. Here are the most common.

Bordetella

Most cases of kennel cough are caused by the bacteria called *B. Bronchiseptia.* Highly contagious, bordetella is passed from dog to dog through coughing and respiratory secretions. Infections are usually quite annoying—your Poodle may have a harsh, unpleasant cough for two to three weeks, although in some cases it may last for eight weeks. However, most dogs never get very ill. Rarely does bordetella infect the lungs and cause pneumonia. If your Poodle acts ill after a kennel cough diagnosis, she should see your veterinarian for a recheck and treatment, if necessary.

Fortunately, two vaccines are useful in the fight against bordetella. The intranasal vaccine is believed to give a more immediate and longer-lasting protection against the disease. Pups living where bordetella is prevalent can be vaccinated when as young as two to four weeks; injection is typically given at 8 to 12 weeks.

Brucellosis

Brucellosis is a condition that is especially feared among Poodle breeders. Caused by the bacteria *Brucella canis,* brucellosis causes reproductive failure in dogs. It results in late miscarriages, stillborn pups, and pups that die shortly after birth. Brucellosis can cause a male or female dog to become sterile with little outward signs of disease. Because the condition can be passed when mating, testing is recommended before breeding.

An active brucellosis infection will cause a dog to have enlarged lymph nodes, fever, and swollen joints. The male's testicles may swell, then atrophy. The bacterian may pass in the urine, aborted fetal tissues, and vaginal secretions present at birthing. People may become infected when handling any of these, and develop serious illness. There

Did You Know?

Dogs see color less vividly than humans but are not actually color-blind.

is no vaccine to prevent brucellosis and no effective long-term treatment for dogs. Antibiotics may be prescribed, but a relapse can occur once the medication is stopped. People generally fare better, and early antibiotic treatment is curative. The best prevention is refusing to allow your Poodle to breed with an untested dog.

Coronavirus

First recognized in 1971, canine coronavirus affects dogs of all ages but is usually only severe to pups. The virus is transmitted via feces, and can spread rather quickly. Symptoms include depression, lack of appetite, bloody vomit, and yellow-orange diarrhea, though most adult dogs may only develop very minor diarrhea.

Dogs or pups who become severely ill with coronavirus are treated with fluid therapy to prevent dehydration, and given medication to stop diarrhea. If secondary infections are present, antibiotics may also be given. Dogs with minor symptoms do not need treatment. They will usually self-cure within one to two weeks.

Vaccines are available to prevent coronavirus, and many vets recommend vaccinating dogs that have frequent contact with other dogs.

Distemper

Distemper is a highly contagious disease that affects pups and dogs. The virus that causes distemper is similar to the virus that causes measles in people. Distemper is most common in unvaccinated pups three to eight months old, but can affect any dog, especially if he is in poor condition.

The distemper virus usually attacks the dog's respiratory tract, the intestines, and the nervous tissue. Symptoms often begin as a mild nasal discharge which looks much like any minor infection. However, both diarrhea and a cough may develop.

Not all dogs respond to the distemper virus in the same way. Some become very ill, some mildly ill. Some dogs will begin to have nervous twitches and seizures. It often depends upon the dog's condition before becoming infected. Secondary infections are common. About 50 percent of infected dogs and puppies die, regardless of treatment.

Treatment for distemper varies, as does the success rate. The earlier the dog is treated, though, the better the chance of a positive outcome.

Fortunately, there are vaccines to prevent distemper.

Hepatitis

Infectious canine hepatitis is a very contagious viral disease that affects dogs of all ages. However, infected pups suffer most severely. Canine hepatitis causes a variety of signs, mild to severe. It is spread easily from dog to dog via urine, feces, and saliva.

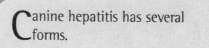

Canine hepatitis has several forms.

Don't confuse canine hepatitis with human hepatitis. Each disease is species-specific, which means that canine hepatitis is transmitted only from dog to dog.

Canine hepatitis has several forms. In the fatal fulminating form, the dog becomes ill suddenly, develops bloody diarrhea, and dies. Pups may die suddenly without apparent illness.

The acute form of canine hepatitis causes the dog to have a fever, bloody diarrhea, and bloody vomit. Jaundice may be present.

Mild cases of canine hepatitis result in a loss of appetite or lethargy.

Dogs that survive canine hepatitis may develop a clouding of the cornea of one or both eyes called blue eye, which usually clears up in a few days.

Canine infectious hepatitis can be prevented with up-to-date vaccination, though blue eye can still occur after a dog is vaccinated.

Infectious Tracheobronchitis

Infectious tracheobronchitis, also called kennel cough or canine cough, can be caused by one or more viruses, and infection results in a harsh, dry cough. The cough may last for weeks and on rare occasions is followed by infectious bronchitis.

Tracheobronchitis earned its name of "kennel cough" due the rapid way it can spread through kennels. Kennel owners are irked by the term, though, preferring not to be labeled as the cause. Canine cough is the current politically correct conversational term. Most kennels require proof of vaccination against the condition before boarding a dog.

The most common causes are bordetella (a bacteria) and parainfluenza (a virus). Vaccines are available, but vaccinated dogs will occasionally develop kennel cough when infected with a less-common virus or bacteria.

Parvovirus

Parvovirus is a highly contagious and potentially devastating disease. It affects both dogs and puppies, but it is especially severe in young pups. The virulent parvovirus is transmitted dog to dog via infected feces, but can be carried on the feet or skin of an infected dog and the shoes and clothing of caretakers. Parvo is most serious in young pups.

The most common signs of parvovirus are lack of appetite, depression, vomiting, and bloody diarrhea. The dog usually has a high fever and appears in pain. Less commonly, parvovirus can attack the heart muscle. This usually occurs in young dogs, rarely in adults. Affected pups will stop nursing, whine, and gasp for breath. Death may come suddenly. Pups that survive often have long-term heart problems.

Parvo can be treated, but the outcome varies depending on the age of the dog and severity of the disease. Treatment is aimed at stopping dehydration due to severe vomiting and diarrhea. The cornerstone of therapy is based on fluid therapy. Medications to stop diarrhea as well as antibiotics may be administered.

Immunization is available and is highly recommended to prevent this devastating disease.

Rabies

The well-known rabies virus can affect any warm-blooded animal, including dogs and people. The virus is usually spread from the saliva of an infected animal through a bite or wound. In the United States, rabies vaccination is required by law for dogs and cats, which accounts for the low incidence of the fatal disease among domestic animals and people. Rabies is found occasionally in wild animals such as skunks, raccoons, bats, and foxes. The only definitive diagnosis of rabies is autopsy.

The average incubation of the virus in dogs is three to eight weeks, but can be as short as a week or as long as six months.

The signs of rabies are caused by inflammation of the brain, which causes a normally friendly dog to become irritable and withdrawn. Shy pets may become overly affectionate. Soon the animal may exhibit any number of odd behaviors, including staring, pacing, aggression, or fear. Dogs may prefer the dark because their eyes become sensitive to light and they may avoid water because it becomes difficult to drink. Fever, vomiting, and diarrhea are common.

Most people associate rabies with "mad dog" behavior. This does occur and is called the furious form. An animal with furious rabies is vicious and aggressive. The animal shows no fear, and will run and snap at the air. Don't count on seeing this behavior, though. Rabid animals can have any range of signs—paralysis, dementia, extreme passivity or extreme aggression, or anything in between. Once an animal shows signs of rabies, it is always fatal.

Rabies vaccination for pets is required by law, and is administered either once a year or every two or three years, depending upon where you live.

Illnesses and Emergencies

Emergencies happen without warning, so a wise Poodle owner will prepare for the unexpected. Following is a list of common emergencies and illnesses you might encounter. Keep your vet's telephone or pager number posted by the phone just in case.

Allergies

There are four common types of allergy syndromes that pets suffer from. Three are aggravating, and one is an emergency situation. First, your Poodle could have an allergic reaction to flea saliva, which causes an itchy condition known as flea bite

dermatitis. Dogs that are allergic to flea's saliva experience a hypersensitive reaction when bitten by fleas. Not only does the dog experience itch-misery, but its skin becomes crusty, red, and thick.

The second type is food allergy in which the pet is allergic to some food such as meat, eggs, fish, or certain grains.

And, like people, pets may become allergic to pollen and other airborne irritants such as dust or mold, as well as to drugs and antibiotics.

What's interesting about pet allergies is how they manifest. Dogs react differently than people. People with allergies generally have runny noses, itchy eyes, sneezing, and congestion. But when dogs are allergic to something, they have itchy skin. Common itchy spots include paws, ears, face, front legs, rump, flanks, and underside. The itchiness can be so bad, and the dog scratches and licks so much, there's hair loss, raw, oozing sores, and bacterial infections develop.

> Common itchy spots include paws, ears, face, front legs, rump, flanks, and underside.

Most seasonal itching problems are flea allergies, or those related to pollens or molds. If the itching season is short for an individual pet, you might be able to control the problem with antihistamines or other medications. If the problem persists, your veterinarian may suggest desensitization to avoid long-term use of medications. Food trials are necessary to rule out food allergies as the cause of seasonal itch.

Not all itching is due to allergies, so it is important to consult your veterinarian to determine the underlying cause of your Poodle's problem. Your veterinarian will ask for a detailed history of your Poodle's symptoms, as well as results from the physical exam. In addition, he or she may conduct basic screening tests (skin scrapings, bacterial and fungal cultures, skin biopsy). Your veterinarian may also recommend more definitive allergy testing so she can make a detailed determination of your pet's immune responses to a number of potential allergens specific to your region. Results from these tests can prove invaluable in developing the best treatment plan for your pet.

How do you spell relief? Although there is no cure for allergies, effective treatments exist that offer substantial relief. Common approaches to the relief of allergy symptoms may include topical products (medicated shampoos, creams, sprays), oral antihistamines (often given in conjunction with fatty acid supplements), and cortisone-type drugs. As an alternative, your vet may suggest immunotherapy, a long-term approach to desensitize your pet through a series of injections (extracts of the offending allergens). Although by no means a quick fix, immunotherapy offers the best opportunity at long-term allergy relief without the potential side effects of certain allergy drugs.

In addition to flea, airborne, and food allergies, pets can experience acute allergic reactions. Insect stings or vaccines are a common cause of an immediate hypersensitivity reaction, with the adverse reaction usually occurring within minutes of exposure and the pet often developing hives and/or facial swelling. An acute reaction can also result in severe problems breathing, collapse, and even death. If you suspect an acute reaction—if you notice hives or facial swelling—head to the vet immediately! Rapid treatment can save your Poodle's life!

Bleeding

If your Poodle is wounded, he will bleed. Bleeding may be arterial (squirting of bright red blood) or venous (oozing of dark red blood). You must stop the bleeding. If bleeding is mild, it will stop on its own within five minutes. To stop bleeding from a severe cut or wound, the best technique is direct pressure.

First, try to control bleeding by using direct pressure. Apply several pads of sterile gauze or even your finger over the wound and press firmly and evenly. Be aware that if your Poodle is wounded, he's in pain. You may need someone to restrain the dog gently but firmly while you apply pressure to the wound. Do not wipe the wound or apply hydrogen peroxide or ointments. If blood soaks through the pad, do not remove it—this could disrupt clotting. Simply place another pad on top and press.

If the bleeding continues and spurts, keep applying direct pressure to the wound while also holding the area just above it (between the wound and the heart) with your hand. If this technique fails, apply a pressure bandage by wrapping gauze around the wound and securing it with tape.

If bleeding on a leg or tail does not stop by applying pressure, it is best to move the dog to your veterinarian's hospital, while continuing to slow the bleeding with continued pressure. If the dog becomes weak or the gums turn pale from blood loss, you may need to try using a tourniquet. Use this only as a last resort, though. A tourniquet that is left on too long can result in limb loss. To apply a tourniquet, wrap the limb or tail with one-inch-wide gauze or a wide piece of cloth slightly above the wound and tie a half-knot. Do not use a narrow band or rope. Place a pencil or stick on top and finish the knot. Twist the pencil slowly until the bleeding stops. Loosen the tourniquet every five minutes to allow blood flow back to the limb, then gently tighten again—just enough to stop or slow bleeding from the wound. Get to the veterinary hospital immediately for treatment.

Did You Know?

The tallest dog on record was 42 inches tall at the shoulders and weighed 238 pounds.

Bloat

Bloat is swelling of the dog's stomach due to gas. Once gas accumulates, the stomach may rotate or twist, causing stoppage of blood flow to the tissue. The combination of bloat and twisting is called "gastric dilation volvulous" (GDV). Both bloat and GDV are medical emergencies. It is estimated that 50 percent of dogs who suffer from bloat die. Signs of bloat include a sudden onset of abdominal pain, vomiting attempts that produce nothing, restlessness, and inability to get comfortable. The dog will often lie on his chest with his rump in the air. The dog's abdomen and/or lower chest will usually be distended and hard to the touch. If thumped with a finger, it may sound like a balloon or a drum.

Bloat most commonly affects dogs in the prime of life, between four and seven years of age. It's more common in male dogs, and in large, deep-chested breeds. Dogs that suffer bloat tend to eat large amounts of kibble, may have a history of digestive upset, and are often of nervous temperament.

> Dogs that suffer bloat tend to eat large amounts of kibble, may have a history of digestive upset, and are often of nervous temperament.

Bloat can be prevented, in some cases, by feeding two to three meals a day instead of one and by restricting exercise for one-half hour after each meal. Certain dogs may also benefit from gastric-motility enhancing drugs. If you suspect bloat, remember that it is always an emergency. Go immediately to your nearest veterinarian or emergency hospital. If your Poodle is merely bloated, he may be treated by passing a stomach tube to relieve the gas. If the stomach has rotated, however, surgery will be required to save his life.

Burns and Frostbite

Burns and frostbite can occur in dogs, just as they can in people. For first- and second-degree burns (redness and slight swelling to blisters and extreme tenderness), immerse small areas of the body in cool water or apply ice packs wrapped in clean towels. Do not apply butter or human medicines. Call your vet immediately for additional treatment.

With third-degree burns, the skin appears white, hair comes out easily, and the pain is severe. In such cases, go to your vet immediately. This is an emergency. Do not apply anything unless directed otherwise by your vet.

Frostbite usually affects the toes, ears, and scrotum. The skin is pale white, but becomes red and swollen when warmed and circulation returns. Frostbite looks very similar to a burn. Move the dog to a warm place and warm the affected area with cloths soaked in warm water or moist, warm packs. Do not rub the area or use anything hotter than barely warm. Call your veterinarian right away.

Choking

Just like people, your Poodle can choke, usually when something becomes lodged in his windpipe. Severe coughing and respiratory distress are the usual symptoms when food or a foreign object is stuck in the windpipe or bronchus. Often these are coughed up quickly; but if not, call your vet and get your Poodle to the clinic immediately.

Diarrhea

It certainly isn't a pleasant subject or sight, but at some time during your Poodle's life, he will suffer diarrhea.

Where Are My Pantyhose!?

Medical emergencies can befall even the most experienced dog owners. So it was for Poodle breeder Grace Blair, M.D., of California-based Cosmic Poodles and co-founder of Versatility In Poodles, a non-profit organization dedicated to the health of the breed.

Dr. Blair had a black female Poodle, Taylor, which she describes as a "driven retriever" who had to have something in her mouth at all times. "One morning before my shower, I laid out my clothes as usual," says Dr. Blair, "then found that I had forgotten to get out my pantyhose—or so I thought. I couldn't find them anywhere."

A few days later 18-month-old Taylor didn't eat her evening meal, but vomited instead. About 11 P.M. she began vomiting again. "I noticed a brown something that would protrude from her mouth and retract back in," says Dr. Blair. "The next time she tried to vomit, I grabbed the brown something and found myself holding the foot of my pantyhose! I couldn't pull it out."

Dr. Blair knew then why she never found the missing pantyhose. Taylor had eaten them. She also knew the Poodle was in danger. "I called the emergency vet hospital—excellent vets and a surgical specialist in the clinic 24 hours a day—and headed down the road," says Dr. Blair. Taylor was taken into surgery immediately. The veterinarians found part of the pantyhose in Taylor's stomach and part in the small bowel. It required one incision in the stomach and three in the small intestine to remove the pantyhose. Following surgery, Taylor was in intensive care for four days and in the hospital for three.

"She came home in fine condition," says Dr. Blair, "and went on to become the mother of two litters, several of which are AKC champions. It was a team of dedicated veterinarians and their staff that saved the life of this lovely girl, and my stupidity that caused the entire problem. Most veterinary emergencies are the result of errors made by the owners."

Frequent, loose, unformed stools are not the sickness, but are a sign of something else. Because diarrhea can be the result of an underlying condition, you should investigate its cause and treat it.

Diarrhea in your Poodle can be due to any of several factors, including a change in his diet or water; stress; eating garbage, toxic substances, food to which he's allergic, or other no-nos; or by infectious disease, kidney failure or other serious system-wide diseases.

Mild diarrhea, lasting no longer than 24 hours, can be treated at home. Consult your vet for exact treatment, but she will usually recommend withholding food or giving the dog water or ice cubes to drink, or medication to stop the diarrhea. Once the diarrhea subsides, she may recommend a bland diet (rice and cooked hamburger, for example).

> Bloody diarrhea, diarrhea with mucus, or diarrhea that lasts more than 24 hours must be treated by a veterinarian.

Bloody diarrhea, diarrhea with mucus, or diarrhea that lasts more than 24 hours must be treated by a veterinarian. And, if the diarrhea is accompanied by other signs of illness such as lethargy or fever, consult the vet right away.

Difficulty Breathing

Your Poodle may have difficulty breathing for any number of reasons, including chest injuries or foreign objects lodged in his windpipe. Signs include gasping for breath, anxiety, weakness, and loss of consciousness.

If your Poodle has difficulty breathing, you must act fast: Head to the vet immediately. If your Poodle loses consciousness, you may need to perform artificial respiration. There are two methods of artificial respiration: chest compression and mouth-to-nose. Keep in mind that you should not attempt artificial respiration on a conscious dog.

Emergency Procedures

Chest Compression Respiration

Chest compression respiration should be performed when the dog's heart is beating, but he is having difficulty breathing. It should only be used in dire emergencies because it can damage the lungs, ribs, and heart.

1. Lay the Poodle on her right side and remove collar and harness.

2. Open your dog's mouth and check for obstructions.

3. Place both hands on her chest and press down sharply. Release quickly.

If done properly, the air should move in and out. If not, perform mouth-to-nose respiration.

4. Continue until your Poodle breathes on her own or as long as her heart beats.

Heart Massage

Heart massage is used when there is no pulse and the dog is not breathing. If she is breathing, the heart is beating even if you cannot detect a pulse.

1. Feel for dog's pulse or heartbeat.

2. Open your Poodle's mouth and check for obstructions.

3. Lay the animal on her right side and remove her collar and harness.

4. Place your thumb on one side of the sternum and fingers on other side just below the elbows. For large dogs, place the heel of your hand on your dog's rib cage behind her elbow, which is directly over her heart.

5. With hands in this position, squeeze firmly to compress her chest. Do so five to six times. Wait five seconds to let the chest expand, and repeat.

6. Continue until the heart beats on its own or until no pulse is felt for five minutes.

Mouth-to-Nose Respiration

1. Lay the Poodle on her right side and remove collar and harness.

2. Open your dog's mouth and check for obstructions.

3. Pull her tongue forward and close the mouth.

4. Place your mouth over your dog's nose and blow in steadily for three seconds. Her chest will expand. Release for exhale.

5. Continue until your Poodle breathes on her own or as long as her heart beats.

Chest compression works by applying force to the chest wall, which pushes air out and allows the natural recoil of the chest to draw air in. It is easier to perform than mouth-to-nose, but can damage the heart and lungs. Mouth-to-nose is forced respiration. It is used when the dog's heart is still beating, when the compression technique fails, or when the chest is punctured (see Emergency Procedures, page 152).

Artificial respiration should not be confused with cardiopulmonary resuscitation or CPR. CPR combines artificial respiration with heart massage for an unconscious animal whose heart and breathing have stopped.

Electric Shock

Poodle puppies are playful, curious, and love to chew on everything. Unfortunately, this makes them prone to electric shock—the result of chewing on electrical cords. A burned mouth is usually the result, but circulatory collapse and difficulty breathing can result. When a puppy bites the cord and gets a jolt, the electric current wreaks havoc on the lung capillaries, which in turn lead to fluid in the lungs. Whether the pup suffers a burned mouth or falls unconscious, immediate veterinary attention is essential.

Prevent electric shock by hiding electrical cords and watching your puppy closely when she is in the house. Never allow her to wander around unsupervised. Teach your Poodle pup to chew only on her toys, and make sure you have plenty of safe, fun chew toys on hand.

Eye Injuries

Your Poodle is squinting and pawing at her eye, or her eye appears teary and red. If this is the case, chances are your Poodle has injured her eye. Probably the most common eye irritation is caused by a foreign object such grass, dirt, or seeds getting stuck in a dog's eye. This can be painful and very irritating. Many times, a veterinary visit is required to remove the object, especially if it becomes lodged behind the third eyelid, a protective membrane that cleans and lubricates the eye.

If a dog has a foreign object in his eye, he will usually suffer corneal abrasion or a scratched cornea. If treated promptly and properly, the eye usually heals quickly. If not, the abrasion can lead to a corneal ulcer, which is very painful and potentially serious. Corneal abrasions, scratches, and ulcers require veterinary treatment to prevent loss of vision.

Trauma can result in eye displacement when the eye comes of out the socket. This is an emergency condition, and veterinary care is required. If this happens to your dog, place moist, clean gauze or towels over the eye and get to a veterinary hospital immediately.

Fishhooks

If your Poodle joins you at the lake, river, or ocean, there is a chance a fishhook could become embedded in his mouth. This will cause the dog to cough, gag, salivate, or frantically paw at his mouth. If you notice this, take a look inside with a flashlight. If he's hooked, call your vet.

Wherever it's embedded, a fishhook must be removed. It's best not to attempt this yourself but to allow your dog's vet to remove it.

Fractures

Fractures or broken bones can occur in dogs, usually as a result of their being hit by a car. Fractures are classified as either simple

First-Aid Kit Essentials

- ○ Your veterinarian's phone number
- ○ An after-hours emergency clinic's phone number
- ○ The National Animal Poison Control Center's hotline number: (888) 426-4435 or (900) 680-0000
- ○ Rectal thermometer
- ○ Tweezers
- ○ Scissors
- ○ Penlight flashlight
- ○ Rubbing alcohol
- ○ Hydrogen peroxide (3%)
- ○ Syrup of ipecac and activated charcoal liquid or tablets (poisoning antidotes)
- ○ Anti-diarrheal medicine
- ○ Dosing syringe
- ○ Nonstick wound pads, gauze squares, and roll cotton to control bleeding
- ○ Adhesive tape
- ○ Elastic bandage
- ○ Styptic powder (in case nails are cut too short)
- ○ Emergency ice pack
- ○ First-aid book
- ○ Latex examination gloves

or compound. A simple fracture doesn't break through the skin, whereas in a compound fracture, the bone is exposed. Young pups tend to suffer what are called greenstick fractures, which are cracks instead of complete breaks.

If you suspect your Poodle has broken a bone, the most important thing you can do is keep him still to prevent further injury. Following that, get veterinary attention. If necessary, you can apply a temporary splint, which you can easily make out of a magazine and masking tape. However, splints can do more harm than good, so most veterinarians prefer you simply bring the dog in right away.

Handling an Injured Poodle

If your Poodle is injured, he may growl or snap when you attempt to touch or move him. Don't be offended by this behavior. Your Poodle is feeling pain, and this is the way he expresses it. You must be aware of this before handling your injured Poodle and take a few steps to prevent injury to yourself.

First, talk to your Poodle quietly and calmly. He may be excited or anxious (aren't you when you're injured?). Move slowly and keep talking in a soothing voice.

Next, muzzle your hurt Poodle. If you don't have a muzzle handy, improvise with a necktie, stocking, or long strip of soft cloth. Loop the cloth over your Poodle's muzzle and tie a half-knot on top of the dog's muzzle, then tie another half-knot under his chin. Wrap the material behind and below the ears and tie a full knot at the base of the dog's head.

To transport a severely injured Poodle to the emergency clinic, use a stretcher. A flat board or a sheet of plywood, for example, will work well. If that isn't available, use a large towel or blanket. To avoid injuring your Poodle more seriously, be very careful moving him onto the makeshift stretcher. Slide one hand under the Poodle's rear and your other hand under the chest. (You may need a helper if your Poodle is especially large or you're especially small.) Slowly inch the dog onto the stretcher and cover him with a towel.

Drive carefully but quickly to the veterinary clinic. Have someone ride next to the Poodle, keeping him calm and still. Call ahead so the staff expects you, and have staff members come out to help carry in the hurt dog.

Surgery, splints, or casts may be necessary treatments for broken bones.

Heat Stroke

Dogs don't cool their bodies like people do. Dogs cool themselves by panting, not sweating, to exchange hot air for cool air by way of their tongues and mucous membranes. When the air tem-

How to Take
Your Poodle's Temperature

If your Poodle is ill, your veterinarian will want to determine her temperature. Your vet may ask you to take a reading at home before bringing the dog to the clinic. For the most accurate reading, the temperature must be taken rectally. You may need an assistant because this can be slightly uncomfortable for the dog. Always use a rectal thermometer and shake it down before using.

1. Lubricate the thermometer with petroleum jelly.

2. Ask the Poodle to stand and have your assistant keep him standing.

3. Raise his tail and gently insert the thermometer.

4. Don't let go! Hold the thermometer in place for about 4 minutes.

5. Remove, wipe clean of fecal matter, and read. Normal should be between 100 and 102.5 degrees Fahrenheit.

6. Clean the thermometer with alcohol and put it away.

perature is close to the Poodle's natural body temperature of 100 to 102.5 degrees Fahrenheit, it's difficult for the dog to cool down. At this point, heatstroke, a potentially serious condition that can lead to death, is possible.

Overheating and heatstroke can happen easily. A dog left in a parked car in hot weather or confined in a hot kennel with no shade is susceptible, as are dogs that exercise in the afternoon heat. (Snub-nosed breeds such as Bulldogs and Pugs are especially prone to overheating.)

The signs of heatstroke include rapid panting, dark-colored gums and tongue, salivating, exhaustion, and vomiting.

If you suspect heatstroke, your immediate goal is to cool down the Poodle. If she seems only mildly affected, move her to a cooler environment, such as an air-conditioned home, or wrap her in moistened towels. Take her temperature, and if it is over 104 degrees Fahrenheit or the dog seems ill, hose her down with cool water (not cold) from a garden hose or immerse her in a tub of cool water. Once wet, head directly to your veterinarian.

Overheating and heatstroke can be prevented quite easily. Give your Poodle the same consideration you do yourself during hot weather. Stay inside in air-conditioning if you have it. Don't exercise at high noon. If you do go out, make sure you carry plenty of water. Don't leave your Poodle in a parked car. Kennel your Poodle in an open-air crate and be aware that darker colored dogs are especially prone to overheating.

Hit by Car

Poodles and cars are no fair match, which is why keeping your Poodle on-leash when you're out is so important. Some dogs are tempted to chase cars, but you must nip this behavior in the bud. The car will always win, and losing is usually disastrous for the Poodle.

What should you do if your Poodle dashes in front of a car and is hit? Get to the emergency clinic as soon as possible. Some dogs get by with minor breaks or bruises after being hit, but chances are good the animal is injured seriously. Treat for shock and transport the dog carefully (see Handling an Injured Poodle page 156).

Insect Bites and Stings

Your Poodle may someday find herself face to face with a wasp, bee, yellow jacket, spider, or other stinging or biting insect. In most cases, the

Shock

Different causes produce different symptoms of shock. When your dog is in shock, she may be weak and subdued. Her body temperature can range from below normal to normal or above normal (in cases of shock caused by a bacterial infection). Her pulse may be rapid and weak, and her gums may exhibit a delayed capillary refill time. (Test capillary refill time by pressing on your dog's gums, removing your finger, and counting the time it takes the gums to change from white back to pink. Normal is less than two seconds.) If your dog's gums seem to respond normally, but she is acting lethargic and confused, she may be in the early stages of shock.

In all cases of shock, immediate veterinary care is imperative. Control any bleeding, wrap your dog in a blanket, towel, or piece of clothing to keep her warm, and rush her to the veterinary clinic.

encounter is benign. But dogs can and do get stung by these critters, and it not only hurts but can cause a severe reaction and illness as well.

The sting of bees, wasps, and yellow jackets swell and are painful. That's usually the extent of the damage, but dogs who are stung repeatedly could experience shock from the venom. Additionally, just as some people are highly allergic to insect bites and stings, some dogs are allergic and react severely to bites and stings.

Spider bites, especially those from the black widow and Missouri brown spider, can be toxic. The bite itself is painful, and can result in fever, difficulty breathing, and shock. Scorpion and centipede stings are no fun either, as they cause your dog pain and can make him very ill.

When it comes to insect bites and stings, the best advice is to identify the attacker and call your veterinarian. Ask for instructions on what to do at home to make your dog comfortable immediately.

The vet may advise you to apply a paste of baking soda or ice packs to the sting, or may wish to examine the dog. If your Poodle shows an extreme reaction, such as facial swelling, difficulty breathing, or weakness, get to the clinic right away.

Poisoning

A poison is any substance that can be harmful to your dog. Poisoning can result when your Poodle ingests or comes in contact with a toxic substance such as household cleaners, antifreeze, rat poison, gasoline, plants, or even chocolate. You must be extremely careful not to allow your Poodle access to potential toxins. Poison-proof your house, and keep your Poodle on a leash when outdoors to minimize any chance of poisoning.

The signs of poisoning vary, but can include an irritated mouth, excessive drooling, vomiting, diarrhea, skin rash, seizures, or coma. If your dog appears to have been poisoned, or you know he has nibbled or licked something toxic, call your veterinarian immediately! There is no time to waste. If possible, identify the poison so you can inform the vet to help him determine the appropriate treatment.

National Animal Poison Control Center: (888) 426-4435, $45 per case, with as many follow-up calls as necessary included. Have name, address, phone number, dog's breed, age, sex, and type of poison ingested, if known, available; www.napcc.aspca.org.

Once you get your vet on the phone, ask for instructions. He may tell you to induce vomiting or give charcoal, which will help eliminate the poison from your dog's system or delay its absorption. Follow doctor's orders carefully because they can mean life or death for your poisoned dog.

Seizures

Dogs can suffer seizures or convulsions very similar to those seen in people. A seizure is a sudden and uncontrolled burst of electrical activity in the brain that results in foaming at the mouth, jerking of the legs, chewing, and collapse. There are two common types of seizures: grand mal and petit mal.

Seizures can be caused by several factors, including head injury, hypoglycemia, heavy internal parasite infestation, poisoning, kidney failure, and liver failure. Frequent or periodic seizures can indicate epilepsy, a recurrent seizure disorder.

What should you do if your Poodle suffers a seizure? Stand aside, wait for the seizure to take its course, and call the vet. That can be scary, but most seizures are over within minutes. Your veterinarian will probably want to examine the dog to pinpoint the cause and determine whether the dog is suffering from epilepsy. If the seizure is prolonged—lasting more than three minutes— you must take the Poodle to your vet immediately.

Shock

Shock is the collapse of the circulatory system, and is usually a secondary result of severe injury, blood loss, or allergic reactions. If your Poodle is injured, he may experience shock. A dog in shock will have a decreased supply of oxygen, which results in unconsciousness, pale gums, weak, rapid pulse or labored, rapid breathing.

Shock must be treated right away because it can be fatal. If you suspect shock, stop any bleeding and administer CPR as necessary. Cover the animal with a blanket or towel, and transport her to the veterinary clinic right away.

Normal Vital Signs

Temperature: 100 to 102.5 degrees Fahrenheit

Pulse: 60 to 169 beats per minute for adult dogs; up to 180 in Toy breeds; 220 for puppies

Respiration: 10 to 30 breaths per minute at rest

Vomiting

Another less-than-pleasant symptom your Poodle is likely to experience during her lifetime is vomiting. Many illnesses and diseases can cause vomiting, so this sign must be investigated.

Common causes of vomiting include overeating and eating too fast. Eating grass or something else irritating to the stomach is another common cause of vomiting.

If the Poodle vomits a few times, appears well, and doesn't vomit again, her vomiting usually isn't cause for concern. Repeated vomiting, vomiting blood, projectile vomiting, or vomiting foreign objects are, however, causes for concern. Pay attention to when and how often vomiting occurs, and call the veterinarian. Vomiting blood, attempting to vomit without any results, or any vomiting accompanied by abdominal pain is an emergency—head to the vet right away.

Health Concerns Specific to Poodles

You should be aware of certain health conditions that more commonly affect Poodles. It's especially important that you know about these conditions when you select a Poodle puppy or adult. That way, you can ask questions regarding the health of the dog, her parents, and other family members. Some of these conditions are genetic and can be tested or screened. You have a right to be an informed buyer. Don't hesitate to ask the breeder whether her dogs are afflicted with any of the following conditions. If you already have a Poodle, the following may help in understanding ailments common to Poodles.

Hip Dysplasia

Hip dysplasia is a common cause of lameness in dogs, most common in large breeds weighing more than 20 pounds. Hip dysplasia is a genetic disorder which manifests itself as the dog develops. As your Poodle grows, the way the head of the femur fits into the hip socket may change. Loose ligaments or poorly formed bones allow the head to slip inside the socket, causing pain, cartilage damage, and arthritis. The dog may have trouble getting up from lying down or sitting, may be lame, and may lose muscle tone in the rear.

Hip dysplasia is considered an inheritable condition. Poodles, primarily the Standard variety, are one of the breeds that have an increased incidence of hip dysplasia as compared to the general dog population. Since hip dysplasia can be genetic, dogs with this condition should not be bred. More importantly, all dogs should be screened before breeding.

Currently, screening is done by taking x rays of a dog's hips. The x rays can be sent to the Orthopedic Foundation for Animals, a non-profit foundation that provides a standardized method of evaluating and registering the x rays. For a fee, the OFA's panel of expert radiologists will review a dog's

Genetic Tests

Versatility In Poodles (VIP) is a non-profit group dedicated to improving the health and promoting the talents of the Poodle. VIP also funds research studies on health and genetic conditions that affect the breed. (The organization's Web site, www.pageweb.com/vipoodle, is a must-see for every prospective Poodle owner. It is loaded with health, performance, and rescue information.)

Testing is essential to improving the health of the breed. VIP recommends the following genetic screening tests for Standard Poodles:

- ○ X rays for hip-joint dysplasia
- ○ Eye examination for progressive retinal atrophy (PRA) and 21 other inherited eye abnormalities found in Poodles, such as juvenile cataracts, entropion, ectropion
- ○ Skin biospy for sebaceous adenitis (SA)
- ○ DNA test for von Willebrand's disease
- ○ Blood test for thyroid malfunction
- ○ Blood test for Addison's disease
- ○ Blood and urine tests for juvenile renal disease

VIP recommends the following genetic tests for Miniature and Toy Poodles:

- ○ X rays for hip joint dysplasia and Legg-Calve-Perthes disease
- ○ Examination for patellar luxation
- ○ Eye examination for progressive retinal atrophy (PRA) and 21 other inherited eye abnormalities found
- in Poodles, such as juvenile cataracts, entropion, ectropion.
- ○ DNA test for von Willebrand's disease
- ○ Blood test for thyroid malfunction

x rays. If the conformation of the hips (or other joint) is shown normal for that breed, the dog is then "certified," and given a number. OFA certifies dogs 24 months or older, and primarily certifies hips and elbows. The Wind-Morgan Program of the Institute for Genetic Disease Control in Animals at the University of California, Davis, School of Veterinary Medicine, is another non-profit program offering registry and screening of orthopedic disorders. Wind-Morgan certifies hips and elbows, but also reviews radiographs of shoulders and hocks.

What is the importance of reviewing X-rays of potential breeding stock of any breed of dog? Genetic studies have shown that breeding radiographically normal dogs produces less joint disease than when affected dogs, or dogs of unknown status, are bred.

Before you buy a Poodle, ask to see certification of both parents from OFA, GDC, PennHip, or all of these organizations. Certification, plus an ethical breeder, means less chance of acquiring a dog with hip dysplasia.

> Genetic studies have shown that breeding radiographically normal dogs produces less joint disease than when affected dogs, or dogs of unknown status, are bred.

Tear Stains

Toy and Miniature Poodles, especially light-colored ones, often develop copper-colored tear stains in the fur beneath their eyes. In most cases, this is not evidence of a serious condition, but it is unsightly. Most owners would prefer to have the fur stay clean and white.

Because tear staining can be caused by a variety of congenital eye problems, such as a blocked tear duct or a malformed eyelid, a Poodle that develops tear stains should always be examined by a veterinarian. These defects can be treated, and the staining will disappear after successful treatment.

In most cases, however, your Poodle's dark circles will have no known cause. You can improve her look by keeping the fur trimmed short, using a groomer-recommended whitener on the fur under the eye during bathing and grooming, and by using certain antibiotic eye ointments. In most cases, the staining will stop entirely if your veterinarian prescribes oral tetracycline antibiotics. These antibiotics interfere with the chemical interactions that cause clear-colored tears to turn copper. However, the staining will return when tetracycline is discontinued.

Progressive Retinal Atrophy

Progressive retinal atrophy or PRA is a disease that eventually leads to blindness in dogs. It manifests itself in many breeds of dogs, including mixed breeds. PRA is prevalent in Toy and Miniature Poodles, but has also been diagnosed in Standard Poodles. This genetically inherited condition affects the entire retina and is the canine equivalent of *retinitis pigmentosa* that occurs in humans.

The PRA in Poodles is usually diagnosed late in life, with the first signs noted after four years of age. An electroretinograph can be used for early detection of PRA. Animals to be tested in this manner are anesthetized while electrodes are placed on the eyes to record the retina's reaction to light. In other cases, visual ophthalmological examination by American College of Veterinary Ophthalmology certified vets can identify cases of PRA and then have them subsequently confirmed with electroretinography.

All dogs affected with PRA eventually go blind. Carriers show no clinical signs. Symptoms are subtle, starting with night blindness and some pupil dilation, and progressing to complete blindness. Annual testing is always recommended, especially for breeding stock.

Prospective buyers should ask to see each parent's "CERF number," which is evidence that the dog has been screened and found free of a heritable eye disease. CERF refers to the Canine Eye Registration Foundation, an organization that works in conjunction with the American College of

Veterinary Ophthalmology (ACVO). Be aware that CERF registration is good only for 12 months from examination date; thereafter the dog must be re-examined by an ACVO diplomate and re-registered to maintain an up-to-date CERF number.

Bloat

Bloat, a condition described earlier, is prevalent in the Standard Poodle and is the filling of the stomach with gas. Gastric dilation volvulous (GDV) includes bloat, but is followed by the twisting or torsion of the stomach, with the dog going into shock. A genetic link is suspected though no testing or certification is currently available. Immediate surgery is essential for a Poodle suffering from GDV. No dog who has had surgery for gastric torsion should be bred. Recent studies at Purdue University suggests that dogs with deep, narrow chests and a nervous temperament are at greater risk.

> Water should be withheld immediately following vigorous exercise and the dog should be rested for one-half hour after eating to prevent bloat.

Preventing bloat is not an exact science, since several factors besides a possible genetic predisposition may cause it. Studies at Purdue University found that happy, easygoing dogs are at less risk than stressed or fearful dogs. Fast eating or a diet of dry kibble may be a factor, as well as eating one large meal a day. Though studies are presently inconclusive, many veterinarians recommend feeding more than one meal per day by dividing the dog's daily portion into several smaller portions. Water should be withheld immediately following vigorous exercise and the dog should be rested for one-half hour after eating. Additionally, dry kibble should be slightly moistened before feeding.

Skin Tumors

Dogs of all breeds often develop tumors of the skin. The Toy and Miniature Poodle, however, seem to make lumps and bumps an art form. Once your Poodle begins to age, don't be surprised to see lots of small skin tumors crop up. These usually look like warts, and may or may not be filled with a thick fluid. In most cases these "old age" bumps are nothing serious. They are likely to be basal cell tumors, hair follicle tumors, or sebaceous cysts—none of which are likely to be malignant. However, it is impossible to tell cancer from benign growths by looks alone, so any new growth needs to be checked by your veterinarian. Ideally, they will be removed with surgery and sent off for a biopsy to confirm that they are benign. In many older Poodles, however, the sheer number of these little wart-like bumps makes removal of them all impossible. Even if your vet says not to worry, they need to be rechecked and removed if they grow, darken, are attached deeply under the skin rather than merely growing from the skin surface, if your dog itches at them, or if they bleed.

Undescended Testicle

Male dogs are born with two testicles. At birth they may be found either in the scrotum, near the body wall, or even inside the body. However, each testicle is expected to descend into the scrotum shortly after birth, normally by two months of age. If a testicle can't be felt after four months, it is extremely unlikely it will descend. A dog with no testicles found is called a "cryptorchid," and a "monorchid" is a dog with only one testicle present.

While undescended testicles occur in any breed, it is very common in the Toy Poodle. Testicles that stay up inside the body are subjected to higher temperatures than those in the scrotum. This can cause disease, including cancer, so they must be surgically removed in order to prevent serious problems later in life.

Undescended testicles in a dog is considered an inherited disorder, although the exact transmission is not yet completely worked out in each breed. Affected dogs should not be bred.

Hypothyroidism

An underactive thyroid gland is frequently diagnosed in the Poodle and is thought to be inherited in many cases. Because thyroid hormone is essential to the working of the entire body—especially the health of the skin, reproductive tract, heart, and nervous system—dogs with underactive thyroids may become seriously ill. In addition, thyroid disease has many different signs, including dry, itchy skin; allergies; difficulty becoming pregnant or siring pups; hair loss—especially on the tail; increased incidence of ear and skin infection; slow heart rate; and weight gain without increased food intake. Low levels of thyroid hormone can also drop the von Willebrand factor in dogs suffering from that condition, increasing the risk of bleeding from minor bumps and scrapes.

Thyroid disease can be difficult to diagnose, but the best first step is a screening test. This should include not just for thyroid hormone itself (T4) but should include T3 levels, autoantibodies against T4 and T3, as well as TSH levels (thyroid

Did You Know?

Dogs and humans are the only animals with prostates.

stimulating hormone). A hypothyroid dog normally has low T4 and high TSH levels.

Treatment of thyroid disease is inexpensive and satisfying—dogs get well quickly. However, it does involve giving medication every day for the rest of the dog's life, and having occasional blood tests done to evaluate the medication and your dog's health.

> Treatment of thyroid disease is inexpensive and satisfying—dogs get well quickly.

Thyroid disease is thought to be heritable, so hypothyroid dogs should not be bred. Responsible breeders will perform a thyroid screening test before breeding; ask to see these results before buying a puppy.

Patent Ductus Arteriosis (Heart Disease)

The heart of a healthy puppy is nearly perfectly formed at birth. However, because the lungs of a puppy don't work until birth, the heart doesn't pump much blood into the fetal lungs. Instead, there is a small hole, called the ductus arteriosis, that lets blood flow between the pulmonary artery (the vessel that pumps blood into the lungs) and the aorta, which pumps blood to the rest of the body. When the puppy breathes for the first few times, this hole should close, which redirects half of the blood to flow to the lungs and the rest to the body.

If the hole does not close, it is called a "patent ductus arteriosis" (PDA). This is one of the most common congenital heart defects in dogs, and occurs frequently in the Miniature Poodle. Puppies with a PDA develop heart failure, and may die within six to eight weeks. In some cases, the hole partially closes, leaving only a very tiny defect. These dogs may live for several years before heart failure occurs.

Pups may show no signs at first, but a PDA puppy's veterinarian will hear a characteristic murmur early in life. Once heart failure begins, the puppy may tire easily on exercise, may cough, and may collapse. In some cases, the gums may look greyish or blue; it is more common, however, for the mucous membrane on the rear of the dog (around the rectum or vagina) to turn blue, while the gums stay pink.

PDA can be definitively diagnosed by echocardiography (ultrasound of the heart), or by using contrast studies of the arteries. The only cure for this problem is surgery. In skilled hands, the prognosis for dogs that undergo surgery is very good. In fact, 95 percent of puppies who undergo surgery in the first few months after birth survive and live a normal life. Because PDA has a hereditary component, dogs born with this defect should not be bred.

Collapsing Trachea

The trachea, also known as the windpipe, carries air from the mouth and nose into the lungs. In some Poodles, especially the Toy and Miniature, the cartilage in the trachea is weak. While the dog can breathe normally most of the time, when the throat becomes irritated from infection, inflammation, or even from overexcitement, the trachea will narrow, making it hard to breathe. In some dogs, even pulling gently on the collar can cause tracheal narrowing or collapse, both of which result in harsh coughing and gagging.

In most cases the problem is mild, and the Poodle suffers no more than occasional bouts of loud and unpleasant coughing. In rare cases, however, the problem becomes severe. These dogs can have serious trouble breathing, and the increased blood pressure caused by frequent tracheal collapse can lead to heart failure.

There are several treatments available for tracheal collapse. In most cases, the dog only needs minimal care, such as swapping the collar for a harness that presses on the chest, not the throat area, or cough suppressants if the dog catches an infectious disease that irritates the trachea. In severe cases, however, surgery may be necessary to make the trachea stay open so the dog can breathe.

It is unknown if this problem is inherited, but it is wise to avoid breeding a dog that is very severely affected.

Epilepsy

Epilepsy is a seizure disorder that may be secondary (acquired after trauma or disease) or primary (occurs with no known cause). It is not congenital in Poodles. To establish a diagnosis of epilepsy, the attacks must be recurrent and unable to be attributed to any known physical reason. All three varieties of the Poodle can be affected by the primary idiopathic epilepsy. This form of epilepsy is considered to be hereditary and affected dogs should not be bred.

An epileptic seizure may include shivering, shaking, loss of bowel or bladder control, loss of ability to stand, unusual behaviors such as biting at the air, and staring off into space as if in a trance. In most cases, however, Poodles with epilepsy will have full-blown convulsions. These may be frightening to watch, but

are very rarely fatal. The condition can usually be controlled with medication such as phenobarbital. However, the earlier in life seizures begin, the more difficult it is to control them. Epileptic seizures are rarely fatal.

Extensive studies of epilepsy in Poodles have just begun at Florida State University. No tests or certification is currently available to pinpoint dogs with epilepsy. However, a wise Poodle buyer will ask a breeder if the breeder's Poodles are affected. There's no guarantee you'll get a straight answer, but if the breeder is ethical and truly cares about the breed, you'll hear the truth.

> In most cases, Poodles with epilepsy will have full-blown convulsions. These may be frightening to watch, but are very rarely fatal.

Sebaceous Adenitis

Sebaceous adenitis (SA) is a skin disease that causes hair loss and thickened skin. For reasons currently unknown, sebaceous glands become inflamed, which leads to progressive loss of hair. SA is prevalent in the Standard Poodle. It is considered a genetic condition, and 50 percent of all Standard Poodles are carriers. Poodles with SA often have excessive dandruff, dark, thick skin, hair loss, and the skin smells musty. Testing by skin biopsy is essential. Diagnosis of SA is made by a microscopic examination of the biopsy sample by a certified dermatologist. Dogs with SA should not be bred.

There is no cure for or definitive treatment for SA.

Addison's Disease

Addison's disease or hypoadrenocorticism is the destruction of the adrenal gland, which produces adrenal hormones. Addison's disease is prevalent in the Poodle. It is seen mostly in Standards, but can be found in all three varieties. Researchers are not sure whether the condition is genetic, but some research suggests that

Addison's may be passed by a recessive gene. A Poodle with Addison's disease may be depressed, lack appetite, vomit, or have diarrhea with abdominal pain.

Addison's disease can be confirmed by several blood tests, including a complete blood count, chemistry tests, and an ACTH test. Dogs with the condition usually receive medication, fludrocortisone acetate and prednisolone, given orally daily for the remainder of the dog's life.

Addison's disease is prevalent in the Poodle. It is seen mostly in Standards, but can be found in all three varieties.

Addison's disease is fatal if left undiagnosed and untreated. Dogs with Addison's may have a crisis during periods of stress, such as boarding or grooming. Poodles diagnosed with Addison's disease should not be used in a breeding program.

Von Willebrand's Disease

Von Willebrand's disease (VWD) is a genetic blood disorder that can affect all three varieties of the Poodle, but is most common in the Standard. It is caused by a decreased level of a clotting factor. This puts the dog at risk for bleeding to death from bumps, bruises, or surgery. DNA testing is recommended even though the condition is not considered a major problem in the breed. The Doberman Pinscher has the highest incidence of VWD, reported at more than 50 percent.

In most cases, bleeding problems in dogs with VWD are mild and appear to lessen with age. Signs include nosebleeds, blood in the urine and stools, oozing from wounds, or hemorrhage beneath the skin. Surgery can be undertaken even in severely affected dogs if diagnosis is made before surgery and proper medications and precautions are used.

Autoimmune Anemia

Immune mediated hemolytic anemia (IMHA) or autoimmune hemolytic anemia (AIHA) is prevalent in Standard Poodles. Poodles
can be genetically predisposed to the condition due to defects in
enzymes or red blood cells. In hemolytic anemia, a loss of red
blood cells occurs due to destruction of the red blood cells. Destruction occurs when antibodies stick to the red blood cells and
cause the body to react, leading to destruction of the cells. This
can be the direct result of a drug, toxin, blood parasite, virus, or
other primary cause, or it can be an unexplained immune-medi-
ated reaction. Dogs with IMHA usually experience a sudden onset
of signs, including depression, lethargy, pale gums, sometimes
jaundice or a heart murmur, and bruising. Vomiting or abdominal
pain may be present. Death can occur rapidly, even with appropriate treatment. Whenever hemolytic anemia is present, it is wise to
first rule out causes that might be treatable. For example, ehrli-
chiosis (a blood parasite), reactions to sulfa or penicillin antibiotics, and zinc toxicosis (which can occur due to the ingestion of
pennies) can lead to hemolytic anemia. If any of these problems
can be identified and treated, the prognosis is much better.

Symptoms plus a Coomb's test to check for antibodies ad-
hered to red blood cells confirm diagnosis. This test is usually
done at body temperature and at a colder temperature (four degrees Celsius). A small percentage of dogs that have
AIHA will not test positive on the Coomb's test.

Dogs with AIHA often respond well to very high
doses of corticosteroids, such as prednisone. Improvement usually occurs within one to three days. If
signs of icterus (jaundice) are present, the prognosis is
usually worse. It is necessary to treat most dogs for a
fairly long time to prevent recurrence of the disease

and some dogs seem to require lifelong use of corticosteroids or other immunosuppressants. A splenectomy is done in resistant cases since the spleen is a major site of red blood cell destruction.

Patellar Luxation

Patellar luxation or slipped stifles is a dislocation of the kneecap, usually due to abnormal structure of the stifle joint. Patellar luxation is most common in Toys and Miniatures, though it has been seen in Standards. It is an inherited disease, although researchers have not yet determined the exact mode of inheritance. In some cases, patellar luxation can be caused by trauma.

The Poodle with patellar luxation will have the kneecap pop out of place when she flexes the affected leg. As long as the knee cap is "out," she can't put weight on it and she will carry the leg off the ground and move on three legs. Most Poodles affected with this condition do not feel much pain until later in life, when arthritis develops.

The goal of treatment is to return the kneecap to a normal position and prevent arthritis. In order to do this, surgery is usually necessary. Surgery may be necessary in severe or chronic cases.

Any Poodle considered for a breeding program should be X-rayed or examined for patellar luxation prior to being bred. Only dogs having normal radiographs and exams should be considered for breeding. Dogs that produce offspring with slipped stifles should be considered carriers and great care should be taken not to breed carriers.

Juvenile Renal Disease

The kidneys are extremely important organs that function to remove waste from and maintain water in the body. When kidneys fail, the body cannot survive. After a lifetime of work, kidney failure is common in geriatric dogs in any breed. However, a young dog is expected to have healthy kidneys designed to work for ten years or more without any sign of failure.

In juvenile renal disease (JRD), the kidneys begin to fail early, often in the first year of life. Puppies may be born with poorly functioning kidneys, resulting in "fading puppies" (puppies that are born strong but die for no easily known cause within weeks after birth). Many puppies are born healthy, with the genetic defect causing kidney failure as they grow into adulthood. In some dogs, signs may not appear until the dog is two years old. These dogs may have parented litters by this time, possibly passing it on to their offspring.

> The signs of JRD in the Standard Poodle include increased urination, increased level of water intake, dribbling urine, and weight loss.

The signs of JRD in the Standard Poodle include increased urination, increased level of water intake, dribbling urine, and weight loss. Not all pups dribble urine and weight loss usually occurs late in the progression of the disease.

The bad news about JRD is that it will inevitably progress, leading to death in a variable amount of time. On a more positive note, if the dog is mildly affected at the time of diagnosis, the progression may be slowed by proper treatment, which may include medications, dietary changes, and fluid therapy as needed.

JRD has been identified in the Standard Poodle and experts feel like it is likely hereditary in the breed, as it has proven to be in other breeds. It has not yet been reported in Miniature and Toys. Currently there are no tests to identify carriers; the best way to avoid the disease is to buy dogs from parents who are over two years of age and to ask the breeder about any occurrence of kidney problems at a young age in the line.

Research Programs

A variety of research programs intent on each of the conditions discussed are underway. Funding for these programs is jointly supported by the Poodle Club of America, Inc., and the AKC Canine Health Foundation, as well as Versatility In Poodles, VIP.

6

Basic Training for Poodles

By Liz Palika

In This Chapter

○ When to Begin Training
○ The Teaching Process
○ What Every Good Poodle Needs to Know
○ Housetraining

All dogs, including Poodles of all sizes, need training to learn how to behave themselves. When your Standard Poodle learns to greet people by sitting still, he won't jump up on them. When he learns what the word "stay" means, he will learn to be still and to control his own actions. Your Toy Poodle can learn to walk nicely on a leash instead of being carried all the time.

In addition, once you learn how to teach your dog, you can train him to follow the rules necessary for good behavior.

Does your Poodle insist on being the center of attention? Does he bark at people outside your yard? If he gets out of the yard, does he refuse to come when you call him?

Does he raid the trashcan? Does he jump on your guests? These are not unusual behaviors for a young, untrained dog, but they are unnecessary, potentially dangerous, and annoying behaviors that you can change (or at least control) through training.

With training, your Poodle can learn to control himself so that he doesn't react to every impulse. He can learn to sit while greeting people rather than covering them with muddy paw prints or ripping their clothes. He can learn to restrain some of his vocalizations and to ignore the trashcans.

Training affects you, too. You will learn why your Poodle

A well-trained Poodle will accept your guidance even when he would rather be doing something else.

does what he does so you can prevent some of his undesirable actions, either by changing your routine or preventing the problems from occurring. Training your Poodle is not something you do to him, but instead is something the two of you do together.

Lana is a lovely, white Toy Poodle owned by Gayle Bryan of Bonsall, California. Gayle first brought Lana to a kindergarten puppy-training class as soon as Lana had her puppy vaccinations. "I've had Poodles before," Gayle said, "and I know how smart they are. I want to make sure this puppy grows up knowing the correct way to do things so I don't have to try to change bad habits later."

Gayle has other plans for Lana, too. "I would like to train her to work as a therapy dog. She is so loving and gentle that I think people would really enjoy her. But I know she must be very well-trained before she can begin therapy-dog training so we'll keep working toward that goal."

Basic Commands Every Dog Should Know

Sit: Your dog's hips should move to the ground while his shoulders remain upright.

Down: Your dog should lie down on the ground or floor and be still.

Stay: Your dog should remain in position (sit or down) while you walk away from him. He should hold the stay until you give him permission to move.

Come: Your dog should come to you on the first call despite any distractions.

Walk on the leash: Your dog can walk ahead of you on the leash but should not pull the leash tight.

Heel: Your dog should walk by your left side with his shoulders by your left leg.

When to Begin Training

Ideally, training should begin as soon as you bring home your new Poodle. If you have an eight- to ten-week-old puppy, that's okay. Your new puppy can begin learning that biting isn't allowed, that he should sit for treats, petting, and meals, and where he should go to relieve himself. By ten weeks of age, you can attach a small leash to his collar and let him drag it around for a few minutes at a time so he gets used to it. Always watch him closely, of course, so that he doesn't get the leash tangled up in something and choke himself. Young puppies have a very short attention span, but they are capable of learning and are eager students.

Don't let your Poodle pup do anything now that you don't want him to do later when he is full grown. For example, if you don't want your Standard Poodle up on your lap when he's 45

What a Trained Dog Knows

A trained dog knows:

- ○ The appropriate behaviors allowed with people (no biting, no mouthing, no rough play, and no mounting).
- ○ Where to relieve himself and how to ask to go outside.
- ○ How to greet people properly without jumping on them.
- ○ To wait for permission to greet people, other dogs, and other pets.
- ○ How to walk nicely on a leash so that walks are enjoyable for both of you.
- ○ To leave trashcans alone.
- ○ To leave food that is not his alone (on the counters or coffee table).
- ○ Not to beg.
- ○ To chew on his toys and not on things belonging to people.
- ○ That destructive behavior is not acceptable.
- ○ To wait for permission to go through doorways.

A trained dog is a happy dog, secure in his place in the family.

pounds of rough paws and hard elbows, don't let him on your lap now. If you don't want your Toy Poodle growing up to be a problem barker, stop the barking when he's a puppy. It will be much harder to change the habit later. Keep in mind as you begin your dog's training that Poodles are an intelligent breed, responsive to training!

If you have adopted a Poodle who is an older puppy or an adult, you can still begin training right away. Although your new dog will need time to get used to you and his new home, early training will help your new dog learn what you expect of him, and as a result, will make that adjustment easier.

Kindergarten Puppy Class

The ideal time to begin group training is as soon as your Poodle puppy has had at least two sets of vaccinations, usually between ten and twelve weeks of age. Many veterinarians may recommend that you wait even longer. Ask your vet what he thinks. Kindergarten puppy classes introduce the basic obedience commands—sit, down, stay, and come—all geared for the young puppy's short attention span. Puppy classes also spend time socializing the puppy with other people and other puppies.

Start teaching your Poodle the rules you expect of him right away. If you don't want him on the furniture, never allow him to do so, and don't make exceptions or explain away his actions. ("Oh, it's cold tonight so I'll let him come up and cuddle!") If you don't want him on the furniture, teach him right away what your rules are. If you aren't consistent, he won't be either!

Is It Ever Too Late?

Although training is most effective when started early in the dog's life and practiced consistently while he grows up, that doesn't mean it's too late to train an adult Poodle. The downfall to starting training later in the dog's life is that you then have to break bad habits as well as teach new commands. With a young puppy, you're starting with a blank slate and you can teach

Start training early in your puppy's life so she learns good behavior instead of bad habits.

Basic Obedience Class

Most obedience instructors invite puppies to begin the basic obedience class after they have graduated from a puppy class or after a puppy has reached four months of age. Dogs or older puppies over four months of age who have not attended a puppy class would also attend a basic obedience class. This class teaches the traditional obedience commands—sit, down, stay, come, and heel. In addition, most instructors spend time discussing problem behaviors such as jumping on people, barking, digging, chewing, and others. A group class such as this helps your Poodle learn to control himself around other dogs and people.

the new behaviors before he learns bad habits. If you've ever had to break a bad habit (smoking, for example), you know it can be difficult. However, with most Poodles up to about eight years of age, you can, with consistent training and lots of patience and positive reinforcements, control most bad habits.

If your dog is older than eight years of age, your success at changing bad habits will be much more limited. You can teach new commands—sit, down, stay, and heel—and your dog will be able to learn these without too much trouble. However, Poodles who have not learned to consistently come when called by the time they are eight years old will probably never be reliable.

Basic Dog Psychology

Archeologists have found evidence showing that humans and the ancestors of today's dogs—wolves—shared a history dating back thousands of years. At some point, for some unknown reason, hu-

Private Training

Private training is normally recommended for Poodles with severe behavior problems, such as biting, growling, dog aggression, or uncontrolled behavior. Private training is done one-on-one either at your home or at the trainer's facility. This training can usually be tailored to your dog's individual needs.

Sometimes the behavior problems are so severe that they are impossible to solve. A habit may be too deeply ingrained or the stimulus causing the behavior is too strong. Some Toy Poodles do have a tendency to bark, sometimes to the annoyance of the neighbors. In very severe cases, the dog doesn't seem to realize he's barking; the sound simply erupts. With these dogs, or dogs with other severe problem behaviors, private training can often help, but sometimes the problem never totally goes away.

mans and some individual wolves decided to cooperate. Perhaps the wolves, being efficient hunters, aided the human hunters. Perhaps the wolves took advantage of the humans' garbage heap. For whatever reason, this cooperation occurred, and the result was domesticated dogs.

Families and Packs

In the wild, wolves live in packs. This pack has some important social rules that are seldom broken. If a youngster breaks a rule inadvertently or on purpose, he is corrected fairly but firmly. The correction may be a growl, posturing over the youngster (by the adult), or even a physical correction that consists of the adult pinning the youngster to the ground. Packs are usually fairly harmonious. Each member knows his or her place and keeps to it. However, when an adult dies, becomes disabled, or leaves the pack, there may be some posturing or fighting until the new pack order is established.

Dogs fit into our family life because they have this pack history. A human family is a social organization similar to a pack, although our families have significant differences from a wolf pack and vary from each other depending upon our culture. We normally have an adult male and female, although today's families more commonly have just one adult. In addition, our family rules are often chaotic. In a wolf pack, the leaders always eat first; but in our families, people often eat any time and in no specific order. These family rules, or lack of rules, can be confusing to our dogs.

Poodles today are primarily pets but retain the desire to please that they inherited from their working-dog ancestors. To satisfy that desire, Poodles need strong leadership; otherwise they are sure to develop problem behaviors. A family with a strong leader—you—can provide the needed guidance.

What Does it Mean to Be "Top Dog"?

Top dog is a slang term for the leader of the pack. In the wolf pack we discussed, the top dog is the dominant male or dominant female, often called the alpha male or alpha female. In your family, there should be no confusion: The top dog should be you, the dog's owner (and leader). Your dog should maintain a subordinate position to any additional human family members.

Often during adolescence, a Poodle with a particularly bold personality may make a

Don't let your dog use his body language to show dominance. Your dog should recognize you (and your children) as above him in the family pack.

bid for leadership of the family. Adolescence usually strikes at sexual maturity, usually between eight and twelve months of age. Luckily, Poodles are usually eager to maintain pack harmony so it is generally fairly easy for most owners to maintain leadership of the family pack. Because eating first is the leader's prerogative and is an action the dog readily understands, the owner should always eat before feeding the dog. You should also go through all doorways first and have your dog follow you. Make sure you can roll your Poodle over to give him a tummy rub without any fussing on the dog's part. A dog who takes over the leadership of the home can make life miserable for all concerned—this is when growling, barking, biting, and mounting behaviors become apparent—so make sure you maintain your position as the dog's leader.

> A human family is a social organization similar to a pack.

Most owners of larger dogs, including Standard Poodles, realize the importance of being their dog's leader. Unfortunately, the owners of small (especially tiny) dogs don't. The tiny dog is allowed to continue obnoxious behaviors a larger dog would never be allowed to do, including mounting, leg-lifting, barking, and growling. The owners of these tiny Poodles often make excuses for their little tyrant's poor behavior, "Oh, he's so tiny!" They don't realize that this little tyrant isn't a happy dog; he's simply assuming the position of leader that his owner hasn't assumed. If his owner acted like the leader and relieved his little dog of the need to demonstrate these behaviors, many of the behaviors would stop. All Poodles—Standard, Miniature, and Toy—need a good leader, and that leader must be you.

Although it is very important that your dog regard you as the leader or top dog, don't look upon every action your dog makes as a dominance challenge. Most of the time your Poodle won't care

You Are the Top Dog!

○ Always eat first!

○ Go through doors and openings first; block your dog from charging through ahead of you.

○ Go up stairs first; don't let him charge ahead of you and then look down on you.

○ Give your dog permission to do things, even if he was going to do them anyway. If he picks up his ball, tell him, "Get your ball! Good boy to get your ball!"

○ Practice your training regularly.

○ Have your dog roll over for a tummy rub daily.

○ Do not play rough games with your Poodle—no wrestling, no tug-of-war.

○ Never let your dog stand above you or put his paws on your shoulders. These are dominant positions.

about his position in the family pack; he knows you're in charge. However, during adolescence, and for more dominant personalities, training is very important.

The Teaching Process

Teaching your dog is not a difficult project, although at times it may seem impossible. Most dogs, especially Poodles, do want to be good; they just need to learn what you want them to do and what you don't. Therefore, most of the teaching process consists of communication. You need to reward the behaviors you want your dog to continue doing and you need to interrupt the behaviors you wish to stop. Let's use barking as an example again. When your dog begins to bark inappropriately, stop him with a verbal correction, "Quiet!" given in a firm, no-nonsense tone of voice. When your dog stops barking, you will then praise him, "Good boy to be quiet!" in a higher-than-normal tone of voice.

Did you notice my emphasis on two different tones of voice? As verbal animals themselves, dogs are very aware of different tones of voice. When the leader of a wolf pack lets a subordinate know that he or she made a mistake, the leader uses a deep growl to convey that message. When things are fine, the pack has hunted, and all is well with the world, the leader may convey that with higher-pitched barks or even yelps. When you copy this technique—using a deep, growling voice to let the dog know he's made a mistake and a higher-pitched tone to reinforce good behavior—your dog doesn't have to stop and translate that information. He just understands.

Don't confuse high and low tones of voice with volume, though. Your dog can hear very well—much better than you can—and it's not necessary to yell at him. Instead, simply sound like you mean what you say.

As you begin teaching your dog, remember that human words have no meaning to your dog until he's taught that they do. For example, he's probably already begun learning some

A treat can be a wonderful training tool to help teach your dog to pay attention to you. When he looks at you, praise him, give him the treat, and then follow through with other training.

words. He may know treat, cookie, ball, toy, walk, car, and bed. He may have already learned leash, outside, go potty, inside, and no bite! But other words are just sounds—gobbledy-gook that have no meaning. As you teach him, he will learn that words like sit, down, come, and heel have meanings that are important to him.

The Training Process

To teach a new command:

○ Show the dog what to do with a lure, your hands, or your voice;

○ Praise him for doing it and reward him with the lure, if you used one;

To correct problem behavior:

○ Prevent the problem from happening when possible.

○ Set the dog up for success by teaching him to do something else and then rewarding it.

○ Correct him for mistakes only when he knows and understands the command and chooses not to do it.

○ Interrupt the behavior when you catch the dog in the act. Let him know he made a mistake.

○ Show him the appropriate behavior.

So how can you teach your dog that these sounds have meanings? First, repeat the word as you help your dog perform the act. As you help your dog to sit, say the word, "Poochie, sit!" You can reinforce it by praising the dog after he has done as you asked by telling him, "Good boy to sit!" By using the word, your dog will learn that the word has meaning, that he should pay attention when he hears that word and do whatever the word requires him to do.

Corrections should be given as the dog is making the mistake, not after the fact.

Just as communication is a big part of the training process, so is your timing. You must use your voice to praise your dog for doing something right—*as he is doing it*—not later, not after the fact. The same thing

Training Vocabulary

Listed below are several terms that will be used to help you train your Poodle.

○ **Positive reinforcement**: Anything your dog likes that you can use to reward good behavior, including treats, praise, toys, tennis balls, and petting.

○ **Praise**: Words spoken in a higher-than-normal tone of voice to reward your dog for something he did right; part of positive reinforcement.

○ **Lure**: A food treat or a toy used to help position the dog as you want him, or to gain his cooperation as you teach him.

○ **Interruption**: When you catch your dog in the act of doing something and stop him. This can be verbal, in a deeper-than-normal tone of voice, or it could be a sharp sound like dropping your book to the floor. An interruption stops the behavior as it is happening.

○ **Correction**: Usually a deep, growly verbal sound or words to let your dog know he made a mistake, preferably given as he is doing it. A correction can serve as an interruption, but also lets your dog know that you dislike what he is doing. This can also be a snap and release of the leash. A correction should be firm enough to get your dog's attention and stop the behavior at that moment and that's all.

applies to letting your dog know that he's making a mistake. Use your voice to let him know he's making a mistake *as* he begins to bark. Don't wait until he's already in full voice. Then, when he stops or decides *not* to bark, praise him for making the right choice. When your timing is correct, there is no misunderstanding; your dog knows exactly what message you are trying to convey.

Don't rely on corrections (verbal or otherwise) to train your dog. We all, dogs and people alike, learn just as much from our successes as we do from our mistakes, and we are more likely to repeat our successes! Don't hesitate to set your dog up for success so that you can praise and reward him. If you want to keep your Poodle off the furniture, have him lie down at your feet and hand him a toy to keep him busy *before* he jumps up on the furniture. You can then reward him for good behavior instead of correcting him for bad.

A properly timed correction will let your dog know when he's making a mistake but doesn't tell the dog what to do instead. If your Poodle is chewing on your leather shoes and you simply correct him, you are conveying to him that chewing on your shoes is wrong; but you aren't teaching him what he can chew on. And since chewing is important for dogs, that's an important lesson. So instead of *just* correcting him (to show him what is wrong), you can walk him to his toys and hand him something of his to chew on (to show him what is right). Then praise him when he picks up one of his toys (to reinforce a good choice).

Teaching Your Dog to Be Handled

One of the jobs that comes part and parcel with Poodles is grooming. With a Poodle's high-maintenance coat, grooming is an ongoing, daily process. In addition, your Poodle needs help caring for himself. You must be able to brush him, comb him, trim him, bathe him, trim his toenails, and clean his ears. When he's sick or has hurt himself, you must be able to take care of him, whether it's cleaning his ears when he has an infection, caring for his stitches after neutering, or washing out his eyes if dirt gets in them.

It's important to teach your Poodle to accept handling before there's an emergency. If you teach him to accept the handling of his body by others early in life (as a puppy or as soon as you bring him home), then when he has a problem that requires special care, you will have already built that bond of trust and he will know to relax and let you, or his vet or groomer, care for him.

A tummy rub can help relax your dog if he's over-stimulated. You can also follow through with any needed grooming. In addition, this is a wonderful time for bonding with your dog.

To introduce this exercise, sit on the floor and invite your Poodle to lie down on the floor between your legs, on your lap, or in front of you. Start giving him a tummy rub to relax him. When he's relaxed, start giving him a massage. Begin massaging at his muzzle, rubbing your fingers gently over the skin, and at the same time, check his teeth. Then move your fingers up his head, touching the skin around his eyes, then his ears. Handle each ear flap, look in each ear, and massage around the base of each ear. As you massage, look for any problems. Look for discharge from the eyes or nose. Look for dirt, excess wax, or redness in the ears. Let your fingers feel for lumps, bumps, or bruises on the skin.

Continue in this same manner all over your Poodle's body. If he protests at any time, go back to the tummy rub for a moment, let him relax, and then continue. Do not let him turn this into a wrestling match; instead, keep it calm, relaxing, and gentle.

Do this exercise daily and incorporate your grooming regime into it. Daily combing and brushing will keep the coat from tangling and matting. In addition, by brushing the dog daily, you can find other things (such as fleas or ticks) before they turn into major problems. If your dog needs medication or first-aid treatments, you can do that while massaging, too. Simply make it part of the massage and don't let it turn into a fight.

There is a side effect of this massage you will enjoy. When you're through massaging your Poodle, he will be totally relaxed, like a limp noodle.

There is a side effect of this massage you will enjoy. When you're through massaging your Poodle, he will be totally relaxed, like a limp noodle. So plan ahead and do it when you want your dog to be quiet and relaxed. If he's over-stimulated in the evening when you would like to watch a favorite television show, sit on the floor, massage him, and then let him sleep while you watch your show!

The Importance of Good Socialization

Socialization is a vital part of raising a healthy, mentally sound Poodle. A young Poodle who has been introduced to a variety of people of different ages and ethnic backgrounds will be a social dog, happy to meet people and unafraid. A Poodle who has been kept in the backyard or house too much will be fearful. He may grow up afraid of children, or of senior citizens. A dog who has never met people of a different ethnic background than his owners may be afraid of different people. A Poodle of any size who is afraid can become aggressive out of fear, and so-called "fear biters" are dangerous. Dogs who bite out of fear often don't think before they act, and most eventually have to be destroyed because of their danger to people.

Introduce your dog to other friendly, well–behaved, healthy dogs. Avoid rowdy, poorly behaved, aggressive dogs; they could scare your dog and ruin the socialization you've done so far.

Socialization also refers to meeting other dogs and pets. Your Poodle should have opportunities to play with other well-behaved dogs so that he learns what it is to be a dog and how to behave around other dogs. Ideally, your Poodle should also meet friendly cats, rabbits, ferrets, and other pets. Always protect your Poodle by introducing him to pets that you know are friendly to dogs, and in addition, protect those pets from your Poodle. Don't let him chase the rabbit, for example, or the cat.

Socialization also includes the sights, sounds, and smells of the world around your Poodle. Let him see and hear the trash truck that comes by each week. If he's afraid of it, have him on-leash when the truck comes by and let the driver offer your Poodle a good dog treat. Let him watch the neighborhood kids go by on in-line skates; just don't let him bark or chase them. Walk your Poodle past the construction crew mending the potholes in the road. He can smell the hot asphalt as he watches the crew work. Take your Poodle to different places so that he can smell new smells and see new sights. The more he sees, hears, and smells, the better his coping skills.

> You can start socialization when your puppy is nine to ten weeks of age by introducing him to calm, friendly family members and neighbors.

Don't overload your Poodle, though, by trying to introduce him to everything at once. You can start socialization when your puppy is nine to ten weeks of age by introducing him to calm, friendly family members and neighbors. Let these people pet and cuddle him, but don't allow rough games; keep the experiences positive. Week by week, you can introduce your puppy to more people and different things.

Should your Poodle puppy be frightened of something, don't hug him, pet him, and try to reassure him—your puppy will assume those comforting words are praise for being afraid. Instead, use a happy tone of voice, "What was that?" and walk up to whatever scared him. Don't force him to walk up to it—just let him see you do it. For example, if your puppy sees a trashcan rolling in the street after the wind has blown it over, and he appears worried by it, hold onto his leash (to keep him from running away) and walk up to the trashcan. Ask your puppy (in an upbeat tone of voice) "What's this?" Touch the trashcan. Pat it several times so your puppy can see you touch it. If he walks up to it, praise him for his bravery!

A Crate Can Help Your Training

Originally designed as travel cages, crates have become very popular training tools for a variety of reasons.

Using a crate to confine your baby Poodle during the night and for short periods during the day helps him learn and develop more bowel and bladder control since his instincts tell him to keep his bed clean. He is not going to want to relieve himself in his crate.

Using the crate to confine your Poodle when you cannot supervise him will also help prevent problems from occurring. Your Poodle can't chew up your shoes, raid the trashcan, or shred the sofa cushions if he's confined to the crate. By preventing problems from occurring, you are also preventing bad habits from developing. As he grows up you can gradually give him more freedom, but not until he's grown up and mentally mature—about two years old for most Poodles.

A crate helps your puppy develop bowel and bladder control, prevents accidents from happening, and becomes your puppy's special place.

Many first-time dog owners resist the idea of a crate, saying it's too much like a jail. But dogs like small,

Choosing the Right Crate

Crates come in two basic types: plastic crates with solid sides originally designed for traveling with the dog and wire crates that look more like cages. Each style has its pros and cons. The plastic crates give the dog more security because of their solid sides. However, those solid sides make these crates bulky and they don't break down very much when you need to store them. The wire-sided cages usually fold down into a smaller, flat package although they are still quite heavy. The wire sides provide more ventilation for the dog but don't provide much security because they are open. To choose the right one, look at your needs. Will you have to move the crate much? Are you short of storage space? And look at your dog's needs. Does he need more air flow or more security? Choose a crate that will give your Poodle room to stand up, move around, lie down, and stretch out.

secure places, especially when sleeping. Most dogs quickly learn to like their crate, and it becomes their special place. My dogs continue to use their crates (voluntarily) on into old age because their own individual crate is their personal space to which they can retreat when tired, overwhelmed, or don't feel well.

Introduce the crate by opening the door and tossing a treat or toy inside. As the dog goes in, say the command phrase you wish to use, such as "Poochie, go to bed!" or "Poochie, kennel!" When he grabs the treat or toy, praise him, "Good boy to go to bed! Yeah!" Repeat this several times. When mealtime comes around, feed your dog his next meal in the crate, placing the food toward the back. Don't close the door yet, but let him go in and come out on his own.

At night, put the crate in your bedroom next to your bed so that your Poodle can smell you, hear you, and know that you are close by. He will be less apt to fuss during the night when he's close to you. You will also be able to hear him if he needs to go outside during the night. In addition, by being close to you, your dog gets to spend eight hours with you—precious time in your busy life!

> At night, put the crate in your bedroom next to your bed so that your Poodle can smell you, hear you, and know that you are close by.

Let your Poodle spend the night in his crate and a few hours here and there during the day. Other than at night, your Poodle should spend no more than three to four hours at a time in the crate. During the day, he needs time to run and play.

What Every Good Poodle Needs to Know

Dogs together have their own rules for social behavior. Unfortunately, those rules are not necessarily the same as yours. For example, in a dog pack, it's normal to sniff each other's rear end, whereas people consider that extremely poor manners—even when a dog does it! Your Poodle needs to learn the social rules you will require him to follow so that life with him is enjoyable rather than embarrassing.

No Jumping

Standard Poodles are not heavy dogs but they are very athletic. Although a Poodle jumping up will probably not knock an adult over, his muddy paws will not be appreciated. In addition, a Poodle jumping on a child or a senior citizen with poor balance could cause harm. Even Miniature and Toy Poodles can scratch skin, rip pantyhose, or muddy clothes. Therefore, it's usually a good idea to teach your Poodle not to jump on people when he greets them.

If you teach your Poodle to sit each time he greets people (anyone, including you, your family, guests, and people on the street), then he cannot jump on them and sit at the same time. Sitting becomes a replacement action for jumping up. We'll talk about the mechanics of teaching the sit later on in this chapter.

You can use the sit to stop the jumping up in several different ways. First, if your dog doesn't have his leash on—such as when you come home from work—make sure you greet him with empty hands. As your dog dashes up to you, grab his buckle collar (which should be on him with his ID tags) and tell him, "Poochie, no jump! Sit!" and with your hand on his collar, help him sit. Keep your hands on him as you praise him for sitting. If he tries to jump up, your hands on him will prevent it and you can continue to teach him.

> The leash is also a good training tool to help you control your dog.

The leash is also a good training tool to help you control your dog. When guests come over, ask them to wait outside for a moment (weather permitting, of course!) while you leash your dog. Once your Poodle is leashed, let your guests in. Make sure your dog sits before your guests pet him. If he jumps up, correct him, "No jump!" and have him sit again. Don't let your guests pet your dog while he's jumping up and misbehaving; if they do, they are rewarding him for bad behavior.

You can do the same thing when you and your dog are out in public. Have him sit before anyone pets him. If he's too excited and cannot hold still, don't let people pet him until you make him sit. If people protest, "Oh, I don't mind if he jumps!" explain that you are trying to teach him good social manners.

Barking

All dogs bark; it's their way of communicating. However, most neighbors do not appreciate a dog that barks excessively. The first thing you need to do is teach your Poodle a command that means "quiet" and enforce it while you're at home. Ask a neighbor to help you. Have her come over to your house and ring the doorbell. When your dog goes dashing to the door, making noise, tell him, "Poochie, quiet!" as you grab his collar. If he stops making noise, praise him, "Good boy to be quiet!" If he continues making noise, gently close his muzzle with your hand as you tell him to be quiet. When he stops, praise him.

Many Poodles will learn this command with repeated training. However, some are a little more persistent about making noise. With these dogs, the correction needs to be a little stronger. Take a spray bottle and put one-eighth part vinegar to seven-eighths parts water. There should be just enough vinegar to smell. If it smells too strong (to your nose), dilute it a little more.

Then, when your Poodle charges to the door barking, follow him and quietly tell him, "Poochie, quiet!" If he stops, praise him. If he doesn't, spray the water/vinegar towards his nose. He will be disgusted by the vinegar smell and will stop barking to think about it. As soon as he stops barking, praise him. The squirt bottle works as an interruption because your dog has a very sensitive sense of smell and he's going to dislike the smell of the vinegar. Therefore it can stop the bad behavior (the barking) without giving an overly harsh correction.

However, this squirt bottle technique needs to be used with caution. Vinegar can sting a dog's eyes, and, at high strengths, even damage them. Be sure that the water/vinegar solution is not too strong, and that you aim the solution only at your dog's nose.

Anti-Bark Collars

Several different types of bark-control collars are available to dog owners. Some give the dog an electric shock or jolt when he barks, some make a high-pitched sound, and one gives off a squirt of citronella. The citronella works on the same principle as the vinegar/water squirt bottle: The smell disrupts the dog's concentration and is annoying enough that he stops barking. This is the collar I recommend for most Poodles, as it is effective for most dogs and is a humane training tool.

If the solution should get into your dog's eyes, immediately flush them with water.

Use the same training techniques (verbal correction, collar, closing the muzzle, or the squirt bottle) to teach your Poodle to be quiet around the house. When he is reliable in the house, move the training outside. If he barks at the gate when the kids are playing out in the front yard, go outside to the gate and correct him with a verbal command and a squirt from the bottle. Always, of course, praise him when he's quiet.

No Begging

Poodles are very quick to pick up on a person who is an easy mark, and with those large eyes and that fluffy coat, who can resist a Poodle? You should! There is no reason any Poodle should beg for food from people who are eating. Begging is a bad habit and one that usually escalates into worse behavior. The dog may start by picking up food that has fallen to the floor, then may start pawing at a hand or leg, trying to solicit a handout. Eventually the

No Exile

I don't like to exile dogs to the backyard while people are eating. Although this is much easier to do—just put the dog outside and close the door—being banished tends to build up more frustration in the dog. He knows you're eating and knows he's been exiled, which is enough to cause frustration. When the dog is let in the house later, he's going to be wild!

However, if the dog is allowed to remain in the house, and is required to behave himself, he learns self-control. He knows he will get something to eat after the people are done so he learns to wait.

dog is actively begging and making a nuisance of himself. Sometimes it goes so far that the dog steals food from the kids' hands or off the table.

Fortunately, this is an easy habit to break although it does require consistency from all family members. Later in this chapter we will teach the down/stay command. When your Poodle has learned the down/stay, simply have him down/stay in a particular spot away from the table (or where people are eating) and make him hold his position while people are eating. By teaching him to lie down and stay in a corner of

Teach your dog to hold a down–stay while you're eating. He will learn that he gets to eat when you are finished so he must be patient.

No Rough Games!

Standard Poodles are not large dogs (as compared to German Shepherds or Rottweilers), but they are athletic dogs who like to play. Unfortunately, some rough games, like wrestling and tug-of-war, give the dog the wrong message about how he should regard or treat people. Wrestling teaches the dog to use his strength against you, to fight you and to protest when you hold him tight. Tug-of-war teaches him to use the strength of his jaws and his body against you. Neither game teaches him to respect or be gentle with you.

After too many of these rough-and-tumble games, every time you try to trim his toenails, a wrestling match will ensue. When you try to hold him still, he will fight you. When you try to take something out of his mouth, he may decide to play tug-of-war with it instead! Bad behavior!

Instead of playing these detrimental games, play hide-and-seek or retrieving games.

the room, so that he's not underfoot and cannot beg under the table, you are breaking the bad habit. When everyone has finished eating, you can then give your dog his meal or a treat in his bowl away from the table.

When you begin teaching this new rule, use the leash and collar on your dog so that if he makes a mistake and tries to beg (and he will initially!), you can lead him back to the spot where you want him to lie down and stay. Correct him as many times as you must until he holds the position or, in a worst-case scenario, the meal is over.

No Biting

All it takes is one bite and your Poodle could be taken from you and euthanized. All dog owners must take this issue seriously

Time Out!

Sometimes when puppies are corrected for what is natural behavior to them (such as mouthing), they will throw a temper tantrum. If your puppy should throw himself around, flail, and act like a cornered wild animal, don't punish him or try to stop it. Instead simply put him in his kennel crate and give him a time out. Don't yell at him, scold him, or try to reassure him—just put him in his crate, close the door, and walk away. In 15 or 20 minutes, if he's quiet and calm, let him out, but don't make a big fuss over him; just open the door and let him out.

Most puppies—just like most human children—will throw one or two tantrums sometime during puppyhood. If you give in to it, your puppy will learn that this horrible behavior works. However, if you give him a time out and put him away, he'll learn that this behavior is not rewarding.

because right now, the legal system works against dogs, not for them. There have been far too many bad dog-bite cases where people, especially children, have been seriously mauled or killed.

A dog bite is legally defined as the dog's open mouth touching skin. Puncture wounds do not require a biting action, nor must the skin be broken. Vicious intent is not necessary either. If your Poodle is in the backyard and decides to grab the neighbor's son (who has the dog's toy), that is a bite, even if the skin is not broken.

It's important to teach all dogs that teeth are not allowed to touch skin—ever! That means the dog is not to grab your hands when he wants you to do something. Nor should he use his mouth to protest when you're taking a toy away from him. To keep your dog safe, never allow him to use his mouth so that teeth (or the mouth itself) ever touch skin.

It's easy to teach young puppies that they should not use their mouth. Take your hand away as you correct the puppy verbally. A consistent, "No bite!" in a deep, growly tone of voice is usually all that is needed. If your Poodle puppy tries to use his mouth during playtime, tell him "No bite!" and get up and walk away, ending the game. If he bites hard, say "Ouch!!!" in a high-pitched, hurt tone of voice, followed by a deep, growly "No bite!" If the puppy is persistent about using his mouth, grab hold of his collar with one hand while you close his mouth with the other hand as you tell him, "No bite!"

> A dog bite is legally defined as the dog's open mouth touching skin.

If you are having trouble teaching your Poodle to stop using his mouth, or your Poodle seems intent on mouthing you, or you have a gut feeling that you may be bitten by the dog one day, call a professional trainer or veterinary behaviorist to help you. Don't wait until a bite has already happened.

Digging

Dogs dig for a number of reasons, all of which are natural to the dog. As pack animals whose ancestors lived in dens, some dogs like a tight, close, snug place to cuddle up and may find a hole in the ground just right. Because digging is so natural, you might offer your Poodle a spot where he can dig to his heart's content—maybe out behind the garage where it won't be too obvious. Dig up this area and make the dirt soft, bury a few dog toys and treats, and invite your dog to dig here.

In the rest of the yard, fill in the holes and spread some grass seed. If he is going back to one or two holes and re-digging them,

Too Many Toys?

If your dog is a chewer, don't try to change his behavior by giving him lots of toys. Too many toys will give him the idea that he can chew on anything and everything because virtually everything is his! Instead, give him just two or three toys at a time. If he likes toys, you can buy him new ones, but rotate the toys so he has only two or three at a time. On Monday, you could give him a rawhide, a squeaky toy, and a Kong toy. On Tuesday, substitute a new rawhide, a rope tug toy, and a tennis ball. By rotating the toys, you can keep him interested in them without overwhelming him.

When your dog picks up one of his toys, rather than something of yours, praise him! Tell him what a smart dog he is and how proud you are of him! Really go overboard. When he learns this is a good choice, he'll be more likely to repeat the behavior later.

Remember that if you find he's chewed something up earlier, don't punish him. After-the-fact corrections don't work.

crumple up some hardware cloth (wire mesh) and put that in the hole. Then fill it in with dirt. When he tries to re-dig that hole, the wire mesh will not feel at all comfortable on his paws thus will discourage him from digging there. Luckily, Poodles are not normally problem diggers.

Destructive Chewing

As with many other undesirable activities, destructive chewing is a natural behavior for puppies. Most Poodle puppies begin to chew when they're teething—losing their baby teeth and getting their adult teeth. The gums are sore, and chewing seems to help relieve the discomfort. Unfortunately, at this point many puppies learn that chewing is fun. Besides being fun for the puppy, chewing can be incredibly destructive and costly for you. In addition, the puppy who chews will inevitably swallow something he shouldn't so chewing also becomes dangerous. For many reasons, this bad habit needs to be controlled.

You can prevent a lot of bad behavior by keeping your puppy close to you when he's in the house. Close doors or put up baby gates so he doesn't have free run of the house. Under your supervision, you can teach him what is okay to chew on and what is not. When he picks up one of his toys, praise him, "Good boy to have a toy! Good toy!" When he picks up something he shouldn't, correct him, take it away, and then walk him to one of his toys, "Here. This is yours." When he picks up his toy, praise him.

As with many other problem behaviors, prevention is very important. Keep your Poodle close to you, close closet doors, keep the dirty clothes picked up, and empty the trashcans. If you can prevent him from getting into trouble as a puppy, when he grows up he won't have any bad habits and won't be tempted to try them.

Other Bad Habits

Poodles are usually pretty good dogs. Their biggest problems are generally barking, jumping on people, and not coming when called. Training can help all three of these problems if you are consistent with it.

If your Poodle has some other behavior problems, you can approach them in the same manner we did these. What is your dog doing? Why is he doing it? Can you use your training to teach him? Can you prevent it from happening?

If you are unable to solve a problem yourself, don't hesitate to call a professional trainer or board certified behaviorist for help. Ask your veterinarian whom he recommends.

Housetraining

Housetraining your Poodle is primarily a matter of taking him outside when he needs to go, making sure he does relieve himself while out there, teaching him a phrase that tells him to try to go, and then restricting his freedom until he is reliably trained.

Using a Crate to Housetrain

When we introduced the crate a few pages ago, I said that a crate is a wonderful tool to help you housetrain your Poodle. Because dogs are born with an instinct to keep their bed clean and will toddle away from their bed as soon as their legs will support them, the crate helps the puppy develop bowel and bladder control. You, of course, must never leave the dog in the crate too long; if you do, he will have to relieve himself and will be upset at doing so in such a confined space.

> Because dogs are born with an instinct to keep their bed clean and will toddle away from their bed as soon as their legs will support them, the crate helps the puppy develop bowel and bladder control.

Housetraining Guidelines

Using a crate is not all that needs to be done to housetrain a baby puppy, older puppy, or adult Poodle. He needs to learn when to go outside and where you want him to relieve himself, and to understand the phrase you wish to use.

Just sending the dog outside won't work. If you send him outside alone, how do you know whether or not he's relieved himself when you let him back in? He may have watched birds at the feeder rather than relieved himself. Then once you let him

Housetraining Timetable

Your Poodle will need to relieve himself after:

○ Waking up
○ Eating
○ Drinking
○ Playtime
○ Every two to three hours in between

Be alert: When your puppy is sniffing the floor and circling, grab him quick and take him outside!

in, he may remember his bladder is full and—woosh!—it's all over your floor!

You need to go outside with him. When he's sniffing and circling, tell him quietly, "Go potty!" (Use whatever word or phrase works for you.) When he does what he needs to do, praise him, "Good boy to go potty!" Once he's done what he needs to do, bring him inside with you but still restrict his freedom. Close doors or put up baby gates to keep him close. Do not consider him reliably housetrained until he's eight or nine months of age and hasn't had an accident in months! If he's younger and hasn't had any accidents, it just means you're doing everything right! Remember, Poodles are usually quick studies. If you follow these guidelines, your Poodle should be easy to housetrain.

When Accidents Happen

If you catch your puppy in the act of relieving himself inside, you can let him know he's making a mistake, "Oh, no! Bad boy!" and take him outside. However, if you find a puddle and he's already moved away, don't correct him. It's already too late.

Keep in mind that your Poodle must relieve himself. The act of urination or defecation is not wrong. Instead, when there is an accident, it is the place he did it rather than the act that was wrong. If you correct him after the fact, he could easily misunderstand you and think that the act of urination or defection is what you're angry about. Then you'll have a dog that sneaks off behind the furniture to relieve himself.

Go outside with him, praise him when he does it outside, and supervise him in the house. Correct only those accidents that you catch happening.

Asking to Go Outside

Because so many dogs have a hard time controlling their barking or howling, it is probably not a good idea to teach any dog to bark to go outside. Why emphasize a behavior that could already be a problem? However, your dog does need a way to let you know he has to go outside so we'll teach him to ring some bells instead.

> Because so many dogs have a hard time controlling their barking or howling, it is probably not a good idea to teach any dog to bark to go outside.

Go to a craft store and get two or three bells (each one to two inches across). Hang them from the doorknob or handle of the door where the dog goes in and out. Make sure they hang at your dog's nose level. Cut up a hot dog into tiny pieces and rub one piece on the bells. Invite your dog to sniff it. When the bell rings, praise him, take him outside, and give him a tiny piece of hot dog outside.

Repeat this three or four times per session for a few days. When he starts ringing the bells on his own, praise him enthusiastically and let him outside!

Five Basic Obedience Commands

Every dog should know these five basic obedience commands. They are the foundation for good behavior and with these commands, your Poodle learns self-control and will be well-behaved at home and when out in public.

Sit

The sit exercise teaches your Poodle to hold still, a hard concept for many young Poodles! When he sits, he isn't jumping on people; you can feed him without him knocking the bowl out of your hands;

Hold a treat in your hand and let your dog sniff it. Then take the treat up and back over his head. As his head comes up, his hips will go down.

and you can get his attention so that he can do other things. This is an important lesson in self-control.

When your dog sits and his hips are on the ground, praise him.

You can teach any dog to sit using any of several different methods, as long as it is humane and works. One of the easiest methods uses a treat as a lure. Tell your Poodle, "Poochie, sit!" as you take a treat and hold it above his nose. Move your hand back toward his tail, over his head. As his head goes up to follow the treat, his hips will go down. As he sits, praise him, "Good boy to sit!"

With one hand on the front of the dog's chest under his neck, push gently up and back as you slide the other hand down his hips. At the same time, tell your dog to sit. Praise him when he does.

Another easy method involves shaping the dog into position. With your Poodle close to you, tell him, "Poochie, sit!" as you place one hand on his chest under his neck and push gently up and back as the other hand slides down his hips and tucks them under. Think of a teeter-totter—up and back at the front and down and under at the rear. As you position your Poodle in the sit, praise him, "Good boy to sit!"

Have your dog sit and then show him a treat. Tell him to lie down as you take the treat from his nose down to the ground in front of his paws.

Down

When combined with the stay command (which will be taught next), the down teaches your Poodle to be still for gradually increased periods of time. You will be able to have him lie down and stay while people are eating so he isn't begging under the table. You can have him lie at your feet while you're watching television in the evening, or you can have him stay quietly while guests are visiting.

As your dog lies down, praise him.

The down/stay is a very useful command.

Start by having your Poodle sit. Once he's sitting, show him a treat in your right hand. As you tell him, "Poochie, down!" take the treat from his nose to the floor right in front of his front paws. Lead his nose to the floor. As his head follows the treat, your left hand can be resting on his shoulders to help him lie down. If he tries to pop back

If your dog doesn't lie down for the treat, just scoop his front legs out from under him and gently lay him down. Praise him even though you're helping him do it.

up, your left hand can keep him down. Once he's down, praise him and give him the treat. If he doesn't follow the treat down, gently pull his front legs forward and shape his body into the down position. Try to help him do the command himself rather than physically positioning him.

Stay

You want your Poodle to understand that stay means hold still. He will do this both in the sit and in the down although he will be able to hold a down/stay much longer than a sit/stay simply because it's an easier position to hold for longer periods of time. In either position, he should hold it until you give him permission to move.

Start by having your Poodle sit. With an open palm toward his nose, tell him, "Poochie, stay!" At the same time, put a little pressure backwards (toward his tail) with the leash so he won't be as apt to follow you when you take a step away from him. When he seems to be holding still, release the pressure of the leash. After a few seconds, go back to your dog and praise him.

As he learns the command (in both the sit and down positions), you can gradually increase the time and distance away from him. For example, for the first few days take one step away and have him hold the stay for ten seconds. Later that

The signal for stay is an open-palmed gesture right in front of the dog's face.

week, have him hold the stay while you take three steps away and have him be still for twenty seconds. Increase it gradually. If your Poodle makes a few mistakes, you'll know you're moving too fast.

Walking Nicely on the Leash

It's no fun to take a dog for a walk when he chokes himself on the leash and pulls so hard your shoulder hurts. That's torture, not fun! However, when your dog learns to walk nicely, without pulling, and pays attention to you when you talk to him, then walks are enjoyable!

Hook the leash up to your Poodle's collar and hold the leash in one hand. Have some good dog treats in your other hand. Show your dog the treats and then back

Use a treat and your happy verbal praise to encourage the dog to follow you on the leash as you back away from him. Praise him when he follows you.

away from him so that it appears you are leading your dog by his nose. When he follows you, praise him. When he's following you nicely, turn so that he ends up on your left side and you're both walking forward together. You can still use the treat to encourage him to pay attention to you. Stop, have him sit, and praise him! Practice this often and keep the walking distances very short,

When your dog is following you nicely, turn so that the both of you are walking forward together. Keep a treat handy to pop in front of his nose should he get distracted. Praise him.

with lots of sits and praise. If, while you're walking, your dog gets distracted, simply back away from him again and start all over.

Come

It is very important that your Poodle understands that "come" means he should come directly to you, on the first call, every time you call him. He isn't to come just when he wants to, or when nothing else is very interesting; he is to come immediately, all the time, every time.

Have your Poodle on the leash and hold the leash in one hand. In the other hand have a box of dog treats. Shake the dog treats, and as you back away from your dog (so he can chase you), call him to come, "Poochie, come!" Let him catch up to you, have him sit, then give him a treat as your praise him, "Good boy to come!"

Make sure your dog will come to you reliably all the time before you try it off-leash.

The box of dog treats is a sound stimulus that makes your verbal command much more exciting. Since this command is so important, use the sound stimulus (the box of treats) often during your training.

When your dog is responding well on the leash, repeat the training with a longer leash (up to 20 or 30 feet in length). Continue using the box of treats, too. Don't be in a hurry to take the leash off your Poodle. Most Poodles aren't mentally mature and ready for off-leash training until they are at least two years old. Some aren't ready for off-leash training even then. Your training on-leash must be very, very good with few mistakes before you should ever try it off-leash and then do so only in a fenced in, secure area.

Training, an Ongoing Process

Training your Poodle can be a lot of work. You need to pay attention to your dog, respond to him, and teach him right from wrong. You may also need to make some changes around the house and be sure other family members cooperate.

The rewards are worth it, though. Silly's owner, Barbara, says that Silly is a joy to spend time with. "Now I even wish I'd given her a different name because she is such a sweet, obedient dog." She added, "But she can still be pretty silly come playtime, so I guess the name still fits!"

A well–behaved dog is a joy to own and a pleasure to spend time with.

Grooming

7

In This Chapter
- Home Grooming Versus Professional Grooming
- Routine Care Every Poodle Needs
- Show Grooming
- Grooming Safety

You probably already know this, but when it comes to grooming, you have chosen a high-maintenance breed. From as early as three weeks to her last days, your Poodle will need grooming every four to eight weeks. Figure on about 12 years of haircuts, based on the average life span of a Poodle. And it's your job to make sure that happens, either by snipping, clipping, and bathing at home or hiring a professional groomer to do it for you.

Perhaps the practice of trimming the Poodle's coat seems peculiar to you. Why is it important, and why all the puffs and outrageous patterns?

As you've learned, Poodles are descended from water-retrieving dogs with curly, water-repellent coats. These heavy coats helped keep early dogs warm while dashing in and out of water for their masters. But once wet, those dense coats could also hamper the dog's movement. Owners solved the problem by cutting the coat shorter to making swimming easier. Hindquarters were shaved, but tufts of hair were left to keep joints warm. Hair was left long on the chest and neck area to help keep the dog afloat and to keep it warm out of the water. The topknot was tied to keep hair out of the dog's eyes, and colorful ribbons added to help masters recognize a particular dog in the field.

So began the practical custom of trimming the Poodle, a heritage you are about to explore.

Your Poodle's Skin and Coat

Your Poodle's skin and curly coat is unique. To be healthy and in good condition, it requires care. First, let's take a look at the basic physiology of the dog's skin and hair.

The dog's skin is comprised of three layers: the epidermis (outer), the dermis (middle), and hypodermis (inner). The skin is designed to protect the body from outward trauma, and it main-

tains the dog's internal body by keeping water and nutrients in. Sebaceous glands secrete oils that lubricate the skin and coat, giving the healthy Poodle a luxurious coat. The skin oils also protect the dog against bacterial and fungal infections.

Skin regulates body temperature and protects against rapid temperature changes outside. Dogs do not sweat through the skin as do people, but rely on panting to cool off.

Dogs' skin is thinner than people's, and is less acidic. That means soaps and shampoos made for you are unsuitable for your Poodle. Use only those shampoos made with your dog's special pH skin balance in mind.

Unlike people, whose hair grows continuously, the dog's hair grows in cycles: growing period, transitional period, and resting period. Hair growth and shedding is controlled by seasonal changes or length of daylight. However, it can be influenced by what the Poodle eats, seasonal temperature, pregnancy, stress, or illness.

Poodles are double-coated with a coarse outer coat and a soft downy undercoat. The breed is sometimes known as non-shedding, but Poodles do shed. Because the loose hair stays firmly in the curly coat, shedding is not as noticeable as with some other breeds.

The Poodle puppy coat is very different from the adult Poodle's coarse, curly coat. It is straighter, fuzzier, and appears wild and out of control. It doesn't hold a trim. The transition from soft, fuzzy hair to a coarser coat starts around eight months and can last anywhere from a year to two years old, depending upon the dog's coat. The transition coat tends to mat heavily, so frequent brushing or a short trim may be a good idea during the change.

> Unlike people, whose hair grows continuously, the dog's hair grows in cycles: growing period, transitional period, and resting period.

Grooming is a *must* for *all* Poodles! There's no getting out of it. It's not a one-time shot, either. Most owners and groomers recommend grooming every four to eight weeks, depending upon the trim. Long-coat styles require more frequent grooming, short styles can go a little longer between groomings. Regardless of style, regular brushing and combing, and sometimes bathing, is necessary between groomings.

What to Look for in a Groomer

The groomer you select for your Poodle should:

○ Possess certifiable knowledge and hands-on experience

○ Treat clients with courtesy and listen to their concerns

○ Handle each dog firmly, but gently

○ Show a genuine love of dogs

○ Never allow puppies who are not fully vaccinated to be around older dogs

The grooming facility should:

○ Be sterile and clean

○ Have an adequate number of crates in all sizes to house clients' dogs

○ Have a special outside area for potty breaks

Home Grooming Versus Professional Grooming

Many owners enjoy grooming their Poodles at home, and perhaps you're interested in learning to groom your dog. "Most Poodle owners, as a natural progression to owning a high-maintenance pet, will attempt grooming," says professional groomer Claudette Vatore. "This is exactly how I started grooming professionally. Grooming is a very intimate process and it fosters trust and bonding. It brings your relationship to a higher level. Poodles really do enjoy the results of being groomed. They are very proud animals and love the attention that grooming brings. I believe that all Poodle owners should groom their own dogs, but I also realize that there is a huge investment in equipment needed to accomplish this task."

Basic Supplies

Here's a list of tools and supplies necessary for grooming your Poodle at home:

- ○ Professional model electric clippers
- ○ Blades
- ○ Grooming table
- ○ Blow-dryer
- ○ Scissors
- ○ Toenail trimmers
- ○ Styptic powder
- ○ Soft slicker brush
- ○ Pin brush
- ○ Curry comb
- ○ Metal comb
- ○ Cotton balls
- ○ Ear cleaner/powder
- ○ Ophthalmic ointment
- ○ Shampoo and conditioner
- ○ Spray detangler
- ○ Towels
- ○ Grooming noose
- ○ Sponge
- ○ Small plastic bucket
- ○ Spray attachment
- ○ Flea-control products
- ○ Toothbrush or gauze, and doggie toothpaste

If you'd like to learn to groom your Poodle, be prepared to invest your money and time. Grooming a Poodle is a highly developed skill—it isn't just grabbing a pair of scissors and cutting. Before you decide you will groom your Poodle at home, consider:

- ○ The cost of equipment (clippers, blades, scissors, grooming books, videos, and so on)
- ○ The time it takes to perfect your grooming technique
- ○ The challenge of learning a new skill
- ○ The reality of bad haircuts!

"The nice thing about grooming a Poodle is that their hair grows back rather quickly," says Vatore, "so one can always start over if a mistake is made. Also, it's fun to experiment with different looks to see which one looks best on a particular Poodle."

A good grooming book and video are a must for the home groomer. Appendix A includes a few of my favorites to get you started.

But not everyone has a knack for dog grooming or is so inclined. You may feel overwhelmed by the idea of bathing your Poodle, trimming her nails, scissoring her coat. No worry! Hire a professional groomer. Besides cash, all that's required of you to hire a pro to do the grooming dirty work is the ability to choose a skilled and kind professional.

The best way to start your search for a groomer is to ask someone you trust—a breeder, rescue volunteer, dog-owning friend, veterinarian—for a recommendation. Ask why they recommend a particular groomer, and whether they've utilized the groomer's services and for how long.

Once you have a few referrals, hopefully pretty close to home, call the salons. Ask about grooming prices and what's included, how far in advance you need to make appointments, how many groomers are on staff, whether or not the groomers are certified (not required by law, but a good indication of professional commitment), and whether the shop sells products such as shampoos or collars and leashes. Keep notes on each shop you query.

Be aware that groomers are usually very busy, so be courteous and let the shop know you'll be stopping by.

The next step is to visit each salon. Be aware that groomers are usually very busy, so be courteous and let the shop know you'll be stopping by. Otherwise, the owner or groomer may be too busy to chat with you for long. Keep visits short, 10 to 15 minutes, but long enough to ask a few questions and form an impression of each shop. Ask yourself:

❍ Is the shop clean? (A few tufts of hair are okay, though)
❍ Is the staff friendly and professional?
❍ Is the shop well-organized with up-to-date equipment?
❍ Do the groomers handle the dogs carefully?

After making the rounds, it's time to make a decision. Consider the recommendations, along with the positive or negative impressions of each salon. Choose one and call to schedule an appointment.

Routine Care Every Poodle Needs

As a new Poodle owner, you'll quickly learn that grooming doesn't take place just at home or at the grooming shop. Because the Poodle requires such high maintenance, it usually takes both you and your dog's groomer to keep up her coat: a professional haircut and bath every four to eight weeks, and you brushing in between, as well as giving a bath every few weeks. At a very minimum, you should know how to brush your Poodle.

Pick Up a Brush!

Plan on brushing and combing your Poodle's coat at least twice a week, more often for a long style. A thorough brushing removes dead hair and dirt, and distributes coat oils. Regular brushing will help keep the coat shiny and the skin healthy.

A favored brush for Poodles is a soft slicker (for pet coats only) or pin brush. A metal comb is essential, too.

Brushing should be done systematically, starting at the head, for example, and working back to the neck, legs, back, tummy, rear end, and tail. Don't start at one place and skip to another. Develop a brushing pattern and do it every time. You won't lose your place, and your Poodle will learn what to expect next. Brush gently on tender areas, such as the Poodle's tummy or legs.

Brushing, then combing, should precede bathing. If you don't brush out tangles and mats before bathing, they will tighten and become more difficult to remove once wet.

Choosing a Style

The Poodle's coat can be snipped, scissored, and shaped into many, many styles and patterns. Which style is best for your Poodle?

The answer is for you to decide. But realize that not all trims are created equal. For example, a long-coat style is a lot more work and requires more maintenance than a short trim. Professional groomers say the best trim for your individual Poodle depends upon how much work you are willing to do at home and how often you are willing to take the dog to the salon for grooming. The bottom line is, the more hair you leave on the Poodle, the more upkeep is required.

Think about your lifestyle when considering a trim. Do you have time for brushing and upkeep? Busy owners are better off selecting a short, easy-care style.

Also consider the cost. Can you afford (and how often) $25 to $100 a pop (depending on your Poodle's size and trim)?

Poodles with Dreadlocks

What happens when you don't brush or trim a Poodle's coat, but let the curls grow and entwine in tangled chaos? You have a Poodle with dreadlocks!

More accurately called a "corded" Poodle, this unusual coat style was the rage 100 years ago. The first Poodle to earn a championship in England was Achilles, a black Standard with a corded coat. You hardly see corded Poodles today, but there is still some interest among enthusiasts. The Poodle Club of America breed standard allows for the showing of corded Poodles.

A corded coat is a controlled matting. The coat is left to grow without brushing. While the coat is still damp after bathing, it is separated and twisted into cords.

A corded coat looks spectacular, and owners don't have to worry about someone petting the Poodle and messing up the coat. The cords do have a few downsides. It takes forever to dry after bathing, sometimes overnight. As a result, the coat can mildew. Also, the Poodle can catch a toe on the cords while scratching an itch and injure a toenail.

One bit of advice: Don't try this at home, unless you have the help of a groomer or breeder who is skilled at creating corded coats. The corded coat isn't the result of neglect. Though brushing is out, it's a carefully planned style that requires as much effort as any other Poodle coat style.

What is your Poodle's conformation? Just as people look better in certain hair styles, your Poodle may look better in a certain trim. Choosing a trim is an individual decision and it really depends on how much work you are willing to do at home, and how often you are willing to take your dog to the groomer.

Pearly Whites

As you learned in Chapter 4, regular tooth brushing should be a part of every Poodle's health care. To make regular brushing easy to remember, many Poodle owners include it as part of their grooming routine. Brush the coat, then brush the teeth. Easy to remember, right?

The Poodle's 12 incisors, 4 canines, 16 premolars, and 10 molars can suffer from plaque or tartar buildup, or from periodontal disease. Normally, plaque, a soft white or yellow substance that consists of organic and inorganic material, along with bacteria, is deposited on your Poodle's teeth. If not removed, plaque hardens and becomes tartar. Tartar is yellow-brown in color and is usually found along the gum line. Unlike plaque, tartar cannot be removed by brushing or wiping. It must be removed the same way it's removed from your mouth—with dental tools in the hands of your veterinarian. Plaque and tartar are perfect hosts for bacteria, and will lead to infection and disease if not removed.

> To make regular brushing easy to remember, many Poodle owners include it as part of their grooming routine. Brush the coat, then brush the teeth.

Take a close look at your Poodle's teeth and gums regularly. Are the teeth white or do you see tartar buildup? Are the gums pink or red and bleeding? Does your Poodle have extremely bad breath or regular doggie breath? Consult with your vet if you notice tartar buildup, red and bleeding gums, broken teeth, or obvious decay.

Brush your Poodle's teeth with a small toothbrush and doggie toothpaste. Don't be tempted to share your toothpaste because human products can make your dog sick. Brush the teeth in the same way you brush your own, with gentle, thorough brush strokes. Brush once or twice a week.

Poodles are usually very accepting of tooth brushing as long as you teach them to accept it when they're youngsters. Still, some dogs just don't like having a toothbrush in their mouth. If this is the case, try wiping the teeth with clean, sterile gauze.

Wrap the gauze around your finger, moisten it with water, add a dab of doggie toothpaste, and wipe the teeth one at a time.

Feeding a kibble diet helps keep teeth clean, too. Soft or canned food can increase plaque, but a crunchy diet actually cleans the teeth. Chewing on hard biscuits or dental toys is also helpful.

Nail Care

At least once a month for adult Poodles and once a week for pups, you must tackle another grooming chore—nail trimming. Failing to trim your dog's nails can result in sore, splayed feet. How can you tell if your Poodle's nails are too long? Listen. Do you hear a *click-click* when she walks across the tile or linoleum floor? If you do, that means the nails are touching the floor—and they shouldn't. Or, take a look at your Poodle's feet while she's standing. Do you see the nails touching the floor? The idea is to keep your Poodle's nails trimmed back short enough so they don't touch.

There are two basic types of nail clippers: the scissors and the guillotine. You also can use a nail grinder, but it may take some time to get your dog used to the noise. If you use scissors or guillotine clippers, keep them sharp and clean. Dull clippers won't make a clean cut, and rusty, dirty ones can infect your dog if you cut the quick and your pet bleeds. The objective when clipping nails is to trim as close to the quick as possible without accidentally nicking it. Dark nails are more difficult to cut than light-colored ones, since it is impossible to see the pink vein. Remove the dry-looking hook at the tip of the nail, cutting off small bits of nail at a time. As you cut the nail shorter, you'll notice it becomes softer and you'll see a small grayish-white dot under the nail, which is the end of the quick. When you reach this point, the nail is short enough; you can now move on to the next one. Keep in mind that the more often you trim, the shorter you can get the nail, since the quick actually recedes with frequent trimming. Cut each nail as quickly and cleanly as possible; cutting slowly tends to pinch the nail and cause your dog discomfort.

> The objective when clipping nails is to trim as close to the quick as possible without accidentally nicking it.

To trim your Poodle's nails, hold one paw firmly in your left hand (if you're right-handed) and place your thumb on top of the foot. Place your fingers underneath the pads so you can spread the toes. With the clippers in your right hand, clip each nail right below the quick with short, decisive strokes. Don't forget the dewclaws if they were not removed when your Poodle was a pup.

Finish trimming the first paw, then file each nail with a metal file to remove sharp, rough edges that could scratch your legs if your Poodle is naughty and jumps up on you. DO NOT file any nails that have bled. Work your way to the next paw, trim each nail, then file.

If you accidentally cut the quick, don't panic. Apply a styptic powder to staunch the bleeding and continue clipping the other nails. Don't stop and make a big fuss over your mistake, as it may make your dog even more apprehensive the next time you attempt to clip his nails.

When clipping your dog's nails, also check the pads of his feet and remove any pebbles or other small debris that may be lodged there, and also be sure to clip and remove any matted fur between the toes. Check your dog's feet frequently during winter to make sure they're not irritated from road salt or ice. Canine booties or petroleum jelly applied to the pads can protect your

Poodle's feet during cold months. If you notice your dog excessively biting at his paws, wash them off thoroughly to keep him from ingesting road salt. Small-size trimmers will work when your Poodle is a pup. Larger-size trimmers are best for adult Poodles.

A word of advice: start early. Poodles, like all dogs, must learn to accept new experiences. Begin nail trimming while your dog is a pup and do it every week. Between trimmings, handle the dog's feet to accustom her to being touched. The Poodle doesn't usually make a fuss about trimming, but it's still wise to teach your dog to accept it from a young age. Before attempting to clip your Poodle's nails yourself, you may want to observe your groomer or veterinarian the first time.

Ear Care

Did you know your Poodle grows hair inside her ears, as well as all over her body? If you lift up your Poodle's ear and look inside, you will see hair growing in the ear canal. In light of this, there are two basic beliefs on ear care for the Poodle: One, the ear hair should be pulled out regularly to provide proper air flow in the ear, thus preventing infections and infestations; and two, hair pulling should be avoided because it irritates the ear, is painful, and can lead to secondary bacterial infection.

"I think the individual dog and his coat should be considered with regards to ear hair pulling," says Vatore. "One of my dogs is very sensitive when it comes to his ears. He will scratch after pulling. His ear hair seems to come from deeper inside his ear. Therefore, I don't remove all the hair from his ears and I do it less frequently. My other dog has a lot more hair growing more to the outside of the ear canal and ear-hair pulling doesn't bother him at all."

Poodle owner Belinda Hankins agrees: "I think it depends on the individual dog. I have two dogs that I must pull faithfully to keep chronic ear infections at bay, and two that I never pull."

Because opinions vary on caring for the Poodle's ears, ask your veterinarian to recommend a plan.

Bathing

At some point, your Poodle may need a bath between groomings. Bathing is a job done easily at home, but the trick to success is to be prepared. Many owners scrub their Poodle right in the family bathtub. Pups, Toys, or Mini Poodles can be bathed in the kitchen sink. A spray attachment is best because you don't want the dog standing in knee-deep soapy water. There are many spray attachments on the market made especially for bathing dogs at home. Check out a local pet-supply store or pet-supply catalog. Don't bathe your dog in the front yard with the garden hose. How would you like to sprayed with freezing-cold water?

You'll need a rubber mat in the tub to prevent the Poodle from slipping and, if possible, a way to secure your dog in the tub. A professional grooming noose or non-leather collar and leash works well. The idea is to keep your Poodle from dashing out of the tub mid-bath if he's less than thrilled about bathing.

Following those preparations, you must have supplies handy before turning on the water. You'll need cotton balls to put in the Poodle's ears, ophthalmic ointment, shampoo, a plastic bucket, towels, and a sponge. Dilute the shampoo with warm or body-temperature water in the bucket and drop in the sponge. Once you've got everything within an arm's reach of the tub, it's time for the big event.

Secure your Poodle in the tub and place a cotton ball in each ear to keep water out. Apply a dab of sterile ophthalmic ointment (available from your vet) in each eye to protect against shampoo irritation. Dampen the dog with warm, baby-bottle temperature water beginning at the top of the head, behind the ears. Remember that dogs are not used to hot water, so keep the water temperature barely warm, or simply not cold. Keep the spray nozzle close to the dog's body, and soak down to the skin. Work back, soaking the back and the tail. Return to the front and soak the dog's neck and chest. Then saturate the tummy and legs. Finally, hold the nozzle on the top of the dog's head and carefully dampen his face, or dampen the face with a sponge. Don't spray directly into the dog's face.

> Remember that dogs are not used to hot water, so keep the water temperature barely warm, or simply not cold.

Make sure you wet the Poodle's coat thoroughly. Once the dog is completely wet, pick up your soapy sponge and apply shampoo from head to tail. Be careful not to get soap in the dog's eyes, but don't skimp on shampoo. You want to get your Poodle clean. Scrub with the sponge or your hands. Rinse well, beginning with the head and working back, and shampoo again.

The final rinse is really important. If you don't get all the soap out of the coat, it can leave the coat dull, the dog's skin itchy, and in dark-colored Poodles, dried shampoo looks like flakes of dandruff. Very unsightly! Rinse until you think all the soap is out, then rinse again. Literally, you want to hear the coat squeak. Squeeze out excess water with your hands, then gently towel-dry.

Fluff-Drying

Fluff-drying—drying while continuously brushing—is next. Fluff-drying is the top-secret method of giving the Poodle a puffy, smooth look. If left to dry on its own, the Poodle's naturally curly coat will dry into ringlets. Proper fluff-drying straightens the coat, making it easier to shape and cut with clippers and scissors.

Tools for fluff-drying include a soft slicker brush and a blow-dryer, preferably one on a stand so you can have both hands free to work. Wrap the Poodle in a towel, except for her head and ears. Direct the air flow at the topknot and brush quickly and lightly. Once the head and ears are completely dry, work down the chest and to the front legs. Keep the towel over the Poodle's hindquarters. Once the forequarters are dry, move to the rear. Fluff the tail, then the hindquarters, one at a time. Fluff the body and stomach.

> Tools for fluff-drying include a soft slicker brush and a blow-dryer, preferably one on a stand so you can have both hands free to work.

Fluff-drying isn't easy, so don't expect your Poodle to look perfect the first time. It's difficult to coordinate the dryer and brush while keeping the Poodle still all at the same time. It's also difficult to brush dry one area quickly before another area dries on its own—and curls.

Show Grooming

There are two approaches to grooming a Poodle: pet grooming and show grooming. Most likely, you're a pet owner and need only concern yourself with keeping your pet Poodle neat and clean. But if you're considering showing your Poodle, your approach to grooming will be completely different.

Caring for a Poodle in show coat is the opposite of caring for a Poodle in a pet trim. With pets, the goal is usually to keep as much hair off the Poodle as possible. With show Poodles, the goal is to grow as much hair as possible on the dog. As one groomer says, grooming the show Poodle is a lot more work than grooming the pet Poodle. There are no shortcuts!

Toward the goal of growing coat, *extreme* care is taken not to damage, break, or tear the hair. Slicker brushes are off-limits to the show Poodle since they pull out undercoat and can tear the coat. Using pin brushes and brushing inch by inch is standard practice and makes certain that the coat isn't ripped out. Additionally, the coat is never brushed while dry. The Poodle show coat is brushed with moisturizer to minimize damage.

To grow a long topknot and ear hair, the topknot and ear feathering are brushed, wrapped, and conditioned daily in plastic or paper to protect against breakage. Collars aren't allowed because they can damage the coat on the neck.

Between shows, coats are "kept in oil." The dog is bathed, an oil/conditioner mix is applied and left to dry in the coat. The oil look isn't attractive, but it helps protect the coat. The oil is washed out before showing.

In addition, the Poodle in show coat is generally:

○ Bathed every week to ten days
○ Brushed gently every two to three days
○ Fluff-dried by hand (though some owners use high-velocity dryers)
○ Clipped once a week

Owners interested in showing their Poodles in an American Kennel Club breed ring must exhibit the Poodle in accordance with the official AKC breed standard, which outlines several specific coat styles. This applies only to Poodles who compete in conformation, not those who compete in obedience, agility, or hunt tests.

According to the breed standard, a Poodle under 12 months may be shown in the Puppy clip. In all regular classes, Poodles 12 months or over must be shown in the English Saddle or Continental clip. In the Stud Dog and Brood Bitch classes and in a non-competitive Parade of Champions, Poodles may be shown in the Sporting clip. A Poodle shown in any other type of clip shall be disqualified. In all clips, the hair of the topknot may be left free or held in place by elastic bands.

> According to the breed standard, a Poodle under 12 months may be shown in the Puppy clip. In all regular classes, Poodles 12 months or over must be shown in the English Saddle or Continental clip.

Puppy Clip   Poodles less than one year old may be shown in the Puppy clip. The coat is long and the face, throat, feet, and base of the tail are shaved. There is a pompon on the end of the tail, and some shaping of the coat is permissible.

English Saddle   In the English Saddle clip, the face, throat, feet, forelegs, and the base of the tail are shaved, leaving puffs on the forelegs and a pompon on the end of the tail. The hindquarters are covered with a short blanket of hair except for a curved shaved area on each flank and two shaved bands on each hindleg. The entire shaven foot and a portion of the shaven leg above the puff are visible. The rest of the body is left in full coat, but may be shaped to ensure balance.

Continental   In this show clip, the face, throat, feet, and the base of the tail are shaved. The hindquarters are shaved with pompons (optional) on the hips. The legs are shaved, leaving bracelets on the hindlegs and puffs on the forelegs. There is a

The Working Continental

Some Poodle enthusiasts, mostly owners of working Standards, are trimming their Poodles in what's loosely called a "historically correct working Continental." This simple trim is what one Poodle enthusiast calls a "re-enactment" of the working Poodle trim of yesteryear.

The pattern many owners use for this working trim is identical to the Continental pattern allowed in the AKC and CKC (Canadian Kennel Club) conformation rings. There's a big difference in coat length, though. Unlike the long, carefully sculpted coat found on Poodles in the ring, the historical Continental is cut short (about two inches) and left curly. It's a great working length for fieldwork, say enthusiasts, and makes good sense. But whether this historical trim is accepted in the conformation ring remains to be seen.

pompon on the end of the tail. The entire shaven foot and a portion of the shaven foreleg above the puff are visible. The rest of the body is left full, but may be shaped.

Sporting   This trim calls for the Poodle's face, feet, throat, and the base of the tail to be shaved, leaving a scissored cap on the top of the head and a pompon on the end of the tail. The rest of the body and legs are clipped or scissored to follow the outline of the dog, leaving a short blanket of coat no longer than one inch in length. The hair on the legs may be slightly longer than the hair on the body.

Mind Your Manners

Good manners go hand in hand with good grooming. A Poodle that accepts grooming graciously is easier to groom than one who puts up a fight. Grooming should be a safe and pleasant experience for all involved, which is why it's essential to teach your Poodle from an early age to accept grooming as a fact of life. If you hire a professional groomer, she will also be teaching your Poodle to accept grooming.

Along with basic obedience training for your Poodle pup or adult, you must teach grooming manners. A Poodle must learn several things to be a good grooming student, including sitting, lying down, or standing still while being brushed; accepting nail trimming; standing quietly while being bathed; sitting patiently while her ears are checked or cleaned; jumping into the tub or onto the grooming table when asked (Standards); and holding still while being blow-dried.

> Poodles are very smart, and they love being pampered, so it doesn't take much to teach them what's expected during grooming sessions.

Poodles are very smart, and they love being pampered, so it doesn't take much to teach them what's expected during grooming sessions. You must remember that dogs learn by repetition, correction, and praise. That means you must be consistent in what you expect and ask while grooming, just as you must be consistent in obedience training. You'll need to be firm, but praise is essential.

Keep your expectations realistic. Don't think a young pup will sit still for hours while you brush and fuss. Keep grooming sessions short for pups, no more than 15 minutes or so. Expect some squirming, whining, or other theatrics. It's all part of learning that the grooming experience is not scary or harmful, which is a primary goal—to teach your Poodle that grooming can be fun! Yes, grooming is a time for business, but it's also a time for your undivided attention.

Pups, or adults not accustomed to being groomed, may be afraid of grooming at first. Speak quietly to the Poodle when you sense she is afraid. The Poodle may nip at the "mean" brush or clippers, pull away from the nail trimmers, or shy from the blow-dryer. You must always be firm and gently correct such antics with "no" or "stop." Gently show the Poodle what you expect, and praise her when she complies.

Poodles are quite capable of learning good grooming manners. Introduce grooming at a young age, keep the sessions short, positive, and fun, and you'll have a Poodle who begs for grooming!

Grooming Safety

You should be aware of a few minor injuries that could occur during grooming.

Clipper Burn   Clipper burn is a phrase commonly used to describe any injury or irritation caused by electric clippers. The most common causes of clipper burn are overheated blades, dull blades, or blades with broken teeth. Some Poodles have highly sensitive skin and even clipping with cool, sharp blades will result in skin irritation. The best treatment should clipper burn occur is to keep the affected area clean and apply antibiotic ointment. Aloe products or topical anesthetics can be helpful, too. Don't allow the Poodle to scratch at or rub the area on the floor or carpeting, which will further irritate the skin.

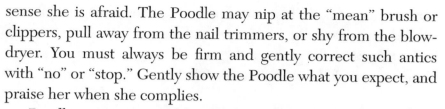

Brush Burn   Brush burn is any skin irritation caused by brushing, usually the result of brushing too hard and too long in one area when the coat is matted.

Cut   The sharp scissors that can so beautifully shape a Poodle's coat can also cut the skin, sometimes severely.

Cuts are uncommon when skilled professionals are doing the grooming and more likely when inexperienced owners are using scissors. If you cut your Poodle, place sterile gauze pads over the wound to stop bleeding and call the vet right away. Stitches may be necessary.

Bleeding Nail   This isn't really an injury, but cutting a nail too short does require attention. If you do cut the quick, don't get upset. It's not serious and the Poodle will be fine. Follow the instructions given on page 228 for applying styptic powder.

Shampoo in the Eyes   Apply sterile ophthalmic ointment before bathing, and always be careful not to get shampoo in your Poodle's eyes. But should you get shampoo or dip in the dog's eyes, flush them with plenty of fresh water or sterile saline (available over the counter for contact lens wearers). Do not apply more ointment. If the eye appears red or if your dog squints or paws at her eyes, give your vet a call. Prevent your Poodle from rubbing and pawing her eyes, which could result in further irritation.

Allergic and Toxic Reactions   If your Poodle seems extremely itchy after a regular bath or her skin is red, she may be allergic to the shampoo or conditioners used. Give your vet a call, especially if your dog develops hives. Medication may be required to stop the allergic reaction. Some Poodles are highly sensitive to the insecticides used in flea shampoos and dips. Signs of insecticide poisoning include vomiting, diarrhea, drooling, and pinpoint pupil size. If your Poodle shows signs of poisoning after being washed in flea shampoo or rinsed in flea or tick dip, call your veterinarian right away. Ask for immediate instructions and be sure to tell your vet what products you used.

Injury   Never leave your Poodle unattended in a bathtub or on a grooming table. A jump off a grooming table or out of a tub could result in a broken leg, hip, or other injury.

Minimizing the Mess

If you don't already know this, you'll figure it out after one home grooming session with your Poodle: Grooming is messy! Figure on hair everywhere, wet towels, and dirty clothes. You can minimize the mess, though, by thinking ahead. Here are a few ideas.

> Grooming is messy! Figure on hair everywhere, wet towels, and dirty clothes.

○ Invest in a quality vacuum cleaner. This is a must for every dog owner, not only to suck up cut hair after trimming, but dirt, fleas, and anything else.

○ Wear an apron, and your special set of dog grooming clothes, when grooming at home. A waterproof apron will help keep you dry while bathing your Poodle. And, if you are wearing old clothes, you'll have no need to worry about how dirty and hairy they are.

○ Have a stack of towels handy for towel-drying your Poodle and to place them underneath while you blow-dry her. Towels don't need to be fancy or monogrammed. Use old ones or pick some up at a thrift store (wash before using, of course).

○ Keep a trash bag nearby while grooming to toss cotton balls or hair. If you clean up as you go, the mess isn't as overwhelming. Keep a roll of paper towels handy, too, for accidents (puppy may get excited and potty) or spills.

○ Machine-wash your grooming clothes and towels in hot water and detergent. Don't mix grooming items with the family laundry or you'll end up with itchy hair all over everything.

○ Rinse the comb and brush after use, especially if you've brushed a muddy dog.

○ Wipe down the grooming table and wash out the tub and mat with disinfectant. Remember to remove hair from the drain.

The Old and the Young

What about grooming the very young or very old Poodle? As noted previously, approach grooming sessions with your Poodle puppy as though they're training sessions. To make grooming a fun and positive experience for puppy, consider the following:

○ Set aside a certain time and place for grooming. The puppy will quickly learn that when she's placed on the grooming table you have set up in the basement, it's time for grooming.

○ Keep sessions short (15 minutes). Pups have short attention spans and tolerance levels.

○ Always praise your puppy for cooperating.

○ Use obedience commands: sit while brushing and stand while bathing, for example.

○ Be realistic in your expectations of your puppy. Learning to sit or stand quietly while being groomed takes time. Don't be surprised if your puppy tries to wiggle away, bites the brush, yelps when you trim her nails, shakes her head wildly as you clean her ears, or disregards your commands. You should expect this.

○ Because puppies can chill easily, it's best to dry them right away with a blow-dryer. Do not let your puppy outside until he is completely dry.

○ Puppy toenails are sometimes soft and very small, which means the nail can tear when you clip. Make sure the trimmers are sharp, or try using human fingernail trimmers when your pup is very young.

Grooming is important for the elderly Poodle as well, but you may notice that your older dog is less patient with grooming, doesn't have the stamina, or is grouchy when her feet are clipped. Don't be surprised by such behaviors; they're very common. You'll just need to find positive ways to work around your older Poodle's quirks. Here are a few tips:

○ Keep sessions short (sound familiar?). While dogs in their prime can tolerate lengthy grooming sessions, the old and young cannot. The older dog may tire more easily or be unable to stand for long periods due to arthritis. Be considerate of your older Poodle's limitations.

○ Be extra gentle when handling the Poodle. Your older dog's joints don't

Did You Know?

The pompon cut used on Poodles was originally developed to increase the breed's swimming abilities as a retriever. The short haircut allowed for faster swimming but the pompons were left to keep the joints warm.

move as well as they used to, or she may be more touch-sensitive.

○ Make sure your older Poodle is comfortable during grooming. Let her lie down to prevent her from tiring too quickly.

○ Pay special attention to her nails. Because older Poodles may be less active, their nails may not wear down. More frequent trimming may be necessary. The nails of older dogs often tend to become brittle. Keep the nail trimmers very sharp to avoid splintering your older Poodle's nails.

○ Be aware of skin and coat changes. Your older dog may become sensitive to coat products, or develop dry skin due to reduced activity of oil-producing glands. Be on the lookout for lumps, bumps, or other signs of illness, too.

What's That Smell?

Someday your Poodle may surprise you with an incredibly bad odor or a sticky, gooey mess. One of the worst offenders is skunk spray. The biting, acidic odor is unforgettable on a dog. One whiff is enough to send you running in the opposite direction! Poodles who live in the country or work in the field are most likely to encounter these smelly, black-and-white critters. What can you do if your Poodle gets sprayed by a skunk? Realize there are no magic cures. Some commercial products and homemade remedies do help reduce the odor, but the bottom line is this: The smell has to wear off, and you'll have to live with it until it does.

Conquering Grooming Disasters

Here are some of the more common grooming problems you may encounter and the best ways to handle them.

Burrs Although romps through fields or wooded areas offer wonderful exercise for your dog, you may pay the price of burrs, seeds, twigs, or other things sticking to your dog. Your Poodle's curly hair is especially attractive to these hangers-on. Try to remove them immediately with a fine-toothed comb. Mink oil conditioners, available at grooming shops or supply stores, can make the coat sleek, which makes it easier to remove burrs.

Skunk Spray You may have heard that tomato juice takes out the smell of skunk. This is not true. Not only does tomato juice not take the smell out, it also leaves you with a pinkish, sticky dog! Instead, use a high-quality skunk shampoo; your pet-supply store or groomer should be able to recommend one. Remember to brush your dog thoroughly before bathing him (plugging your nose if need be) since any dead, loose fur just retains the smell and prevents the shampoo from penetrating all the way down to the skin.

Another option that comes highly recommended is a special "recipe" you can easily prepare at home. Include in your dog's bath one quart bottle of 3% hydrogen peroxide, 1/4 cup of baking soda (sodium bicarbonate), and one teaspoon of liquid soap. Follow the bath with a tap-water rinse.

No matter what you use, though, your dog may continue to smell slightly skunky every time he gets wet for several weeks or even months.

Paint Before it hardens, immediately wash out any latex paint your dog brushes against or rolls in. This paint, which is toxic, thankfully is water soluble. If your dog gets into oil paint, you'll have to cut away the fur with paint on it. Never use varsol or turpentine, and never let your dog chew at the paint.

Gum You discover a bright pink wad of bubble gum stuck to your Poodle's fur! Don't rush for the scissors yet. First, try rubbing the gum with ice cubes to make it brittle. If the gum is stuck only to the ends of the hairs, you should be able to break or lift it off. If it's down in the coat, however, try using peanut butter as a solvent. If your dog steps in gum, try rubbing it with ice and then peeling it off the pads. If the gum is attached to the hair on the paw, cut it away.

Tar Hot tar can scald your dog. If your pet comes in contact with hot tar, apply cold water immediately and see your veterinarian. If your Poodle encounters cooled, sticky tar, apply ice cubes to harden the tar and then cut it away with scissors.

There are several high-quality skunk shampoos you can choose from should your dog ever encounter and be sprayed by a skunk. Be sure to thoroughly brush your dog before bathing her, removing the dead hair and tangles that can prevent the shampoo from going skin deep. Your pet-supply store or groomer can recommend a good shampoo for this situation.

Another favorite is a mixture of one quart of 3 percent hydrogen peroxide, a quarter-cup baking soda, and one teaspoon of liquid soap. Apply the mixture to your dog's coat and let stand for 10 minutes or so. Shampoo and rinse thoroughly.

If you opt to try a commercial product, follow directions carefully.

Your Poodle may also roll in something dead (very smelly) or have a party in someone's stinky garbage. If either is the case, a thorough bath, with two or three shampoos, is in order.

Gum, tar, and oil could find a home in your Poodle's coat, too. The problem is how to get them out once they're firmly attached! When it comes to gum, groomers favor two old-fashioned remedies: ice and peanut butter. Freeze the gum with an ice cube to make it less sticky and easier to pry out of the coat. If that doesn't work, apply a little peanut butter and work it around and underneath the gum. The oil in the peanut butter loosens the gum from the hair shaft.

Tar is another matter. It can be difficult to remove and may take several treatments. Soak the tarry area in vegetable oil for 30 to 60 minutes (yes, it's very messy!) then shampoo with dishwashing detergent, which is formulated to remove oils and is used to clean oil from animals saturated in oil spills. Follow up with a regular dog shampoo to restore the pH balance. Avoid using petroleum products to remove tar, such as gasoline or turpentine. These are highly toxic to your Poodle. Tar can be toxic to your dog and cause serious burns so you may want to let your veterinarian exam your dog.

Grease or oil isn't easy to remove either. One method is to shampoo with dishwashing detergent, followed by a regular pet shampoo. Another method is to apply baby powder or cornstarch to the oily area, then shampoo with pet shampoo.

Anal Glands

Every dog has two anal glands, or sacs, near the rectum. These sacs are sometimes called scent glands, and may be a way dogs identify each other. Hence, the propensity for nose-to-rear sniffing. The anal sacs normally empty when the dog defecates. The secretion that comes out is liquid and brownish. Anal sacs can also be emptied as the result of a sudden contraction of the anal sphincter—when the dog is frightened or upset, for example.

In some Poodles, the anal sacs fail to empty normally. Though most common in Toy Poodles, it can happen to any Mini or Standard Poodle as well. Soft stools are a primary cause of malfunctioning glands. When the sacs do not empty normally, they can become impacted and infected. Your Poodle may be giving you a clue that she is having anal gland trouble if she scoots on her rear, or bites her tail, rump, or rear as though in pain. If you notice these signs, take your Poodle to your veterinarian. Over-full glands can be relieved by a quick (but smelly) expression of the fluid by hand; infected glands will require antibiotic therapy. Some dogs, especially Poodles, get their anal glands expressed at every grooming.

Did You Know?

Nose prints can be used to identify dogs just as fingerprints are used to identify humans.

Good, Clean Fun

While caring for and grooming your Poodle takes a lot of time—either actual grooming time or taking her to her grooming sessions—the results are a beautiful, happy, and stylish Poodle.

The several styles and variations you can choose from keep the repetition of grooming fresh and exciting for both you and your Poodle. If you plan on grooming your Poodle yourself, there are endless resources for you to choose from to assist you with your grooming sessions. If you plan on taking your Poodle to a grooming professional, rest assured your Poodle will always have a wonderful Poodle style to show you when you pick her up. Either way, whether you plan on home grooming or professional grooming, enjoy!

8

Family Life

In This Chapter

❍ Playtime
❍ Playing Nicely with Children
❍ Making Your Poodle a Good Neighbor
❍ Traveling with and Boarding Your Poodle

S mart, beautiful, and talented. In a nutshell, that's the Poodle. To make the grade as an owner of such a delightful breed, you must be willing to satisfy your Poodle's need for love, attention, and direction, and challenge her high intelligence. That can seem overwhelming if you're a novice Poodle owner. No worry. The following will help you do all that, and more.

Playtime

Given the Poodle's history as a working dog—water retriever and, later, land retriever and truffle hunter—your

Poodle needs activities; formal or informal, to keep her mind busy and her body active. Here are several activities popular with Poodle enthusiasts to get you started. Have fun!

Agility

Racing against time, agility competitors must maneuver a series of jumps and obstacles in which they are judged on accuracy, as well as speed. Dogs race against the clock as they jump hurdles, scale ramps, travel through tunnels, traverse a seesaw, and weave through a line of poles. This fast-paced, athletic sport is demanding and fun—a great challenge for the quick-witted and agile Poodle.

Any dog with good physical ability and energy is a strong candidate for agility. Though some breeds appear more naturally adapted to the sport, more than 100 breeds and mixed breeds have participated in the sport. Agility is open to all dogs regardless of pedigree—mixed-breed and purebred dogs alike are welcome to compete in United States Dog Agility Association (USDAA) events. Though agility is a competitive, athletic sport, the USDAA promotes dog agility as a community sport, a fun way for individuals and families to spend time with their dogs.

It's also great fun for the dogs, says Poodle enthusiast Julie Borst. "My dogs love agility and the exciting obstacles so much they are smiling the entire time."

Agility competitors may earn certification titles, such as agility dog, advanced agility dog, and master agility dog, as well as titles offered through the USDAA Junior Handler Program and Basic Performance Program.

If you're interested in agility, attend a few events. Contact a local obedience club and ask for information on agility classes. Find a trainer or coach who is experienced in teaching agility.

Canine Good Citizen

Would you like to show off your Poodle's good manners? And would you like your Poodle to be considered a good citizen? A program sponsored by the American Kennel Club does just that. Administered by dog clubs, obedience clubs, private trainers, or 4-H clubs throughout the United States, the Canine Good Citizen program aims at encouraging all owners to train their dogs.

What does it take to earn a citizen seal of approval? To earn a Canine Good Citizen Certificate, dogs are graded pass/fail on such things as allowing a stranger to approach, walking on a loose lead, walking through a crowd, sitting for examination, and reacting to another dog or other distraction.

"I believe that most of the Poodles I know, of any size, naturally have the fundamental characteristics needed to pass the AKC CGC test," says Poodle enthusiast Deb Johnson.

Conformation Competition

Conformation competition aims at judging the Poodle's structure, looks, and movement against the breed's "standard of perfection." Dogs who most closely adhere to the standard (whether it be the AKC, UKC, registry, and so on) are considered the best dogs for breeding. There are two types of conformation dog shows: specialty and all-breed. Specialty shows are limited to a designated breed

Did You Know?

According to the American Animal Hospital Association, more than 40 percent of pet owners talk to their pets on the phone or through the answering machine.

Versatility In Poodles

"In every Poodle puppy lies versatility. It is up to you to develop and enjoy it."
—Versatility In Poodles web page

In the fall of 1992, several Poodle fanciers attended the same obedience workshop. As they compared notes, they found to their dismay that each had at least one Poodle with a serious health problem. Everyone agreed that something needed to be done. The result was Versatility In Poodles, a non-profit organization dedicated to Poodles. VIP's primary purpose is to improve the health and promote the many talents of this remarkable breed.

To accomplish its goal, VIP encourages Poodle enthusiasts to become members. The organization produces and distributes a wide range of free educational materials, ranging from general care information to pamphlets with suggested disease-screening tests. VIP members receive a bimonthly newsletter.

VIP offers a versatility certificate program designed to encourage Poodle owners and breeders to develop their Poodles' talents. The program gives formal recognition to Poodles that achieve high marks in areas such as obedience, tracking, field, agility, conformation, temperament, and health. Dogs can earn a versatility certificate (VC) for high achievement or versatility certificate excellent (VCX) for outstanding achievements.

or grouping of breeds. All-breed shows include all breeds. Poodles entered in conformation competition must be shown in specific coat styles as defined by the Poodle Club of America.

Dogs competing in conformation shows are working for points toward a championship. To become an AKC champion of record, a dog must earn 15 points. A dog can earn from one to five points at a show. The 15 points required for a championship must be won under three different judges and include two majors (wins of 3, 4, and 5 at one show) under different judges.

AKC conformation shows are divided into five classes: puppy (subdivided by 6 to 9 months and 9 to 12 months), novice, bred-by-exhibitor, American-bred, and open.

Conformation showing of the Poodle is competitive and requires dedication. "I have a cream Standard Poodle that I am showing in conformation," says Johnson. "It was my dream 20 years ago to someday own a show Standard Poodle and now Bear is making my dream come true. It is very hard work, and not an activity to be taken on by the thin-skinned. The harsh realities of what it takes for a dog to get a championship, if you aren't a big breeder, sometimes slap you in the face. But the feelings you get when your dog does well keep you going."

If you're interested in conformation showing, the best place to start is a breeder with show-quality pups for sale. Following that, contact a local Poodle club for experienced conformation show enthusiasts and handlers.

Flyball

Flyball is a team sport for dogs that was invented in California in the 1970s. In this exciting, fast-moving sport, dogs compete in timed relay teams with four dogs on a team. The course consists of a starting line, four hurdles spaced ten feet apart, and a spring-loaded box that shoots out tennis balls.

The first hurdle is six feet from the starting line and the box is 15 feet from the last hurdle for an overall length of 51 feet. Each dog jumps the hurdles, then steps on the spring-loaded box that shoots out a tennis ball. The dog catches the tennis ball and then runs back over the four hurdles. When the dog crosses the starting line the next dog goes.

The first team to have all four dogs run without errors wins the heat. Tournaments are usually organized in either a double-elimination or round-robin format. Double elimination is usually best of three or best of five. Round robin is usually best three out of five, and the first team to win three heats receives one point toward their standing in the tournament.

Flyball competitors earn points toward flyball titles based on the team's time. Less than 32 seconds, each dog receives one point. Less than 28 seconds, each dog receives five points. Less than 24 seconds, each dog receives 25 points. Dogs can earn titles ranging from flyball dog (FD) to flyball grand champion (FDGCH).

Hunt Tests

Retriever hunt tests are noncompetitive examinations of a dog's ability to retrieve waterfowl and upland game. Dogs in a hunt test are judged against a standard, and either pass or fail. Hunt tests evaluate a dog's ability at three levels, and each succeeding level is more difficult. Dogs that complete each level successfully can earn titles of junior hunter (JH), senior hunter (SH), and master hunter (MH). Master hunters that successfully pass five master hunter tests in one year are invited to test at the Master National Hunting test.

The Poodle is a relative newcomer to the world of modern hunt tests. In June 1998, the AKC board of directors voted unanimously to allow Standard Poodles into AKC retriever hunt tests. In September 1998, Standard Poodles first entered these tests. Poodle enthusiasts are now at work to have the Miniature Poodle accepted. The first Standard Poodle to attain AKC junior hunter title is Am./Can. United Kennel Club Ch. Oakwind's Time to Burn (George), owned by professional groomer Jaci Bowman.

Hunts tests are available to owners and dogs through organizations other than the AKC. The United Kennel Club and the National American Hunting Retriever Association also offer noncompetitive hunt tests for retrievers.

Obedience Competition

Every civilized dog should know at least five basic commands: heel, sit, down, stay, and come. Obedience training is essential for Poodles. You might say it's the glue that holds together all owner-dog activities. A Poodle who knows and obeys basic commands is a trustworthy, agreeable companion.

Obedience competition is a team activity whereby dog and owner perform a prescribed set of exercises (or commands) on which the dog is scored. AKC obedience competition is divided into three levels and titles: novice, companion dog (CD); open, companion dog excellent (CDX); and utility dog (UD).

The novice obedience competitor must heel on-leash, stand for examination, heel free, recall, and perform an extended sit and down. The stakes are higher for the open competitor, who must heel free, drop on recall, retrieve on flat, retrieve over the high jump and broad jump, and perform an extended sit and down. The advanced utility competitor must perform signal exercises, pass two scent discrimination tests, perform a directed retrieve and directed jumping, and undergo group examination.

> Obedience training is essential for Poodles. You might say it's the glue that holds together all owner-dog activities.

To obtain an obedience title, a dog must earn three "legs." To be credited one leg, the dog must score at least 170 points out of a possible 200, and get more than 50 percent on each exercise. Dogs that have earned a UD title can earn points toward an obedience trial championship. To become an obedience trial champion, the dog must win 100 points that include a first place in utility with at least three dogs in the competition, a first place in open B with at least six dogs in competition, and a third first place in either of these competitions.

> Interested in obedience competition? Begin with basic obedience classes, and then find a trainer who is experienced in competition.

Poodle enthusiast Winona Kuhl has first-hand experience in the obedience ring. "I personally train and take part in obedience and agility work with my Poodles. My Standard Poodle, Puff, is now retired from the obedience ring, and my Miniature, Beau, will soon be competing in both obedience and agility. I became interested in obedience work when my children were young and involved in 4-H. I have been a 4-H advisor now for 29 years, and am also involved with an adult training club. It is my belief that obedience-trained dogs are much happier dogs because they are admired and accepted just about anywhere they go."

Interested in obedience competition? Begin with basic obedience classes, and then find a trainer who is experienced in competition. There are many different options and organizations to choose from.

Therapy Dogs

You might call Poodles and owners who participate in this activity goodwill ambassadors. Therapy dogs are those who make regular visits along with owners to nursing homes, hospitals, day-care centers, and assisted-living facilities. People who are lonely welcome a visit from a friendly dog, especially a Poodle, who brings joy and friendship in a special canine way. Pet visits are not only emotionally uplifting to nursing-home residents and hospital patients, but they can promote healing. Studies have shown that petting an animal can actually lower blood pressure. Also, many people, especially those feeling withdrawn or isolated, respond to pets when they do not respond to people.

Not just any Poodle can be a therapy dog. Most therapy dogs are certified by an organization such as the Delta Society in Renton, Washington. Therapy dogs must pass physical and temperament tests to prove they're safe and friendly with strangers. Owners and pets attend training.

Tracking Tests

Tracking tests require a dog to follow a trail by scent. Under the AKC, dogs can earn several tracking titles: tracking dog (TD), tracking dog excellent (TDX), variable surface tracking (VST), and champion tracker (CT). Dogs either pass or fail the tests, and do not compete against each other or against the clock. The purpose of a tracking test is to demonstrate the dog's ability to recognize and follow human scent.

A TD test is 440 to 500 yards in length, and must include at least two right-angle turns. The track must be one to two hours old. The individual laying the track must be unfamiliar to the dog. A scented article is dropped at the end of the track, which the dog must recover.

The TDX track is lengthier (800 to 1,000 yards) and three to five hours old. It's more complicated, going through varied terrain such as tall grass or ditches. Dummy scents are placed along the track.

A VST test challenges a dog's ability to follow a track in a more developed area. The VST rack is 600 to 800 yards over at least three types of surfaces. The track must be three to four hours old and include up to eight turns.

A CT title is awarded to the dog that earns all three titles.

Poodles Just Wanna Have Fun!

Formal canine sports are wonderful, but they're not the only way to get active with your Poodle. Be creative! Poodles love to do just about anything. Here are a few informal ideas to get you started:

○ *Water activities.* Whether it's a boat ride—life jackets for your Poodle and you, please—a walk along the seashore, or a dash in and out of a lake, most Poodles love to swim and be near water (short, easy-care haircuts advised).

○ *Frisbee.* Tossing and catching a Frisbee is a favorite pastime for many owners and Poodles. Be aware, however, that this activity can damage a dog's teeth. Soft, nylon Frisbees made especially for dogs are much safer than the hard, plastic, generic ones.

○ *Neighborhood stroll.* A daily walk is good for you and Poodle, so pull out the leash and get going. More strenuous hikes are great, too.

○ *Tricks.* As past (and some present) circus performers, Poodles are a quick study for tricks. How about teaching your Poodle

Circus Performers

It's true that the Poodle has an "air of distinction," as described by the American Kennel Club breed standard. But there's a flip side to this breed's sophisticated personality. According to those who know and love the breed, the Poodle is a natural entertainer, clownish, a dog with a "sense of humor." The Poodle is also a quick study, able to learn to do most anything. So not surprisingly, the Poodle has put these entertaining abilities to work over the centuries as a performer and circus animal.

The story of the Poodle as entertainer begins in France. In 1700, a troupe of Poodles from France reportedly performed in London for King George III. These Poodles, and other troupes like them, delighted audiences by dancing, jumping through hoops, tumbling, or pushing a wheelbarrow while walking on hindlegs. One Signor M. Girmondi presented his dogs to royalty throughout Europe, in Berlin, Paris, Vienna, and Madrid. By 1800, the Poodle and shows spotlighting the breed were popular in England.

The Poodle as entertainer has continued, with modern circuses incorporating Poodles into the act. Unfortunately, the Poodle's success as a circus star has typecast the breed somewhat as a trick dog—and only a trick dog—rather than as a smart, hardworking hunting companion. The truth be known, the Poodle is both and much more.

For more information on the subjects, organizations, and activities discussed in this chapter, please see Appendix A, Resources.

the traditional "shake," "roll over," or the not-so-traditional "high five"?

Playing Nicely with Children

"Poodles make wonderful family pets," says Winona Kuhl. "My current Poodles have grown up with my grandchildren, and absolutely love all children."

Common-Sense Rules for Kids and Poodles

○ Parents must supervise all interactions.

○ Never leave a baby or small child alone with any breed of dog.

○ Teach children to never go into the dog's crate because the crate is the Poodle's special, private room.

○ Teach children to never bother the Poodle when he's eating or sleeping.

○ Teach children to never tease and always be gentle, and that yelling, feet stomping, or arm-swinging are not appropriate near the dog.

○ Don't allow children to poke or pull the Poodle's eyes, ears, nose, or tail.

○ Don't permit your dog to steal snacks from kids. Place the Poodle in his crate or another room with his own doggie snack during little-people snack time.

Poodles and children can be excellent companions. The well-bred Poodle's good disposition makes him a trustworthy playmate, and his sense of humor makes him a child's favorite entertainer. That's not to say every Poodle will be accepting of children. Some Poodles, the result of careless breeding, inherit less-than-sunny dispositions. Proper socialization and adequate training helps determine how accustomed a Poodle is to children. Health status, too, can affect the Poodle's attitude toward kids. Older dogs, for example, can be grumpy due to illness.

Also consider the Poodle's size. The diminutive Toy Poodle is much more delicate than the Miniature and Standard, thus less able to withstand the rough-and-tumble antics inevitable with children.

For the most part, if you have kids, a Poodle is a good choice. *But be prepared to supervise all Poodle-child interactions.* That's the key to any successful dog-kid relationship: Adults must supervise to ensure the safety of both child and dog.

The degree of supervision varies, depending upon how old the child is and how old and well-socialized the Poodle. Babies and toddlers need constant supervision when with pets. Never leave toddlers alone with animals (or another child!). As the child grows and shows maturity, supervision may be decreased. While babies and young children should never be alone with the Poodle, older children (ages seven, eight, or nine) can, for example, play in the yard with the Poodle. Parents need not be right in the midst of the game, but should stay close by.

Along with supervision, parents should provide ongoing instruction for children in how to treat a pet kindly. Kids are not born knowing how to pet nicely; they must be taught. The best way to do that is for parents to model the desired behavior. Show the child how to pet with an open hand and not grab. Talk to the child as you demonstrate, explaining what you're doing and why. Keep your lessons short and simple.

Kids will be kids, though, and will forget your instruction. That's where constant supervision comes in. You can observe how the child interacts with your Poodle and correct as needed.

Sometimes the creative Poodle takes correction into her own paws. "I recall a time a number of years ago," says Kuhl, "when my youngest grandchild, Christine, was visiting with her family. Christine was quite fascinated with Puff's [the Standard Poodle] toys and had carried most of them into the living room. It was obvious that Puff was not pleased with this kid having her toys, but she would not try to take them. However, as Christine finished playing with each toy, Puff disappeared from the living room. After a while when all the toys, and Puff, were absent, I went to investigate.

Ten Great Games
Kids Can Play with a Poodle

Children should avoid playing certain games with your Poodle, such as tug-of-war or wrestling, which can put your dog in a position of power, or chase games, which can lead to your child getting nipped. Here are ten safe games your child and your Poodle can enjoy together. An adult must supervise all play. Also watch your dog during certain games, such as doggie soccer, to be sure he isn't getting too possessive of the ball.

Hide-and-Seek. Start teaching this game with your child "hiding" in plain view across the room, then gradually make the game more difficult by having her hide behind furniture, in another room, etc. It helps for your dog to know your family members by name. For example, you can hold onto your dog while your child hides and then release him with an encouraging, "Go find Susie!" Susie can reward the dog's find with praise and/or treats.

Marco Polo. While your dog searches the house for your child, Susie can "bark" or make another noise to help your Poodle find her. Many dogs will respond with a bark of their own, with the barking continuing back and forth until the dog finds the child. It's best to "bark" when the dog is in another part of the house; otherwise, the game becomes too easy!

Freeze Tag. This game requires several children and one dog as players. The children get to call the dog using whatever verbal or body language they want, but then they must freeze before the dog gets close enough to touch them. The child commands the dog to sit, then praises, and the game continues. The dog moves from child to child. Whereas younger children may not understand that they should stand still when a dog chases them, they understand how to freeze in a game setting.

Fetch or Frisbee. Make sure your children play this game properly, with the dog actually retrieving the object, rather than turning it into a game of Keep Away, which undermines your child's authority. Throw a Frisbee close to the ground. While the leaps and twists of Frisbee-catching dogs are breathtaking to watch, they can lead to serious spinal injuries.

Tricks. Teaching tricks provides a way for your child to bond with your dog as well as enforce your child's alpha position.

Chase the Flashlight/Bubbles/Hose. When playing the game with a flashlight, the child simply shines the beam on the ground and quickly runs it back and forth, in circles, or in figure-eights while the dog chases it. Just make sure your child lets your dog see her take out and put away this toy. Since flashlight beams have no smell, appear out of nowhere, and can never be caught, they can turn a Poodle intense, with the dog constantly searching for the elusive beam, even when the game has long been over. The hot new variation of this game uses laser toys to the same effect. As with flashlight beams, let your dog know when the laser game is starting and stopping, and take care never to shine the laser beam in his eyes. This chase game can also be played with blown bubbles or water streaming from a hose. If you find your dog gets too obsessive about this game, however, try another, less intense game on the list instead.

Find the Toy. Help your child teach your dog to know his toys by name and to retrieve them on command. You can do this by associating a name with each toy as your dog picks it up. For example, if your dog picks up his tennis ball, say, "Ball" and then praise him. When he picks up his stuffed mailman say, "Mailman," again followed with praise. If you tell him to get his mailman and he instead picks up his ball, say "Wrong. Get the mailman!" Reward a correct find.

Doggie Soccer. Your child will love passing a soccer ball back and forth with a canine friend. However, teach your dog a "Leave it" command or your dog may control the ball and not let anyone else play with it. Also, don't play this game with a Poodle who is extremely dominant, as such frenzied ball-playing may bring out aggressive tendencies.

Backyard Agility. With a few homemade jumps, a fabric tunnel from a toy store, and garden stakes pushed into the ground to form weave poles, you can make an agility course. Make sure obstacles are sturdy and safe.

Red Light, Green Light. The game is played with several children and your dog. One child turns her back and calls "Come," and then "Red light, green light, one, two, three." On the count of three, the child turns to face the rest of the players and commands "Down," at which point the children must all freeze and the dog must drop in place. The game continues until one of the children or the dog reaches the child who is "it."

I found Puff in the computer room, lying in a sphinx position with all her toys between her legs."

Having a young child and a Poodle can be a lot of work. But if you're willing to put in your time, it's a wonderful opportunity for parents to show children how to be kind to animals. That experience helps children develop empathy for creatures other than themselves.

Given the fact that children are most commonly bitten by their own family pets, according to the American Humane Association, the problem of biting can be a concern to parents. Overall statistics show that 60 percent of dog bite victims are children, over half of them age 12 or under.

Poodles are usually good-natured and not prone to biting. However, you can help prevent this problem by acquiring a Poodle with a trustworthy temperament. Buy only from a reputable breeder who is as concerned about temperament as conformation. Scrutinize the temperament of your pup, her parents, and her other adult relatives. Following that, socialize and train your Poodle by setting clear limits for acceptable behavior. Teach your Poodle to be a trustworthy member of the family and community.

Do not encourage mouthing or biting by allowing kids to play rough, aggressive games with the Poodle. Though they are favorite games, tug-of-war and wrestling can encourage aggression. A family pet should never have its mouth on any person, for any reason.

Make sure kids know never to disturb the Poodle when he's eating or sleeping. Kids should also learn never to approach a strange or loose dog, and to remain motionless and avoid eye contact if approached by one.

Be on the lookout for trouble, such as occasional growls or snaps. Be honest with yourself as to the Poodle's nature and don't make excuses for bad behavior. Learn to recognize aggression and dominance, and contact an experienced trainer right away for help.

Making Your Poodle a Good Neighbor

No matter the size, the Poodle is a great family dog. She will entertain and humor you, and you'll be amazed at her intelligence. (Many Poodle enthusiasts say the breed seems "human-like" in their thinking.) Hopefully, your neighbors will appreciate your Poodle as much as you do.

We've all known of, or lived next to, bad-doggie neighbors. You know, those folks who put their dogs in the backyard and let them bark from 1 to 3 A.M. Or those who take their dog for a walk to defecate in *your* yard. Then there are those neighbors who allow their dog to wander and make mischief in every yard— digging, scattering garbage, and chewing up kids' toys. Are you a good-doggie neighbor? Are you considerate of those living nearby? Let's hope so! Make it your goal to be a good neighbor and teach your Poodle to be a good neighbor, too.

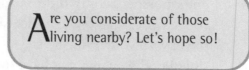

Are you considerate of those living nearby? Let's hope so!

Basic obedience classes are the starting point for the Poodle's introduction to Neighbor Relations 101, followed by the Canine Good Citizen Program sponsored by the AKC. A dog that knows and understands basic obedience commands is on the road to becoming a trustworthy companion. For example, as you're taking a walk through the neighborhood with your Poodle, she walks quietly beside you then sits nicely as you chat with Bill from across the street without jumping up and whining.

Suffice to say, basic obedience training, along with your sensitivity to others, is essential if you want your Poodle known as a good neighbor. Here are some simple good neighbor rules:

○ No incessant barking.
○ No wandering. Keep your Poodle in the house, yard, or kennel run at all times.
○ If you leave the premises, make sure the Poodle is on-leash.
○ If your Poodle defecates while out for a walk, clean it up.

Traveling with and Boarding Your Poodle

Are you snowed in? Rained out? Sick and tired of the day-to-day grind? If your answer is yes, you probably need a vacation. There is nothing like getting away from the details of life to freshen one's perspective, is there? But before you book airline tickets, you have to make a few decisions about your Poodle. Will she travel with you? Will she stay at home? Now that you're a responsible Poodle owner, you have to think ahead.

To Go or Not to Go

Hopefully, the question isn't whether or not you will plan a vacation, but will you take your Poodle along or leave her at home? The answer to that depends upon the type of vacation and your personal preference.

In general, Poodles are good travelers and adapt anywhere quite easily. But not all vacations are cut out for Poodles—a honeymoon on a tropical island, for example. Use common sense to figure this one out. Visualize the vacation and place your Poodle in the picture. If it's an easy fit, take your Poodle along. If not, leave your Poodle at home.

Stay, Girl

If your holiday plans don't include staying at a hotel that accepts pets, then you have some arranging to do. Someone has to take care of your Poodle while you're away. You have three good choices:

○ Leave the Poodle at a reputable boarding kennel.
○ Hire a trustworthy pet sitter.
○ Ask Grandma (or another trusted relative or friend) to babysit.

Boarding Kennel   A boarding kennel is a business that houses dogs and cats, for a fee, while owners are away. Dogs are usually kept in large indoor-outdoor kennel runs, cats in an indoor cattery. The average cost per night to board a dog is $10.63, according to the American Boarding Kennels Association (ABKA) survey of its members. However, boarding costs usually vary by the size of the dog, so boarding a Toy Poodle will most likely be cheaper than boarding a Standard. There are some 9,000 boarding kennels in the United States and Canada—some good, some not as good. Your goal in choosing a kennel to care for your Poodle while you're sipping drinks on a Caribbean beach is to find one that's clean, well-supervised, secure, and adequately staffed.

> The average cost per night to board a dog is $10.63, according to the American Boarding Kennels Association (ABKA) survey of its members.

Of the many kinds of kennels, some are large, some small; some are plush, others basic. Which one you select depends on what you want and can afford. Good basic kennels will house dogs in an indoor-outdoor run; provide food and water; give medication as needed; clean runs daily; require that pets be current on all vaccinations, including canine cough; and may require that pets be flea-free or dipped for fleas before they can stay in the kennel. More luxurious kennels provide plush beds and daily walks or play sessions, even swimming. Whether you are interested in basic care or some degree of frills, don't hesitate to ask questions about the care your pet will be given. Tour several kennels before you make your choice.

To ensure your Poodle the best of care while you're away, tell the kennel staff as much as possible about your dog: his level of training, likes and dislikes, bad habits, and eating schedule. Drop off your Poodle and pick him up as scheduled, and notify the kennel of any change of plans.

Just as a mother will pack an overnight bag for her preschooler spending the night with Auntie, so must you pack a bag for your Poodle. Include medication, a favorite sleeping blankie, toys, or special food. To find ABKA kennels in your area, visit www.abka.com.

Pet Sitter   A petsitter is a person who comes to your house, for a fee, to care for your Poodle. This individual may water plants or pick up mail as well. Services average $10.50 per visit. According to the National Association of Professional Pet Sitters, keeping the pet at home in its familiar environment, eating its regular diet, and enjoying its exercise routine is best for the pet. Being at home eliminates the stress of being away and minimizes exposure to illness.

If you opt to have a professional pet sitter come into your home, make sure the individual you choose is licensed and bonded. Since he or she will have full access to your home, it's essential that you obtain references. Ask for the names of clients as references. Meet with the individual who will be coming to your home and introduce him or her to your Poodle before you leave your dog (and home) in his or her care.

Hi Grandma!   This may be your least likely option. However, for those blessed with a parent, family member, or trusted friend who knows and loves your Poodle, who better to look after him while you're away? Either the Poodle can stay at home while Grandma stays at your house, or you can take the dog to her home. Be sure to offer payment or at least bring home an expensive souvenir!

The Travel Bug

Because Poodles are so adaptable, they make good travelers. What you must know before adding your Poodle to the holiday head count is that you'll need to plan ahead to make the trip go smoothly.

Before you leave home, you'll have some packing to do. You'll need food, bottled water, dishes, collar, leash, bedding, toys, and identification tags with vacation addresses and phone numbers added. You may also need a current health certification, which you should keep along with your other important travel papers. And, make sure your

Did You Know?

In Homer's The Odyssey, the only one to recognize Odysseus when he arrived home disguised as a beggar after a 20-year absence was his dog Argos, who wagged his tail at his master and then died.

Poodle is wearing an up-to-date rabies tag. Don't forget plastic bags so you can clean up after your Poodle. Since you never know when an emergency will arise, it's also a good idea to pack a doggie first-aid kit. Bring along anything you can think of that will help keep your Poodle happy and comfortable.

Car travel is a great way to take your Poodle along on a trip. But before starting on a 300-mile journey, take time to accustom your Poodle to traveling in the car. Take short trips around town, to the park, the store, the veterinary clinic, or the grooming salon. That way, your Poodle will be less anxious on a longer ride.

> Many Poodle enthusiasts transport their dogs in crates or use canine safety restraints. Dogs can be injured in a crash just like people can.

Many Poodle enthusiasts transport their dogs in crates or use canine safety restraints. Dogs can be injured in a crash just like people can. A crate or safety restraint also makes driving safer for you since the Poodle is unable to jump into the front seat and startle you, which could result in an accident. "When I travel anywhere with my Poodles in my car, they ride in a seatbelt," says Winona Kuhl. "They are accustomed to this, and when they see their seatbelts, they get excited. This habit not only assures that my dogs won't move about in the car and distract me while I'm driving, but they are safer."

Do not feed your dog or give her water for about two hours before driving to help prevent motion sickness, and carry paper towels for cleanup in case your dog does get car sick. Stop every few hours for water and a "nature break." Take along a few toys and chews to keep your Poodle busy while driving. However, you'll find that Poodles, like children, tend to fall asleep while riding in the car.

Never leave your Poodle alone in the car, even parked in the shade or with the windows cracked, in warm weather. The interior of the car can get hot quickly, resulting in heatstroke and, possibly, death.

Almost anywhere you can fly on commercial airlines, you can buy a ticket for your Poodle (only a few airlines refuse pets). In the United States, service animals (guide dogs, signal dogs, and assistance dogs) travel free of charge on all airlines. Proof of disability may be required.

The United States Department of Agriculture sets minimum rules and guidelines regulating pet travel, though each airline makes its own rules regarding pet travel. Pets travel either in the cabin in a carrier that stores under the seat or as cargo. Depending upon her size, your flying Poodle will travel in a crate placed in the plane's cargo area or in the cabin with you.

Call the airline to determine specific pet travel policies. Some experienced air travelers recommend calling the airline several times to make sure you're getting accurate information. For domestic flights, make an appointment with your veterinarian about a week before you leave to get a current health certificate for your dog and an updated certificate of vaccination. For international travel, contact the U.S. Department of Agriculture, Animal, Plant, Health, and Inspection Service, Veterinary Services at least a month before travel. Many countries have strict guidelines that take time to fulfill. Some county and national park officials, as well as border patrols, may require a proof of health certificate. Additionally, most destinations require rabies shots, and a few destination sites, such as Hawaii, have quarantines that make vacationing with pets difficult.

Pets must travel in USDA-approved kennels. Airlines usually have several sizes available for rent, though you can buy one on your own. If you opt to purchase, ask the airline for the specific USDA requirements. Put extra food and water in a pack on top of the crate. Mark the crate carefully with your flight information; luggage tags work well for this. The Poodle should wear a collar with an identification tag that lists your name, address, and telephone number, along with vacation information.

Avoid feeding your Poodle for several hours prior to a flight to minimize air sickness. Exercise him before kenneling and boarding, too (a brisk walk and a nature break). Sedatives and tranquilizers are usually not necessary, and they should only be used under veterinary supervision.

Fly direct when possible. If there is a plane change, check to make sure your dog is boarded on the next aircraft. If you have a layover of 30 minutes or more, try to physically check on your Poodle, particularly if it is hot or cold outside. In hot weather fly at night, in cold weather fly during the day. Upon arrival, tell the gate attendant there is a live animal onboard and request that your Poodle be unloaded first. As soon as you know your Poodle is unloaded, head to the baggage claim.

Before traveling, you have to find out if the destination accommodations you've chosen will be happy to see your Poodle. Not all motels, hotels, bed and breakfasts, and campgrounds allow pets, though many do. Just make sure you plan ahead. See Appendix A for some books and online sites that include specific information on hotels, motels, and campgrounds that accept pets.

Wherever you go, you and your Poodle must be considerate guests. Don't allow your Poodle to sleep on the hotel bed and avoid leaving her alone in the room. If you must, leave her in a crate—but only if she doesn't bark when left alone in it. Clean up after your dog and keep her on-leash.

9

A Lifetime of Love and Good Health

In This Chapter

○ Your Aging Poodle—What to Expect
○ How to Keep Your Older Poodle Comfortable
○ Saying Goodbye
○ A New Beginning

No matter how healthy and active your senior Poodle is, and no matter how hard you work at keeping her that way, there's a day in the future that will be tough to face. Inevitably, old age or an illness associated with old age will catch up with your furry friend, and you will have to say goodbye. Along the way, you may notice changes in her activity level, ability to hear, and ability to smell. While you cannot change the inevitable, you can help your Poodle enjoy her golden years by understanding the aging process.

Fall, Poodles, and Memories

How many of us as kids rolled in the fall leaves that blew off the trees? When did we stop? Why did we stop? I recall raking them into big piles and jumping dead center, then crawling under to see who could hide their entire body under the pile of gold, orange, lemon, brown, and red leaves. Sometimes we pretended the leaves were gorgeous jewels, other times the leaves were houses with leaf walls. We'd sit in the "living room" and talk to each other about the mansions we would someday own. Amazing how those childhood mansions we once dreamed of turned into small houses nowhere near mansion size. I watched my Poodles enjoy the first leaves of fall. Oh, how they enjoyed chasing them. As a leaf would tumble downward carried by the wind, they would sight their "catch" and leap with joy in the air. More often than not, the breeze carried it inches away from their snapping mouths. Jumping in the air with such obvious pleasure, you can see the dogs' expressions and body language screaming, "So many leaves! So little time!"

So many wonderful childhood memories of fall! I think I'll make time this year to roll in the leaves once more. The memories that this spectacle of color and elation bring to me are endless. The Poodles become children of yester-year, haunting memories that bring smiles of remembrance. I wonder what my old childhood friends are doing now?

—Rhonda Le'Bilron, Poodle owner

Your Aging Poodle—What to Expect

What changes can you expect as your Poodle grows older? "If they are black, they will likely turn gray here and there," says Poodle enthusiast Sandy Marshall. "All Poodles will slow down and probably like to sleep more. Some may be arthritic and have sore joints. They may need a diet change, as their digestion may become different. They need to be monitored more closely by a vet for any unusual lumps or out-of-the-ordinary health conditions."

Dogs age differently and at a different rate. Generally, large breeds, such as the German Shepherd or St. Bernard, tend to age more rapidly than small breeds such as the Toy Poodle, Pug, or Chihuahua. According to experts at Tufts University, the point at which a dog qualifies as "aged" varies. Veterinarians generally consider small dogs such as Toys and Minis to be senior citizens (roughly corresponding to the 55-plus category in people) at about 12 years of age, while large dogs such as the Standard reach the senior stage at about eight years of age.

Your individual Poodle's biological age is determined by genetics, environment, disease, and nutritional status. A good diet and good veterinary care throughout her life greatly contribute to her good health as a senior. Certainly the better care your Poodle receives the happier life she will live, and most likely, a healthier life, too.

Generally, older dogs are less active, less curious, and more complacent than they were in their youth. The older dog can be forgetful, sleepy, resistant to change, a picky eater, or an excessive barker. While this is not always the case, older dogs can be grumpy and irritable, usually when they suffer from poor health.

Musculoskeletal As your Poodle gets older, so does her musculoskeletal system. You may notice a decrease in muscle mass and tone. The neck and body may appear bulky and the extremities appear thinner. Your Poodle's tummy may sag, her back may sway, and her elbows stick out. Many Poodles develop arthritis in their joints and spine. If arthritis is present, your older Poodle might limp or hold up the affected limb, or her joints may be painful to move or touch.

The musculoskeletal changes your Poodle experiences as she ages can be painful. While some dogs show little evidence of discomfort, others become downright cranky toward family members. Depending upon your Poodle's condition, your veterinarian can prescribe medication or therapy to decrease her pain.

Vision   It's not uncommon for the older Poodle to experience changes in vision. A common change in all dogs is nuclear sclerosis, a hardening of the central portion of the lens that results in a clouding of the lens. While overall vision appears to be unaffected even in advanced stages, your dog may have minor problems seeing objects close up.

Cataracts can affect dogs of any age, but are most commonly associated with oldsters. Some cataracts are caused by heredity.

Another common age-related visual change is the formation of cataracts, which is the loss of the normal transparency of the lens. Any spot on the lens that is opaque, regardless of size, is considered a cataract. The eyes appear to have a milky gray or bluish-white cast. Cataracts can affect dogs of any age, but are most commonly associated with oldsters. Some cataracts are caused by heredity.

Cataracts can result in vision loss, which makes it difficult for the Poodle to navigate her surroundings. However, most dogs adjust well to the gradual loss of vision if they are still able to hear. Surgery is available to remove cataracts, if necessary.

Hearing   Deafness from the gradual loss of hearing is another common condition in aging dogs. Senile deafness usually comes on gradually at about ten years of age. It may or may not be noticeable at first, though your dog may seem less active and responsive. Hearing loss in the older Poodle can cause problems. Since your Poodle cannot hear your commands such as "sit" or "no," discipline may be difficult. A dog that was previously well trained may become difficult to control. If necessary, your Poodle can be taught hand signals for common commands such as sit, down, and come.

A Poodle who cannot hear like she used to cannot detect the sound of an oncoming vehicle, especially in her own driveway, so she is at an increased risk of being hit. An older Poodle with poor hearing must be watched carefully when she is outside. Of course, not all hard-of-hearing seniors have permanent loss. Just as in younger dogs, infections and dirty ears can decrease hearing. Always consult with a vet when you suspect your dog is no longer hearing well.

Kidneys and Bowels   More seriously, kidney function declines with age. The Poodle may urinate more frequently because the kidneys have lost the ability to concentrate waste. An older Poodle with failing kidneys may be unable to keep from wetting in the house, especially at night. While kidney failure is common in older dogs, it is often treatable if caught early. Left alone, however, it is usually fatal. Any change in your older dog's urination habits should signal an immediate trip to the veterinarian. In some cases, house soiling may be the result of lower urinary tract problems such as a weak urinary sphincter. These dogs often dribble, especially in their sleep. For many of these dogs, a simple medication can keep them dry. For some older dogs, frequent nature breaks outside are helpful in controlling house soiling. If you must leave your dog alone for long periods, you might consider reverting to paper training or use disposable diapers, as some owners do. Defecation can also be a problem due to loss of sphincter control. Dogs also respond to stress by soiling the house with stool. If the stress can be identified, the animal can be acclimated to the change, and hopefully the house soiling will subside.

Teeth and Gums   Although it is just a best guess, your veterinarian can roughly determine your Poodle's age by looking at her teeth. Though this examining teeth to determine age is most reliable for dogs from four to six months of age, a vet with a trained eye can detect subtle changes in the teeth from years of biting and chewing. For example, by age three and a half, all cusps are usually worn flat on the upper middle incisors. As time goes on, incisors are worn flat and the canine teeth are blunted.

Tooth and gum disease is common in older dogs, and can interfere with the dog's ability to eat. No teeth, no chewing, and bad health! That's why proper dental care throughout the Poodle's lifetime, beginning when she is a puppy, is essential to ensure healthy teeth during her senior years. Regular brushing and periodic cleaning are especially important for your older Poodle. Ask your veterinarian to recommend a dental plan for your senior, then stick with it.

Skin and Coat   Because of reduced activity of oil-producing glands, the aging Poodle's skin and coat may become dry or scaly. You may also notice the geriatric dog has a stronger doggie odor, which you may help minimize by grooming her more frequently. Poodle enthusiasts recommend trimming senior Poodles in a short, easy-care trim. Additionally, older dogs' nails often need to be trimmed more frequently because less active seniors don't wear them down.

Heart   Geriatric Poodles can suffer from weakened heart muscles. Acquired valvular heart disease is a common cause of heart disease in dogs, usually affecting dogs over age 12. As your dog ages, the heart valves change and degenerate. Toy Poodles are at high risk for degeneration of the mitral valve. A dry cough is often the first sign of valvular heart disease in an older dog. Loss of energy, muscular weakness, and shortness of breath are also common symptoms. While heart disease is rarely cured, there are several medicines that can treat symptoms, improve heart function, and extend the life of these dogs.

Cognitive Dysfunction   Several age-related changes in dogs fall under the heading of canine cognitive dysfunction syndrome (CDS). These behaviors include circling; tremors; stiffness or weakness; inappropriate vocalization; compulsive behaviors; and changes in sleep patterns, housetraining, interest in food, attention and activity, and awareness of surroundings. An older dog may exhibit separation-related behaviors, uneasiness with visitors, and other problems for the first time. If your elderly Poodle exhibits these signs, discuss it with your veterinarian. If another disease is ruled out, CDS can be treated with medication.

Older dogs can be very resistant to change. New routines, locations, or social situations—visitors, children, workers in the home, boarding kennel staff—can be overly stressful to an elderly Poodle. Old dogs adjust poorly to emotional and physical stress since their hearts, livers, kidneys, and metabolism

Did You Know?

The old rule of multiplying a dog's age by seven to find the equivalent human age is inaccurate. A better measure is to count the first year as 15, the second year as 10, and each year after that as 5.

are often unable to meet the increased demands placed upon them if physically challenged.

How to Keep Your Older Poodle Comfortable

Now that you have an idea of what to expect as your Poodle advances in years, how can you best care for your geriatric Poodle every day?

"Give your Poodle whatever she wants to keep happy," suggests Poodle owner Tracy Raby. "She deserves it for being such a loyal and loving companion."

You can start by giving your Poodle a softer place on which to rest her aching bones and joints. Perhaps in her youth she was content to nap on a hard floor, but in old age a comfy bed is in order. Stiffness from osteoarthritis is made worse by sleeping on cold, damp ground or hard surfaces. You can purchase a soft bed at a pet-supply store or make one yourself with thick foam rubber (easily found at thrift stores) covered with a machine-washable, snug blanket. Place the bed in a dry, draft-free area of the house. Older dogs are sensitive to the extremes of heat and cold.

Additionally, reduce stiffness by drying off your Poodle if she gets wet. Dry her thoroughly after bathing or an outing in wet weather. Make sure she doesn't get wet and stay damp.

An arthritic Poodle may find it difficult to bend down to eat and drink from bowls on the floor. Consider buying an eating table—a neck-level table with special cutouts for food and water bowls—for her. This will be more comfortable for the senior Poodle who is hesitant to bend her neck due to the stiffness of arthritis.

While an arthritic Poodle may wish to avoid activity because it's painful, there's nothing more beneficial to an older dog than a regular exercise program, according to Delbert G. Carlson, D.V.M., and James M. Giffin, M.D., authors of the *Dog Owner's Home Veterinary Handbook*. Exercise improves muscle tone and strength, keeps joints moving, and keeps weight on target. The veterinarian can prescribe medication to reduce arthritic pain to make exercise possible.

Activity is essential, but you'll need to protect your arthritic Poodle from injury by modifying exercise and not allowing the oldster to overdo. Avoid jumping and other activities that wear down the joints more. Lift your older Poodle in and out of the car. Avoid stairs and rough play. Let her choose the pace she wants.

The aging Poodle needs more rest than she did in her younger years. If the Poodle is exercising on a regular basis and wishes to nap more, allow that. Just make sure you have a comfy bed handy!

The older Poodle is a creature of habit. She is not likely to appreciate sudden changes in routine, bed placement, food dishes, and activity. Keep such changes to a minimum, changing only what you must.

> Activity is essential, but you'll need to protect your arthritic Poodle from injury by modifying exercise and not allowing the oldster to overdo.

If you're planning a vacation, consider hiring a pet sitter to care for your Poodle at home rather than take her to a boarding kennel. Older dogs don't tolerate drastic changes in their routine such as being away from home in a boarding kennel no matter how nice the place is. Keeping your old dog at home while you're away in the care of a trusted pet sitter is often your best option.

Consider hiring a mobile groomer rather than taking your elderly Poodle to the grooming shop. The mobile groomer comes right to your house, greatly reducing grooming time and reducing your Poodle's stress from driving to and from the salon and being left for several hours. Mobile grooming services are more expensive than salons, but well worth it. Of course, if his favorite groomer is the highlight of his life, he should continue visiting where he's most comfortable.

Reduced hearing and failing eyesight are realities with the older dog. For a Poodle who doesn't hear as well as she used to, teach hand signals for obedience commands. You can also get her attention by stomping on the floor so she can feel the vibrations. Additionally, be careful not to startle your deaf dog. Approach slowly. If you have a Poodle with failing or loss of sight, don't move the furniture! Dogs without sight are amazingly adaptable, as long as everything in their physical environment stays the same. To a great extent, dogs rely on their sense of smell and hearing to navigate the world. These senses become even more acute when sight fails. Never allow a blind dog to run free, however, and reinforce basic obedience commands when possible. Calling to a blind Poodle (who can still hear) to "stop" or "sit" could very well save her life.

The older Poodle's misbehaving kidneys and bowels can be troublesome and frustrating to owners. It can be like a return to puppyhood, with cleaning up accidents in the house. Be patient and take it in stride. Take the Poodle out for nature breaks frequently, place newspaper or pads in the house, and consider using diapers. Also, make sure to ask your veterinarian to examine your senior Poodle at the first sign of urination changes. He or she may be able to prescribe medication to help reduce the problem, and if your dogs kidneys are failing, may be able to save his life.

Senior Health Care

Your veterinarian will probably recommend a geriatric screening exam for your elderly Poodle. A geriatric screening usually includes a physical exam, blood tests, an electrocardiogram, or specialized tests for your Poodle's specific health conditions. Diseases can occur in older dogs that are not usually seen in young dogs, such as arthritis, diabetes, Cushing's disease, cancer, and kidney, heart, and liver diseases. Blood tests will screen for many of these diseases.

Since dogs age at different rates, screening begins at different ages for Toy, Miniature, and Standard Poodles:

Up to 15 pounds   Begin geriatric screening at age 9 to 11

16 to 50 pounds   Begin geriatric screening at age 7 to 9

51 to 80 pounds   Begin geriatric screening at age 6 to 8

Over 80 pounds   Begin geriatric screening at age 4 to 6

Your veterinarian may recommend semi-annual visits once your Poodle becomes a senior. Between visits, be alert to changes that could indicate serious illness and require immediate veterinary attention. Here are several common symptoms:

❍ Sudden loss of weight

❍ Serious loss of appetite

❍ Increase in appetite without increase in weight

❍ Diarrhea or vomiting

❍ Increased thirst, without a change in activity level, and increased urination

❍ Excessive fatigue

❍ Extreme limited mobility

❍ Coughing and excessive panting

What Should I Feed My Senior Poodle?

Your senior Poodle may require a special diet, or at least a diet different from what he ate during his prime. Generally, older dogs tend to be less active, which means fewer calories are needed to maintain target weight. Feed a diet too high in calories and you'll have an overweight Poodle. Since obesity is unhealthy, you've got to keep your Poodle at his optimum weight.

Many veterinarians recommend feeding older dogs a commercially prepared "senior" diet. Senior diets generally contain a reduced concentration of fat and calories, and some foods also contain extra fiber to further reduce caloric density. Ask your veterinarian if a senior diet is appropriate for your older Poodle.

According to current research, a diet rich in protein is also important for older dogs. Do remember, though, that too much protein is not good for seniors—those super high-protein diets are for athletes, not seniors. Seniors are less efficient in metabolizing protein than younger dogs, hence older dogs need more protein to maintain good health. The additional protein is needed to maintain protein reserves and support protein turnover, which help maintain a dog's immune system. Dogs who don't eat enough protein are more prone to stress. The specific amount of protein required for senior dogs varies among individuals, though veterinary researchers recommend that protein comprise 20 to 26 percent of the calories for older dogs. Many veterinarians recommend a senior diet that contains about 25 percent protein.

The added need for protein contradicts a belief by some dog breeders and owners that older dogs should not eat a diet high in protein because it can result in kidney failure. While a protein-restricted diet may be recommended for a dog suffering from kidney failure, there is no evidence that protein at an appropriate level in a nutritionally complete and balanced diet causes kidney problems in dogs.

Besides a good diet, don't feed table scraps or excess treats. Make sure your elderly Poodle gets enough exercise and don't supplement his diet unless your veterinarian advises you to do so.

Don't be surprised if your elderly Poodle has a diminished appetite. This is not uncommon in senior dogs. As a dog ages, his sense of smell or taste may decrease, making food less appealing. However, a sudden loss of appetite could be a sign of serious illness, so be sure to check with your vet if your dog's appetite decreases. Ways to encourage your senior Poodle to eat are to warm his food or add a little water and unsalted beef or chicken broth. Sometimes all the senior Poodle needs is a little variety (don't we all?). Instead of the same old kibble slightly moistened, add a tablespoon or two of canned food, beef or chicken broth, and a few lightly cooked veggies. Add variety in small amounts to prevent digestive upset.

> Ways to encourage your senior Poodle to eat are to warm his food or add a little water and unsalted beef or chicken broth.

A senior Poodle can be picky about drinking enough water. Older dogs often forget to drink or, due to arthritis pain, avoid getting up and going to the water bowl. Dehydration is not good for any dog, but is especially harmful to seniors. Encourage your senior Poodle to drink, and make it easy by placing several water bowls throughout the house and yard. Don't allow your older dog to drink impure water. While a few licks of rainwater in his youth didn't do any harm, the older Poodle's aging kidneys are less tolerant.

Saying Goodbye

While sad to think about, realizing that one day you'll be without your devoted canine companion is healthy. And, that last day may

Leaving Your Pet in Your Will

Who will care for your pet if you die before she does? Many people neglect to think this could happen, with the result of their beloved pet being placed in an animal shelter after their death. Talk with family and friends and find someone who is truly willing and able to take care of your Poodle if you should pass. Then speak with your lawyer and include your pet in your will. You may also want to specify a certain amount of money to go to the person caring for your dog to offset the costs of food, veterinary care, and other pet-related expenses.

be a matter of choice. Some old dogs die naturally in their sleep, while others are euthanized when owners believe their dogs no longer enjoy a quality life.

What is euthanasia? Commonly called "putting to sleep," euthanasia is an intravenous injection of a barbiturate anesthetic in a large enough dose to cause immediate loss of consciousness and a painless end of life. Euthanasia can be performed by a veterinarian in the office or sometimes as a house call. Many consider it a kind way to help a pet die easily and without pain.

Perhaps your elderly Poodle has been getting along okay, with special considerations for limited mobility, some medication to reduce pain, and a daily routine that doesn't change. Then one day you realize he is no longer enjoying anything, is restless, and seems to be in great pain. Your vet can't offer any more help. Or, perhaps your Poodle is very ill, though young, and her chances for improving are slim. Is it time to consider euthanasia?

The decision to euthanize a pet is a highly individual and personal decision. Two Poodle owners faced with the same circumstances will make different choices, for different reasons, at different times. Unlike a math problem, there's no one right answer. "In pets . . . I think euthanasia is a viable alternative when the quality of the pet's life is not good and there is no chance for it to improve," says Poodle owner Deb Johnson. "Animals can't always tell us when they are in pain. We need to look at the signs they do give us and try to help where we can. Pain management in pets is nowhere near where it is in humans and probably never will be. I feel that if you really love your pet, if she is in pain and there is little hope of that changing, either with time or pain management, then euthanasia is best for your pet and you."

It is wise to never make a quick decision either for or against euthanasia. Get the facts on your Poodle's health status from your veterinarian. Know his chance of improvement and survival, the estimated quality and length of his life. Are there any treatments, surgeries, or medications that might help him? Is hospitalization required? Is your Poodle suffering and how much? Can you care for him at home?

> It is wise to never make a quick decision either for or against euthanasia. Get the facts on your Poodle's health status from your veterinarian. Know his chance of improvement and survival, the estimated quality and length of his life.

Once you get the facts, think carefully over the decision of whether to euthanize or treat, or how much to treat. Talk with a friend who knows you and your dog. It's also helpful to chat with other Poodle owners who have faced the same decision. (You can find plenty of support, thoughts, and ideas from members of online Poodle mailing lists.) Even though you get the facts and talk it over, don't expect the decision to be easy.

How about letting the Poodle pass on naturally? Richard H. Pitcarin, D.V.M., author of *Natural Health for Dogs & Cats*, suggests in his book that if the pet appears close to death, seems reasonably comfortable and peaceful, go ahead and allow the

Do Dogs Go to Heaven?

Do dogs go to heaven? That's a question many owners think about when a pet dies. Will they someday be reunited with their Poodle in the afterlife?

Theologians and philosophers have explored that question for eons with, of course, no definitive answer. How can there be? No one really knows. But depending upon whom you ask—a priest, rabbi, pastor, monk—you'll hear a different perspective, even within religions.

The Jewish view, for example, is that everything—humans and animals—is endowed by the Creator with a spirit, and every spirit someday returns to the Creator and is rewarded in the afterlife for its life on Earth.

Catholicism teaches that heaven was designed for people, but dogs may be part of the heavenly realm because of their connection to humans. However, people and dogs are different because humans have a soul made in the likeness of God; animals do not.

Southern Baptists teach that dogs do not have souls. And, scripture does not show anything specific about animals in heaven, other than some references in the Old Testament that might suggest there are animals in heaven.

The Buddhists believe in reincarnation, meaning death is not the end of our existence. Humans and animals alike take another life form and that can be another human or dog. There is a heaven, according to Buddhist thought, and we and dogs go there if we are in the right condition. Actions, called karma, determine where we end up.

Do dogs go to heaven? Only God knows.

process to unfold naturally. It is natural, after all. If the pet is restless, crying, has difficulty breathing, or is experiencing convulsions, euthanasia is probably best.

Growing into Grief

Whether you make the decision to euthanize your Poodle, or he dies naturally of old age or from illness at a young age, you will feel sad. Your bond with your Poodle is real, and when he dies you will experience real grief and a sense of loss. Normal responses to grief include crying, lack of appetite, insomnia, depression, loneliness, and tightness in the chest and throat.

Just as you experience different stages of grief when a beloved person dies, so might you experience the following stages of grief when your Poodle passes on.

Denial is a very common first stage of grief. You might have the feeling that this isn't real, that your Poodle isn't really dead. You might feel like you're in shock or numb. Denial is a way that people deal with severe trauma until they can prepare emotionally and intellectually.

The *bargaining* stage can occur even before your Poodle has died. You might "bargain with God," promise to take really good care of your beloved pet. You will buy only the best food, products, health care—in exchange for his life.

Next, comes *anger.* You may wish to blame someone—the veterinarian didn't do enough, for example. You may blame yourself, or even blame God. Anger is sometimes turned inward and manifests itself as guilt. Perhaps you feel you didn't do enough or make the right decision.

In time, you will *accept* what has happened. You may still feel very sad and miss your Poodle friend, but you accept that he is truly gone. Good memories of him fill your mind, rather than feelings of loss. You can bear the thought of your loss. You may even think about getting another Poodle someday.

Grief is a process. The length of each stage of grief varies for each person. There is no normal time period of grief, and there is no one correct way to grieve. It's very helpful to be able to share feelings of loss with another who understands your sadness. Many

Rainbow Bridge

The Rainbow Bridge Web site (www.rainbowbridge.tierranet.com/bridge.htm) is based on the story below, which was written by an unknown animal lover. Rainbow Bridge is a site of tributes and photos of deceased pets, a message board, and grief support. For owners who are sad from the loss of a pet, from dogs to guinea pigs, "the Bridge" is the place to go for understanding, sympathy, and help. If you've recently lost a beloved pet friend, be sure to check out this very popular Web site, run by Kathie Maffit and a host of volunteers.

But don't forget a hankie!

Just this side of Heaven is a place called Rainbow Bridge. When an animal dies that has been especially close to someone here, that pet goes to Rainbow Bridge. There are meadows and hills for all our special friends so they can run and play together. There is plenty of food, water and sunshine, and our friends are warm and comfortable. All the animals who had been ill or old are restored to health and vigor; those who were hurt or maimed are made whole and strong again, just as we remember them in our dreams of days gone by. The animals are happy and content, except for one small thing; they each miss someone very special to them who had to be left behind.

They all run and play together, but the day comes when one suddenly stops and looks into the distance. His bright eyes are intent; his eager body quivers. Suddenly he begins to run from the group, flying over the green grass, his legs carrying him faster and faster. You have been spotted, and when you and your special friend finally meet, you cling to each other in joyous reunion, never to be parted again. The happy kisses rain upon your face; your hands again caress the beloved head, and you look once more into the trusting eyes of your pet, so long gone from your life, but never absent from your heart.

Then you cross Rainbow Bridge together.

—author unknown

pet grief counseling groups, hotlines, and Web sites offer opportunities to connect with others who have suffered the death of a pet. Many have trained counselors to assist you in walking through grief.

If your Poodle is a family dog, you may be faced with explaining illness, death, or euthanasia to children. What do you say to a child when the Poodle dies? Generally, explain the Poodle's death simply and sincerely. But how and what you say really depends upon the child's age. Young children understand and view the world differently than older children. For children under the age of five, there's a fine line between reality and make-believe. At this age, children need literal, concrete explanations to understand. "Our Poodle has died. He won't be coming home any more." Children from five to ten have a better grasp of the life cycle. They will typically ask more questions. Answer them honestly, but spare any gruesome details that might be more upsetting. Teenagers understand the concept of death, and may find it frightening. Because they are more mature, they are most vulnerable to feelings of grief.

Grief counselors advise against lying to a child about a pet's death. Telling a child that the Poodle has gone to live on a farm doesn't really answer the child's questions about why the Poodle is no longer at home, and it could cause the child to develop fears about being taken away to a farm. It's best to be honest and allow the child to feel sad, too.

Final Plans

Burial plans are a part of accepting the loss of your Poodle. You can select from several options, including burial or cremation at a pet cemetery, burial by your veterinarian, or burial at home.

If you prefer not to deal with burial, ask your veterinarian to take care of the body. Be aware there might be a fee, and

Did You Know?

The oldest dog ever documented was an Australian cattle dog named Bluey, who was put to sleep at the age of 29 years and 5 months.

Veterinary Teaching Hospital Grief Hotlines

○ University of California, Davis, California, (530) 752-4200, 6:30–9:30 P.M. PST, Monday through Friday

○ Colorado State University, Fort Collins, Colorado, (970) 491-1242

○ University of Florida, Gainesville, Florida, (352) 392-4700 (ext. 4080), takes messages 24 hours a day; someone will call back between 7:00 and 9:00 P.M. EST

○ Michigan State University, East Lansing, Michigan, (517) 432-2696, 6:30–9:30 P.M. EST, Tuesday, Wednesday, and Thursday

○ Ohio State University, Columbus, Ohio, (614) 292-1823, takes messages 6:30–9:30 P.M. EST, Monday, Wednesday, and Friday

○ University of Pennsylvania, Philadelphia, Pennsylvania, (215) 898-4529

○ Tufts University, North Grafton, Massachusetts, (508) 839-7966, 6:00–9:00 P.M. EST, Monday through Friday

○ Virginia-Maryland Regional College of Veterinary Medicine, Blacksburg, Virginia, (540) 231-8038, 6:00–9:00 P.M. EST, Tuesday and Thursday

○ Washington State University, Pullman, Washington, (509) 335-4569

that practices vary among clinics, depending upon local regulations. If you have a large yard and city ordinances permit pet burial in residential areas, consider burying your Poodle at home. While it's painful to take care of this yourself, it's also a good way to come to terms with the loss.

A New Beginning

The empty spot in your heart after losing a beloved Poodle can actually be very positive. Your loss can drive you to adopt another

Poodle. True, you won't ever have your old friend back, but you can open your heart to another Poodle who desperately needs a loving responsible owner—you!

Of course, this takes time. Don't immediately try to fill the void. Let the feelings of loss come and subside. Accept your Poodle's death. In time, consider acquiring another Poodle puppy or adult.

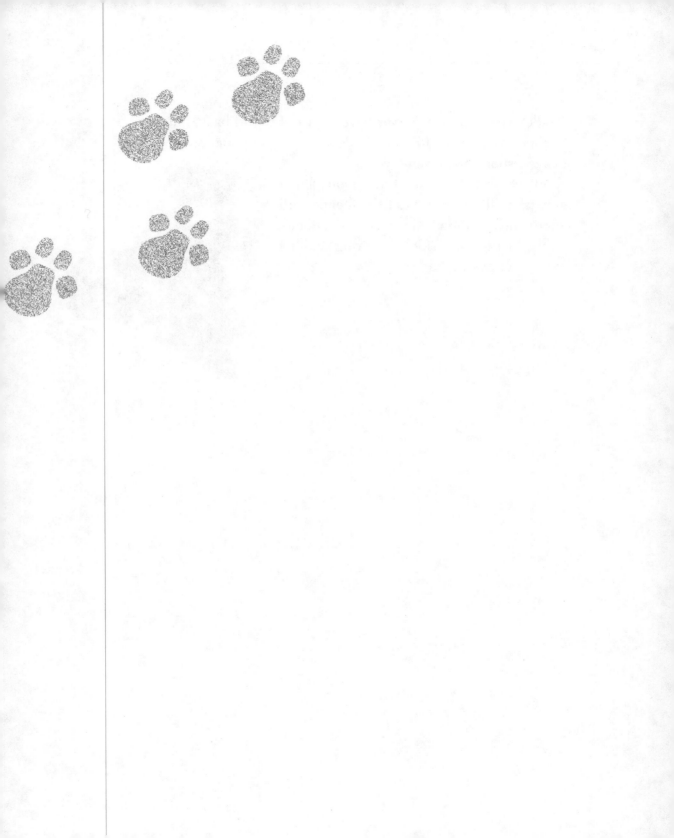

Appendix A: Resources

Boarding, Pet Sitting, Traveling

books

Dog Lover's Companion series,
Guides on traveling with dogs
for several states and cities
Foghorn Press
P.O. Box 2036
Santa Rosa, CA 95405-0036
(800) FOGHORN

*Take Your Pet Too!: Fun
Things to Do!,* Heather
MacLean Walters
M.C.E. Publishing
P.O. Box 84
Chester, NJ 07930-0084

Take Your Pet USA,
Arthur Frank
Artco Publishing
12 Channel St.
Boston, MA 02210

*Traveling with Your Pet 1999:
The AAA Petbook,*
Greg Weeks, Editor
Guide to pet-friendly lodging
in the U.S. and Canada

Vacationing with Your Pet!,
Eileen Barish
Pet-Friendly Publications
P.O. Box 8459
Scottsdale, AZ 85252
(800) 496-2665

...other resources

The American Boarding
Kennels Association
4575 Galley Road, Suite 400-A
Colorado Springs, CO 80915
(719) 591-1113
www.abka.com

Independent Pet and Animal
  Transportation Association
5521 Greenville Ave., Suite 104-310
Dallas, TX 75206
(903) 769-2267
www.ipata.com

National Association of Professional
  Pet Sitters
1200 G St. N.W., Suite 760
Washington, DC 20005
(800) 286-PETS
www.petsitters.org

Pet Sitters International
418 East King Street
King, NC 27021-9163
(336) 983-9222
www.petsit.com

U.S. Department of Agriculture
Animal and Plant Health Inspection
  Service
Import/Export rules, forms, and news

Breed Information, Clubs, Registries

books
The Complete Poodle, Del Dahl
IDG Books Worldwide 1994

*Your Poodle, Standard, Miniature
  and Toy,* Frank T. Sabella
Denlingers 1999

...other resources
American Kennel Club
5580 Centerview Drive
Raleigh, NC 27606-3390
(919) 233-9769
www.akc.org/

Canadian Kennel Club
Commerce Park
89 Skyway Ave., Suite 100
Etobicoke, Ontario, Canada
  M9W 6R4
(416) 675-5511
www.ckc.ca

Hunting Retrieving Club
P.O. Box 3179
Big Spring, TX 79721-3179
(915) 267-1659
www.hrc-ukc.com

InfoPet
P.O. Box 716
Agoura Hills, CA 91376
(800) 858-0248

The Kennel Club
(British equivalent to the American
    Kennel Club)
1-5 Clarges Street
Piccadilly
London W1Y 8AB
ENGLAND
www.the-kennel-club.org.uk/

National Dog Registry
Box 116
Woodstock, NY 12498
(800) 637-3647
www.natldogregistry.com/

North American Hunting Retriever
    Association
P.O. Box 1590
Stafford, VA 22555
(540) 286-0625
www.starsouth.com/nahra

Poodle Club of America, Inc.
418 W. 2nd
Maryville, MO 64468-2233
(660) 582-4955
www.swdg.com/pca/

Poodle History Project
www.poodlehistory.org

Poodle World
www.poodle.org

Tatoo-A-Pet
6571 S.W. 20th Court
Ft. Lauderdale, FL 33317
(800) 828-8667
www.tattoo-a-pet.com

United Kennel Club
100 East Kilgore Rd.
Kalamazoo, MI 49001-5598
(616) 343-9020
www.ukccdogs.com

Versatility In Poodles
P.O. Box 1615
Diamond Springs, CA 95619
www.pageweb.com/vipoodle/

Dog Publications

AKC Gazette and AKC Events
    Calendar
51 Madison Avenue
New York, NY 10010
Subscriptions: (919) 233-9767
www.akc.org/gazet.htm
www.akc.org/event.htm

Direct Book Service
(800) 776-2665
www.dogandcatbooks.com/direct-
    book

Dog Fancy
P.O. Box 6050
Mission Viejo, CA 92690
(949) 855-8822
www.dogfancy.com

Dogs on the Web, Audrey Pavia and
Betsy Siino
MIS: Press 1997

DogGone
P.O. Box 651155
Vero Beach, FL 32965-1155
(561) 569-8424
www.doggonefun.com

Dog World
500 N. Dearborn, Suite 1100
Chicago, IL 60610
(312) 396-0600
www.dogworldmag.com/

Dog Writers of America
173 Union Road
Coatesville, PA 19320
www.dwaa.org

K9web
1669 Woodland Ave.
Palo Alto, CA 94303
Phone: (240) 359-8136
Fax: (240) 359-8136
www.k9web.com

Poodle Variety Magazine
4401 Zephyr Street
Wheat Ridge, CO 80033-3299

Whole Dog Journal
1175 Regent Street
Alameda, CA 94501
(510) 749-1080

Fun, Grooming, Obedience, Training

books
Clipping and Grooming Your Poodle,
Pearl Stone
Arco Publishing Co.

American Kennel Club, *The Complete Dog Book*
Howell Book House

*The Complete Idiot's Guide to Fun
and Tricks with Your Dog,*
Sarah Hodgson
Alpha Books

*The Complete Poodle Clipping and
Grooming Book,*
Shirlee Kalstone
IDG Books Worldwide

Dogs and Kids, Parenting Tips,
Bardi McLennan
Howell Book House

How to Raise a Puppy You Can Live With,
Clarice Rutherford and David H. Neil, MRCVS
Alpine Publications

Old Dogs, Old Friends: Enjoying Your Older Dog,
Bonnie Wilcox, Chris Walkowitz
IDG Books Worldwide

Pet Care on a Budget, Virginia Parker Guidry
Howell Book House

Pet Grooming Basics: Bathing and Drying &
Pet Grooming the Poodle (videos),
Sonnen Productions
P.O. Box 137
Cranfills Gap, TX 76637
(800) 486-3456
www.k9video.com

Surviving Your Dog's Adolescence, Carol Lea Benjamin
Howell Book House

...other resources
American Dog Trainers Network
161 W. 4th Street
New York, NY 10014
(212) 727-7257
www.inch.com/~dogs/index.html

American Herding Breed Association
1548 Victoria Way
Pacifica, CA 94044
www.primenet.com/~joell/abba/main.htm

American Kennel Club (tracking, agility, obedience, herding)
Performance Events Dept.
5580 Centerview Drive
Raleigh, NC 27606
(919) 854-0199
www.akc.org/

Animal Behavior Society
Susan Foster
Department of Biology
Clark University
950 Main Street
Worcester, MA 01610-1477

Association of Pet Dog Trainers
P.O. Box 385
Davis, CA 95617
(800) PET-DOGS
www.apdt.com/

The Dog Agility Page
www.dogpatch.org/agility/

Intergroom
76 Carol Drive
Dedham, MA 02026
www.intergroom.com

PETsMart
www.petsmart.com

Pet Warehouse
P.O. Box 752138
Dayton, OH 45475-2138
(800) 443-1160

National Association of Dog
   Obedience Instructors
PMB #369
729 Grapevine Highway
Hurst, TX 76054-2085
www.nadoi.org/

National Dog Groomers Association
   of America
P.O. Box 101
Clark, PA 16113
(724) 962-2711

North American Dog Agility Council
HCR 2 Box 277
St. Maries, ID 83861
www.nadac.com

North American Flyball Association
1400 W. Devon Ave, #512
Chicago, IL 60660
(309) 688-9840
www.muskie.fishnet.com/~flyball/

SIRIUS Puppy Training (videos)
Ian Dunbar, PhD, MRCVS
James & Kenneth Publishers
2140 Shattuck Avenue #2406
Berkeley, CA 94704

United States Dog Agility Association, Inc.
P.O. Box 850955
Richardson, Texas 75085-0955
(972) 231-9700
www.usdaa.com/

United States Canine Combined
   Training Association
2755 Old Thompson Mill Road
Buford, GA 30519
(770) 932-8604
www.siriusweb.com/USCCTA/

Grief Support

books
*Preparing for the Loss of Your Pet:
   Saying Goodbye With Love, Dig-
   nity and Peace of Mind,* Myrna M.
   Milani, DVM
Prima Publishing

...other resources
Chicago Veterinary Medical
   Association
(630) 603-3994

Cornell University
(607) 253-3932

International Association of Pet
  Cemeteries
P.O. Box 163
5055 Route 11
Ellenburg Depot, NY 12935
(518) 594-3000
www.iaopc.com

Michigan State University
College of Veterinary Medicine
(517) 432-2696

Petloss.com
Ed Williams
P.O. Box 571
Roseland, NJ 07068
www.petloss.com

Tufts University (Massachusetts)
School of Veterinary Medicine
(508) 839-7966

University of California, Davis
(530) 752-4200

University of Florida at Gainesville
College of Veterinary Medicine
(352) 392- 4700

Virginia-Maryland Regional College
  of Veterinary Medicine
(540) 231-8038

Washington State University
College of Veterinary Medicine
(509) 335-5704

Humane Organizations and Rescue Groups

American Humane Association
63 Inverness Drive E
Englewood, CO 80112-5117
(800) 227-4645
www.americanhumane.org

American Society for the Prevention
  of Cruelty to Animals (ASPCA)
424 East 92nd Street
New York, NY 10128-6804
(212) 876-7700
www.aspca.org

Animal Protection Institute of America
P.O. Box 22505
Sacramento, CA 95822
(916) 731-5521

Friends of Animals
P.O. Box 30054
Hartford, CT 06150-0054
(800) 321-PETS
www.animalconcerns.org/

Humane Society of the United States
2100 L St. NW
Washington, DC 20037
(301) 258-3072, (202) 452-1100
www.hsus.org/

Massachusetts Society for the Prevention of Cruelty to Animals
350 South Huntington Avenue
Boston, MA 02130
(617) 522-7400
www.mspca.org/

Poodle Club of America Rescue
Sandy Malicote, national rescue
chair
(713) 526-9619

SPAY/USA
14 Vanderventer Avenue
Port Washington, NY 11050
(516) 944-5025, (203) 377-1116 in
Connecticut
(800) 248-SPAY
www.spayusa.org/

Medical and Emergency Information

books

The Allergy Solution for Dogs,
Shawn Messonnier, DVM
Prima Publishing 2000
3000 Lava Ridge Court
Roseville, CA 95661
(800) 632-8676
www.primalifestyles.com

The Arthritis Solution for Dogs,
Shawn Messonnier, DVM
Prima Publishing

*Dr. Pitcairn's Complete Guide to
Natural Health for Dogs and Cats,*
Richard H. Pitcairn, DVM, PhD,
and Susan Hubble Pitcairn
Rodale Press, Inc. 1995

*Dog Owner's Home Veterinary
Handbook,*
Dr. Delbert Carlson and Dr. James
Griffin
Howell Book House

*Infectious Diseases of the Dog and
Cat,* Craig E. Greene, Editor
W B Saunders Company

Pet First Aid: Cats and Dogs, Bobbi
Mammato, D.V.M.
Mosby Year Book

Skin Diseases of Dogs and Cats: A Guide for Pet Owners and Professionals,
Dr. Steven A. Melman
Dermapet, Inc.
P.O. Box 59713
Potomac, MD 20859

...other resources

American Academy on Veterinary Disaster Medicine
4304 Tenthouse Court
West River MD 20778
(301) 261-9940

American Animal Hospital Association
P.O. Box 150899
Denver, CO 80215-0899
(800) 252-2242
www.healthypet.com

American Holistic Veterinary Medicine Association
2214 Old Emmorton Road
Bel Air, MD 21015
(410) 569-2346
www.altvetmed.com

American Kennel Club Canine Health Foundation
251 West Garfield Road, Suite 160
Aurora, OH 44202
(888) 682-9696
www.akcchf.org/main.htm

American Veterinary Medical Association
1931 North Meacham Road, Suite 100
Schaumburg, IL 60173-4360
(800) 248-2862
www.avma.org/

Canine Eye Registration Inc. (CERF)
Veterinary Medical Data Program
South Campus Courts, Building C
Purdue University
West Lafayette, IN 47907
(765) 494-8179
www.vet.purdue.edu/~yshen/cerf.html

Centers for Disease Control and Prevention
1600 Clifton Road NE
Atlanta, GA 30333
(404) 639-3311 (CDC Operator)
(800) 311-3435 (CDC Public Inquiries)
www.cdc.gov

Institute for Genetic Disease/Wind Morgan
P.O. Box 222
Davis, CA 97617
(530) 756-6773
www.vetmed.ucdavis.edu/gdc/gdc.htm
www.working-retriever.com/library/windmorg.shtml

National Animal Poison Control
  Center
1717 S. Philo, Suite 36
Urbana, IL 61802
(888) 426-4435, $45 per case, with as
  many follow-up calls as necessary
  included. Have name, address,
  phone number, dog's breed, age,
  sex, and type of poison ingested, if
  known, available
www.napcc.aspca.org

Orthopedic Foundation for Animals
  (OFA)
2300 E. Nifong Blvd.
Columbia, MO 65201-3856
(573) 442-0418
www.offa.org/

PennHip
c/o Synbiotics
11011 Via Frontera
San Diego, CA 92127
(800) 228-4305

Pet Assure Inc.
10 South Morris Street
Dover, NJ 07801
(888) 789-7387
www.petassure.com

Senior Dog Project
www.srdogs.com

U.S. Pharmacopeia
vaccine reactions: (800) 487-7776
customer service: (800) 227-8772
www.usp.org

Veterinary Medical Database/Canine
  Eye Registration Foundation
Department of Veterinary Clinical
  Science
School of Veterinary Medicine
Purdue University
West Lafayette, IN 47907
(765) 494-8179
www.vet.purdue.edu/~yshen/

Veterinary Pet Insurance (VPI)
4175 E. La Palma Ave., #100
Anaheim, CA 92807-1846
(714) 996-2311
(800) USA PETS, (877) PET
  HEALTH in Texas
www.petplan.net/home.htm

Nutrition, Natural Foods, Treats

books
Dog Treats, Kim Campbell Thornton
Main Street Books

Home Prepared Dog and Cat Diets,
  Donald R. Strombeck
Iowa State University Press
(515) 292-0140

...other resources

California Natural, Natural Pet
    Products
P.O. Box 271
Santa Clara, CA 95052
(800) 532-7261
www.naturapet.com

Home of the Doggie Cookbook
www.dogcookbook.com

PHD Products Inc.
P.O. Box 8313
White Plains, NY 10602
(800) 863-3403
www.phdproducts.net/

Sensible Choice, Pet Products Plus
5600 Mexico Road
St. Peters, MO 63376
(800) 592-6687
www.sensiblechoice.com/

Two Dog Press
(888) 310-2DOG
www.twodogpress.com/dogfood.html

Search and Rescue Dogs

National Association for Search and
    Rescue
4500 Southgate Place, Suite 100
Chantilly, VA 20151-1714
(703) 622-6283
www.nasar.org/

National Disaster Search Dog
    Foundation
323 East Matilija Avenue, #110-245
Ojai, CA 93023-2740
www.west.net/~rescue/

Service and Working Dogs

Canine Companions for
    Independence
P.O. Box 446
Santa Rosa, CA 95402-0446
(800) 572-2275
www.caninecompanions.org/

Delta Society National Service Dog
    Center
289 Perimeter Road East
Renton, WA 98055-1329
(800) 869-6898
www.petsforum.com/deltasociety/dsb
    000.htm

Foundation for Pet Provided Therapy
P.O. Box 6308
Oceanside, CA 92058
(760) 630-4824

Guiding Eyes for the Blind
611 Granite Springs Road
Yorktown Heights, NY 10598
www.guiding-eyes.org/

The National Education for
Assistance Dog Services, Inc.
P.O. Box 213
West Boylston, MA 01583
(508) 422-9064
www.chamber.worcester.ma.us/neads
/INDEX.HTM

North American Working Dog
Association
Southeast Kreisgruppe
P.O. Box 833
Brunswick, GA 31521

The Seeing Eye
P.O. Box 375
Morristown, NJ 07963-0375
(973) 539-4425
www.seeingeye.org/

Therapy Dogs Incorporated
2416 E. Fox Farm Road
Cheyenne, WY 82007
(877) 843-7364
www.therapydogs.com

Therapy Dogs International
6 Hilltop Road
Mendham, NJ 07945
(973) 252-9800
www.tdi-dog.org/

United Schutzhund Clubs of America
3704 Lemay Ferry Road
St. Louis, MO 63125

Appendix B:
Official Breed Standard for the Poodle

The Standard for the Poodle (Toy variety) is the same as for the Standard and Miniature varieties except as regards heights.

General Appearance, Carriage and Condition

That of a very active, intelligent and elegant-appearing dog, squarely built, well proportioned, moving soundly and carrying himself proudly. Properly clipped in the traditional fashion and carefully groomed, the Poodle has about him an air of distinction and dignity peculiar to himself.

Size, Proportion, Substance

Size   *The Standard Poodle* is over 15 inches at the highest point of the shoulders. Any Poodle which is 15 inches or less in height shall be disqualified from competition as a Standard Poodle.

The Miniature Poodle is 15 inches or under at the highest point of the shoulders, with a minimum height in excess of 10 inches. Any Poodle which is over 15 inches or is 10 inches or less at the highest point of the shoulders shall be disqualified from competition as a Miniature Poodle.

The Toy Poodle is 10 inches or under at the highest point of the shoulders. Any Poodle which is more than 10 inches at the highest point of the shoulders shall be disqualified from competition as a Toy Poodle.

As long as the Toy Poodle is definitely a Toy Poodle, and the Miniature Poodle a Miniature Poodle, both in balance and proportion for the Variety, diminutiveness shall be the deciding factor when all other points are equal.

Proportion   To ensure the desirable squarely built appearance, the length of body measured from the breastbone to the point of the rump approximates the height from the highest point of the shoulders to the ground.

Substance   Bone and muscle of both forelegs and hindlegs are in proportion to size of dog.

Head and Expression

(a) Eyes—very dark, oval in shape and set far enough apart and positioned to create an alert, intelligent expression. *Major fault: eyes round, protruding, large or very light.*

(b) Ears—hanging close to the head, set at or slightly below eye level. The ear leather is long, wide and thickly feathered; however, the ear fringe should not be of excessive length.

(c) Skull—moderately rounded, with a slight but definite stop. Cheekbones and muscles flat. Length from occiput to stop about the same as length of muzzle.

(d) Muzzle—long, straight and fine, with slight chiseling under the eyes. Strong without lippiness. The chin definite

enough to preclude snipiness. *Major fault: lack of chin.* **Teeth**—white, strong and with a scissors bite. *Major fault: undershot, overshot, wry mouth.*

Neck, Topline, Body

Neck well proportioned, strong and long enough to permit the head to be carried high and with dignity. Skin snug at throat. The neck rises from strong, smoothly muscled shoulders. *Major fault: ewe neck.* The **topline** is level, neither sloping nor roached, from the highest point of the shoulder blade to the base of the tail, with the exception of a slight hollow just behind the shoulder.

Body

(a) Chest deep and moderately wide with well sprung ribs.

(b) The loin is short, broad and muscular.

(c) Tail straight, set on high and carried up, docked of sufficient length to insure a balanced outline. *Major fault: set low, curled, or carried over the back.*

Forequarters

Strong, smoothly muscled shoulders. The shoulder blade is well laid back and approximately the same length as the upper foreleg. *Major fault: steep shoulder.*

(a) **Forelegs** straight and parallel when viewed from the front. When viewed from the side the elbow is directly below the highest point of the shoulder. The pasterns are strong. Dewclaws may be removed.

Feet

The feet are rather small, oval in shape with toes well arched and cushioned on thick, firm pads. Nails short but not excessively shortened. The feet turn neither in nor out. *Major fault: paper or splay foot.*

Hindquarters

The angulation of the hindquarters balances that of the forequarters.

(a) Hindlegs straight and parallel when viewed from the rear. Muscular with width in the region of the stifles which are well bent; femur and tibia are about equal in length; hock to heel short and perpendicular to the ground. When standing, the rear toes are only slightly behind the point of the rump. *Major fault: cow-hocks.*

Coat

(a) Quality—(1) Curly: of naturally harsh texture, dense throughout. (2) Corded: hanging in tight, even cords of varying length; longer on mane or body coat, head, and ears; shorter on puffs, bracelets, and pompons.

(b) Clip—A Poodle under 12 months may be shown in the "Puppy" clip. In all regular classes, Poodles 12 months or over must be shown in the "English Saddle" or "Continental" clip. In the Stud Dog and Brood Bitch classes and in a non-competitive Parade of Champions, Poodles may be shown in the "Sporting" clip. A Poodle shown in any other type of clip shall be disqualified.

(1) "Puppy"—A Poodle under a year old may be shown in the "Puppy" clip with the coat long. The face, throat, feet and base of the tail are shaved. The entire shaven foot is visible. There is a pompon on the end of the tail. In order to give a neat appearance

and a smooth unbroken line, shaping of the coat is permissible. (2) "English Saddle"—In the "English Saddle" clip, the face, throat, feet, forelegs and base of the tail are shaved, leaving puffs on the forelegs and a pompon on the end of the tail. The hindquarters are covered with a short blanket of hair except for a curved shaved area on each flank and two shaved bands on each hindleg. The entire shaven foot and a portion of the shaven leg above the puff are visible. The rest of the body is left in full coat but may be shaped in order to insure overall balance. (3) "Continental"—In the "Continental" clip, the face, throat, feet, and base of the tail are shaved. The hindquarters are shaved with pompons (optional) on the hips. The legs are shaved, leaving bracelets on the hindlegs and puffs on the forelegs. There is a pompon on the end of the tail. The entire shaven foot and a portion of the shaven foreleg above the puff are visible. The rest of the body is left in full coat but may be shaped in order to insure overall balance. (4) "Sporting"—In the "Sporting" clip, a Poodle shall be shown with face, feet, throat, and base of tail shaved, leaving a scissored cap on the top of the head and a pompon on the end of the tail. The rest of the body, and legs are clipped or scissored to follow the outline of the dog leaving a short blanket of coat no longer than one inch in length. The hair on the legs may be slightly longer than that on the body.

In all clips the hair of the topknot may be left free or held in place by elastic bands. The hair is only of sufficient length to present a smooth outline. "Topknot" refers only to hair on the skull, from stop to occiput. This is the only area where elastic bands may be used.

Color

The coat is an even and solid color at the skin. In blues, grays, silvers, browns, cafe-au-laits, apricots and creams, the coat may show varying shades of the same color. This is frequently present in the somewhat darker feathering of the ears and in the tipping of the ruff. While clear colors are definitely preferred, such natural variation in the shading of the coat is not to be considered a fault. Brown and cafe-au-lait Poodles have liver-colored noses, eye-rims and lips, dark toenails and dark amber eyes. Black, blue, gray, silver, cream and white Poodles have black noses, eye-rims and lips, black or self colored toenails and very dark eyes. In the apricots while the foregoing coloring is preferred, liver-colored noses, eye-rims and lips, and amber eyes are permitted but are not desirable. *Major fault: color of nose, lips and eye-rims incomplete, or of wrong color for color of dog.*

Parti-colored dogs shall be disqualified. The coat of a parti-colored dog is not an even solid color at the skin but is of two or more colors.

Gait

A straightforward trot with light springy action and strong hindquarters drive. Head and tail carried up. Sound effortless movement is essential.

Temperament

Carrying himself proudly, very active, intelligent, the Poodle has about him an air of distinction and dignity peculiar to himself. *Major fault: shyness or sharpness.*

Major Faults

Any distinct deviation from the desired characteristics described in the Breed Standard.

Disqualifications

Size—A dog over or under the height limits specified shall be disqualified. *Clip*—A dog in any type of clip other than those listed under coat shall be disqualified. *Parti-colors*—The coat of a parti-colored dog is not an even solid color at the skin but of two or more colors. Parti-colored dogs shall be disqualified.

Value of Points

General appearance, temperament, carriage and condition.......30
Head, expression, ears, eyes and teeth.......20
Body, neck, legs, feet and tail.......20
Gait.......20
Coat, color and texture.......10

Approved August 14, 1984
Reformatted March 27, 1990

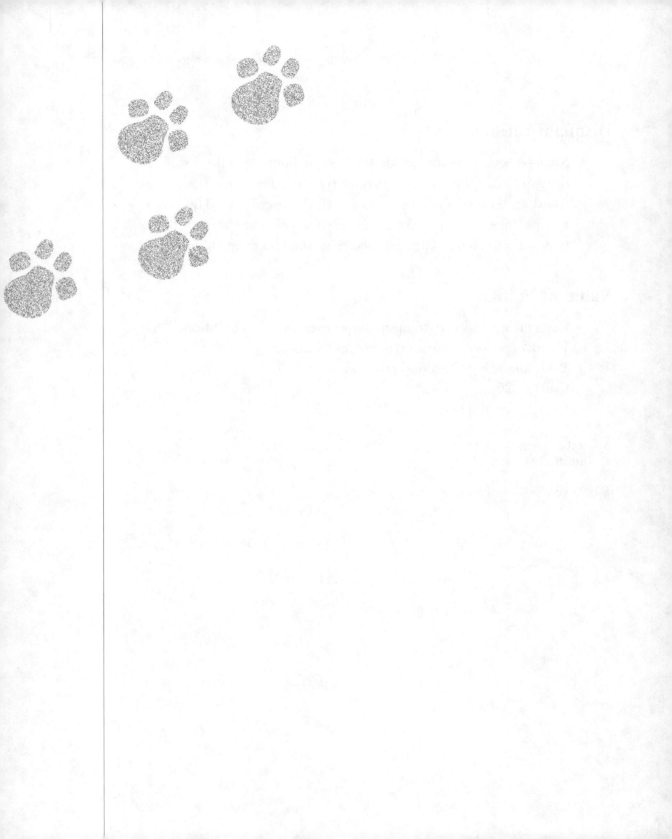

Index

Meet Your Poodle Care Experts

Author **Virginia Parker Guidry** is a long-time animal enthusiast, writer, and editor. A graduate of Berea College in Berea, Kentucky, with a B.A. in English, her editorial experience includes several staff positions on newspapers and magazines, including *Pet Health News* and *Horse Illustrated,* and she is currently a contributing editor for *Dog Fancy* magazine. Guidry is a former professional small-animal groomer and horse groom, and has worked as a veterinary assistant. A member of Dog Writers Association of America, she writes regularly for many pet-related publications and lives in Southern California with her husband and son.

Trainer **Liz Palika** has been teaching classes for dogs and their owners for over twenty years. Her goal is to help people understand why their dogs do what they do so that dogs and owners can live together successfully. Liz says, "If, in each training class, I can increase understanding and ease frustration so that the dog doesn't end up in the local shelter because the owner has given up, then I have accomplished my goal!" She is the author of 23 books and has won awards from both the Dog Writers Association of America and the ASPCA. Liz and her husband, Paul, share their home with three Australian Shepherds: Dax, Kes, and Riker.

Series Editor **Joanne Howl, D.V.M.,** is a graduate of the University of Tennessee College of Veterinary Medicine and has practiced animal medicine for over ten years. She currently serves as president of the Maryland Veterinary Medical Association and as secretary/treasurer of the American Academy on Veterinary Disaster Medicine. Her columns and articles have appeared in a variety of animal-related publications. Dr. Howl divides her time between family, small-animal medicine, writing, and the company of her two dogs and six cats.

Prima's YOUR PET'S LIFE™ Series

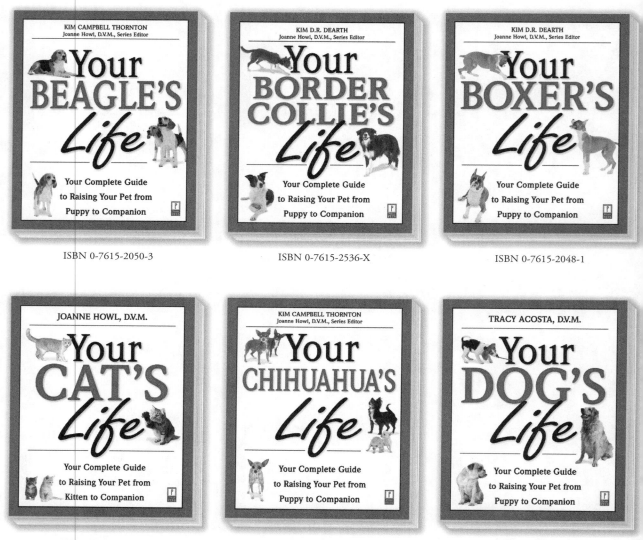

ISBN 0-7615-2050-3

ISBN 0-7615-2536-X

ISBN 0-7615-2048-1

ISBN 0-7615-1361-2

ISBN 0-7615-2051-1

ISBN 0-7615-1543-7

AUDREY PAVIA
Joanne Howl, D.V.M., Series Editor

Your GERMAN SHEPHERD'S *Life*

Your Complete Guide to Raising Your Pet from Puppy to Companion

ISBN 0-7615-2052-X

BETSY SIKORA SIINO
Joanne Howl, D.V.M., Series Editor

Your GOLDEN RETRIEVER'S *Life*

Your Complete Guide to Raising Your Pet from Puppy to Companion

ISBN 0-7615-2047-3

VIRGINIA PARKER GUIDRY
Joanne Howl, D.V.M., Series Editor

Your LAB'S *Life*

Your Complete Guide to Raising Your Pet from Puppy to Companion

ISBN 0-7615-2046-5

VIRGINIA PARKER GUIDRY
Joanne Howl, D.V.M., Series Editor

Your POODLE'S *Life*

Your Complete Guide to Raising Your Pet from Puppy to Companion

ISBN 0-7615-2537-8

KIM D.R. DEARTH
Joanne Howl, D.V.M., Series Editor

Your ROTTWEILER'S *Life*

Your Complete Guide to Raising Your Pet from Puppy to Companion

ISBN 0-7615-2049-X

ELAINE WALDORF GEWIRTZ
Joanne Howl, D.V.M., Series Editor

Your YORKSHIRE TERRIER'S *Life*

Your Complete Guide to Raising Your Pet from Puppy to Companion

ISBN 0-7615-2535-1

YOUR PET'S LIFE™ series is written with one purpose in mind—to give owners the most up-to-date information and guidance they need about the health, nutrition, training, and care of their pet.

To Order Books

Please send me the following items:

Quantity	Title	Unit Price	
_____	The Allergy Solution for Dogs	$ _____	$ _____
_____	The Arthritis Solution for Dogs	$ _____	$ _____
_____	Your Beagle's Life	$ _____	$ _____
_____	Your Border Collie's Life	$ _____	$ _____
_____	Your Boxer's Life	$ _____	$ _____
_____	Your Cat's Life	$ _____	$ _____
_____	Your Chihuahua's Life	$ _____	$ _____
_____	Your Dog's Life	$ _____	$ _____
_____	Your German Shepherd's Life	$ _____	$ _____
_____	Your Golden Retriever's Life	$ _____	$ _____
_____	Your Lab's Life	$ _____	$ _____
_____	Your Poodle's Life	$ _____	$ _____
_____	Your Rottweiler's Life	$ _____	$ _____
_____	Your Yorkshire Terrier's Life	$ _____	$ _____

Subtotal	$ _____
7.25% Sales Tax (CA only)	$ _____
7% Sales Tax (PA only)	$ _____
5% Sales Tax (IN only)	$ _____
7% G.S.T. Tax (Canada only)	$ _____
Priority Shipping	$ _____
Total Order	$ _____

FREE
Ground Freight in U.S. and Canada

Foreign and all Priority Request orders:
Call Customer Service
for price quote at 916-787-7000

By Telephone: With American Express, MC, or Visa,
call 800-632-8676 ext. 4444, Monday–Friday, 8:30–4:30
www.primapublishing.com
By E-mail: sales@primapub.com

il: Just fill out the information below and send with your remittance to:
Publishing • P.O. Box 1260BK • Rocklin, CA 95677

_____

_____

_____ State _____ ZIP _____

_____ Exp. _____

_____ Payable to Prima Publishing